Life at the Wrinkle Ranch

By
Virginia Key

To Sheree & Tom,
Now that you have
experienced the Ranch
as guests, learn what it
is really like, to live here!
Virginia

Foreword

In life there are few opportunities to cross paths with an individual who truly understands how their presence impacts and influences those with whom they come in contact. Through a classy yet surreal approach, the author shares her experiences from a vantage point of an engaged resident of life at a continuing care retirement community. The stories in each chapter provide a panoramic view of such a community, illustrating the variety of ways through which many residents, coming together with different and amazing experiences, vividly impact the quality of life of others, including the team members who have the privilege of working for a time in the forever home of residents. The expansive journey is enriching, and the stories provide a perspective laced with details that enrich and serve as a resource for the process of considering a move to such a community. I have had the privilege to lead several such places and recognize the challenges, joys, and pains that the author so dramatically reveals through the stories and experiences that were the genesis of this book. The author touched my life, and I can only aspire to achieve as she has.

K.S. Knopf
Regional Operations Director
Lifespace Communities

Acknowledgements

This book would never have come to fruition without the encouragement of a number of people. My "Recipients" have for years received my stories and essays in their e-mail in-boxes and have continued to encourage me to write this book.

Thanks are due to both the local and the corporate management of our splendid provider of Senior Living, who, when I "confessed" I was writing a book about my life at the "Wrinkle Ranch," not only reconfirmed their dedication to the First Amendment but also strongly affirmed their support of Seniors who move into wrinkle ranches and continue to be creative and to live life to the fullest!

Of course, all writers are extremely dependent on their editors, and my editor demonstrated patience, above and beyond the call of duty as he advised, fact checked, and rooted out my grammatical sins, which were myriad. Any errors a reader may encounter in this book were likely included at my insistence and over the editor's objections. Louis, you are a gem!

Most of all, I want to recognize My Hero, the most wonderful person I have ever known. He has used his outstanding computer skills to assist me at every turn in my adventure of writing this book, just as he has tirelessly used his splendid life skills to make my existence beautiful every day of our life together – including our life at the "Wrinkle Ranch."

Virginia

2016

Life at the Wrinkle Ranch

Introduction

The term, "Wrinkle Ranch," is a slang expression used to designate a Senior Community. Just as I never set out to move to a Wrinkle Ranch, I never set out to write a book, and then I did both of those things. Once My Hero and I moved to a Senior Community, our Wrinkle Ranch, I had planned to go on living my life and doing the things I had always done and enjoyed, and that did not include writing a book! Well, a wise man once said, "Life is what happens while you are making plans," and so as the days went on, I began to write essays and stories about what I observed at the Ranch. I recorded my frustrations, my disappointments, my triumphs, and the vignettes of life all around me. In the process I discovered that Life at the Wrinkle Ranch, like life everywhere, is inherently funny.

Not having any real outlet for my writing – goodness knows I did not want my new neighbors or the Management to know that I was watching them and then writing about it – I began to e-mail my efforts, one small story at a time, to my old friends and family, most of whom were safely far, far away.

Eventually those people began to say, "You should write a book…." I was flattered, but I was busy and besides, how many little essays and stories does it take to fill a book? But as time went on, while I watched, the essays and stories began to weave themselves into a book.

Then I realized people who want to decide where to spend the last chapter of their life need real information about Wrinkle Ranch living, not just something written by a financial analyst or someone who specializes in actuarial tables, not even something written by a qualified gerontologist or an executive who works for a Life Care provider, but a book written by a person who is a "Rancher," someone who will tell it like it is from a resident's perspective.

Since I had never written a book before, I was not sure just what to do with what I had created. I decided against turning it into a novel – concepts like character development and plot devices just seemed beyond my grasp. Instead I produced a love story – no, not a traditional love story about two people who fall in love with each other but one about how we love living at the Wrinkle Ranch. Like any love story there are some rough patches, and sometimes we and the Ranch have to disagree before we can kiss and make up, but do not misunderstand; this is a love story. We love life at the Wrinkle Ranch.

So here it is, a book that seeks to explain why two perfectly happy, healthy Seniors would move to "A Place Like That" (as so many people outside the Ranch refer to this type of community), a book that is about our lives and the lives of our fellow Ranchers and how we interact with each other and with the people who work here. It's *Life at the Wrinkle Ranch*!

Table of Contents

Table of Contents (continued)

Table of Contents (continued)

Table of Contents (continued)

VIRGINIA KEY

CHAPTER
1

The Most Important Decision

We make important decisions throughout our lives – decisions about our education, our careers, and our mates. If we decide to buy a house or a car, over a lifetime we may make those decisions many times. The need to make choices goes on and on, but regardless of how important and serious a decision is, it usually can be changed given a little time. If you enter the military, you can choose to leave once you serve your commitment. You can change your career, sell your house, even replace your spouse. In America, perhaps more than in any other country in the world, we are free to make decisions and then to change our minds and do something entirely different.

As we grow older, some of our decisions become more important, in part because of the very fact that we are older. We don't have as much time as we once did to change our minds and reroute our lives, and we don't have the same energy we did when we were younger. Making major decisions takes energy, and at some point changing those decisions may take more energy than we have left.

Those factors mean the most important decision we ever make could be choosing where and how we live as we age and transition from a state of complete independence to whatever level of care we may require before our life ends. Whether we decide to stay in our own home, move in with "the kids," or relocate to a Senior Community, once we implement that decision, it can be difficult to change it.

For that reason, My Hero and I thought long and hard about what choice we were going to make for our "Forever Home." Even though neither of us had any diagnosed medical issues, we wanted to plan for that eventuality. We investigated various Senior Living Communities and explored the different types of options available to us at our income level.

Since we are golfers, we want to be able to play year 'round and to use every possible day to play, while we still could. We had already moved south from Virginia to North Carolina when we retired the first time - still too cold in the winter. We checked out California – too expensive; Alabama – too many storms and tornados. Eventually we looked at Florida and discovered that the West Coast of Florida really appealed to us.

Then we began to investigate specific Senior Communities in earnest. We wanted to control our future costs as much as possible so a Life Care Community was our preferred solution. At many Life Care Communities, once you qualify for Independent Living and have a Life Care Contract, you may not pay more if you move to higher levels of care; your monthly fee may not go up, even if one of you remains in Independent Living while the other moves. Furthermore, much of your upfront costs and the monthly fees are deductible as health care expenses on your tax returns.

We did not wait until we "had" to move or until some family member had the burden of choosing our last home for us. We have always made our own decisions, and after much research *we* chose our own "Forever Home."

Our friends and neighbors in North Carolina thought we were crazy. They were sure that one of us had been secretly diagnosed with cancer or some other serious illness. Rumors were spread that My Hero had developed Alzheimer's.

Mostly these well-meaning people created these ideas because they had no idea what an Entry Fee Continuing Care Retirement Community is. They said things like, "Why are you moving to *a place like that?*" Not knowing what "a place like that" was, they assumed we were moving into a nursing home! And yes, there is a nursing home component here. We hope we will never need it. But if we do, it is here – on our campus and right across the street.

So we made our decision. As we drove up to our new home, I looked at My Hero and said, "Here goes the next chapter in our lives. It's *Life at the Wrinkle Ranch.*"

The first chapter of this book contains essays and stories about people we have met who were considering a decision about their "Forever Home," but first I start by presenting "The Committee," which introduces the reader to the way I think about things. I have learned I do not always see the world in quite the same way other people do.

Next, "Are You Ready?" addresses the first question we all must ask ourselves in the process of making this choice. The next story is entitled, "But What Will I Say to the Kids?" and probes the family dynamics of making the decision to move to the Ranch. "Not Good Prospects" recounts a visit to the Ranch by some interesting people who, thankfully, did not become our Forever Neighbors.

The last story in this chapter is "Fear of Aging," which describes the state of mind of a woman whose spouse was "Ready," and she was not. She was suffering from one of the worst human disorders ever diagnosed, Denial! We explore the dangers of Denial several times in this book. Denial is the biggest health risk we ever face. Although Denial is the enemy of people everywhere, it is especially devastating to Seniors and always gets in the way of rational behavior.

Life at the Wrinkle Ranch: The *Committee*

We live in a beautiful Senior Community nestled on a scenic, 140 acre campus, much of which is covered by native trees and other natural Florida flora. There are palm trees, palmettos, live oaks, all manner of colorful shrubs, and wonderful ferns, with plenty of Spanish moss for decoration.

As you might expect, natural Florida flora is accompanied by natural Florida fauna, and although I have yet to see a Florida cougar or a black bear in my exploration of our campus, I have encountered plenty of other critters including alligators, armadillos, raccoons, squirrels, snakes, and a wide variety of birds — egrets, ibises, and the large and elegant Sand Hills Cranes, who move about at will. Gulls and crows are everywhere, even songbirds stop by on their annual migration, and there are plenty of sparrows for Him to keep His eye on here.

Mother Nature, being a wise woman, did not create this beautiful area, teeming with life, without providing a cleanup crew. We have a large complement of turkey buzzards at the Ranch. They take every opportunity to "clean up," but when there is nothing else to do, they sit around just roosting and watching, or eyeing our garbage compactor longingly.

Since I have always been interested in birds and animals, I sought to discover what one called such a group. I went to my Internet search engine and typed in, "What is a group of vultures called?"

Back like a flash came more information that I ever imagined, "A **group** of vultures is called a *wake, committee, venue, kettle,* or *volt*.

3

The term *kettle* refers to vultures in flight, while *committee, volt,* and *venue* refer to vultures resting in trees. *Wake* is reserved for a group of vultures that are feeding."

Now that you understand the situation, let's get down to it. Let's say that you are interested in moving to a Senior Community and you drive through our gates and down the lovely tree-lined boulevard to the Marketing and Sales office, and what do you see perched on every light stanchion and tree in sight but the *committee*!

Maybe you are already a little nervous about the idea of moving to your earthly "Forever Home." Maybe you don't think *you* are ready for the Wrinkle Ranch. Well the sight of a *committee* waiting for you may just be the impetus it takes for you to turn around and head for the hills.

I for one have visited Management a number of times to encourage them to chase away the *committee,* to send our *venue* to another venue, and to inspire our *kettle* to take up residence in someone else's kitchen! Management, however, told me vultures, like so many annoying critters these days, are a protected species. Who knew?

Maybe Management was wrong; they have been wrong before. I rushed to my computer and typed, "Are turkey buzzards a protected species?"

Instantly came the reply, "The black vulture and the turkey vulture are protected by Federal law and cannot be killed without proper permits from the U.S. Fish and Wildlife Service."

Surely there is a bright side to this situation; after all what golfer on our golf course wants to look for his ball in the palmetto bushes only to encounter instead a long dead and stinky animal carcass? And what about those squirrels the Ranchers keep running over on the boulevard; is it not better to have a *wake* to clean up the remains quickly and not have to rely on getting maintenance out there in a timely manner?

No matter how assiduously I try to look at the positives, somehow other issues come to mind: There was the time that an associate demanded Management repair her car because the "lookout" for the *committee* perched daily on the roof of her car and pecked the molding around her windshield so repeatedly that it needed to be replaced.

And then there was the incident we experienced when the inner lining of the compactor rusted through. Until it could be repaired, we had to put our garbage in a temporary dumpster. The entire *crew* convened a serious *committee* meeting and decided to hold a *wake* right on top of the dumpster. They tore open garbage bags and tossed likely tidbits to the ground while their fellow *committee* members swooped down to fight for each beak full like a, well, like a *volt* of lightening.

Even if we were to decide the positive activities of the *committee* and the *wake* outweigh their negatives, there is still the image thing. Surely nothing could be more appealing to the Senior looking for his earthly "Forever Home" than the beautiful vistas provided by our campus.

On the other hand, what could be more off-putting than these watchful avian squatters? It's just "Life at the Wrinkle Ranch: The *Committee!*"

Life at the Wrinkle Ranch: Are you Ready?

One of the thorniest issues for many people is deciding when is the "right time" to move into a Continuing Care Retirement Community (CCRC). Ideally one moves into one of these stages of life communities while still in the Independent Living stage. Many people, however, who are still fully independent, do not fancy the idea of any type of communal life style. They have lived in their own homes for years, eaten on their own schedule, taken care of their own home maintenance chores, and do not want to change. At least – not now. They do not see why they should; after all, aren't they doing fine on their own?

There is a catch-22 inherent in this thinking. If suddenly one needs the care and convenience of a CCRC, there is a myriad of conditions that may preclude entry into such a community. Granted at the time we moved, a recent economic downturn seemed to make many Senior Living providers less stringent in their entrance health requirements, but even then a single person unable to care for himself fully because of stroke, ambulation issues, or a diagnosis of early Alzheimer's found the available options reduced and the cost of those options increased substantially. In some cases even the impaired person with a healthy spouse who can provide support for many of the daily living aspects of the partner's life may not be welcome in Independent Living.

The majority of Americans over sixty-five have one or more medically diagnosed conditions such as high cholesterol, blood pressure issues, diabetes, macular degeneration or other vision problems, heart problems, COPD, or a variety of other maladies. Even if these conditions are under control with proper diet, exercise, and medication, that situation can change overnight. A fall, a stroke, or any other unexpected or undiagnosed problem can be catastrophic as can the rapid progression of some disease such as Parkinson's.

Many thoughtful people resolve this "am I ready?" question by getting on the "waiting list" of a particular community and reviewing their "readiness" periodically when their number comes to the top of the list. Unfortunately others deal with it by ignoring the issue entirely; however, as economic pressures make Senior care organizations more aggressive in their marketing, few Seniors with the resources to consider the CCRC option and who live in an area with a Senior Care Community have missed the reach of that company's marketing arm. Post cards with invitations to dinner and discussions of options and health care come into their homes regularly.

The town that houses our Wrinkle Ranch is such a place. The town is itself an over-55 retirement community. Many of the residents who live at our Ranch stayed in the homes they purchased in town as long as they possibly could, and finally in some stage of impairment, they moved across town to this CCRC. Many needed special moving services to accomplish their relocation, since they were no longer physically able to pack, lift, unpack, and accomplish all the other tiring physical, emotional, and mental chores associated with that daunting task.

Only once, over twenty years ago when the developers of our Ranch pioneered this relatively new and innovative approach to Senior Living, did a large number of very healthy and active people from "across the street" leave their homes and move in here, ready to enjoy the excellent food, the golf course, the pool, the dances, activities, the transportation provided to many cultural and sporting events, entertainment organized by the Activities staff, and the chauffeur driven trips to doctors and financial advisors.

One day a lady at my country club asked where I lived, and I told her. I was not at all surprised when my answer was met with a retort I had heard before, "I've been there a number of times, the food is excellent and it's very nice, but I'm not ready," she said emphatically. It was, by now, a familiar refrain.

But this time I was prepared for it, "How do you know when you're ready?" I asked innocently "Well," said my new golf companion, who looked a lot older than I and was not nearly so nimble, "I guess, when you never want to cook again!" "Damn," I said. "I waited ten years too long!" It's just "Life at the Wrinkle Ranch: Are You Ready?"

Life at the Wrinkle Ranch: But What Will I Say to the Kids?

People who know they need to take charge of the rest of their lives and people whose health has already taken a turn down the mountain will, even in the face of an oncoming flood of medical issues, still practice denial and work assiduously to find reasons not to leap the arroyo and get to the safety of a Wrinkle Ranch.

Take for example our friends Fred and Jennifer. They can certainly afford to live here. They have lots of money; at least compared to us they have lots of money. And since Fred had a six way by-pass some years ago, suffers from gout, and until recently was a three-pack a day smoker and a pretty heavy drinker, and since Jennifer has Parkinson's, tends to fall easily, and is still a smoker, you would think that they would be hightailing it to the Ranch like the entire Apache nation was in hot pursuit. But no!

7

First they had to come for a visit. OK, makes sense: they met great people, saw terrific apartments, and admitted they needed to be here. And then they decided they should compare our community to every one within a fifty-mile radius of their current home town. OK, makes sense.

They did that and admitted that not one was so nice, or so cost effective, or offered such large apartments as our Ranch.

Then they had to take yet another river boat trip up the Rhine to remind themselves that people with Parkinson's can't hike around the countryside successfully.

Then Fred had to get sick and spend a month in a French Hospital just to remind himself that he was not up to international travel either.

And when we persisted in asking if they had finally decided to move here, they said, "We know it's the right thing to do, but what will we say to the kids?"

Now let me see. Fred and Jennifer have been essentially supporting their daughter, her husband, and their children ever since we have known them. Currently they all live in a huge house for which the kids pay nothing, and for which, as far as I can tell, the kids *do* nothing either. Oh yes, the adult "kids" have jobs, but the initial idea was if they all lived together, there would never be any need for Fred and Jennifer to move to a Wrinkle Ranch because the kids would take care of them. Fred and Jennifer bought the 10,000 square-foot house, and they all moved in together, and when Jennifer fell and broke her leg, she had to go to a rehab hospital because the kids were not available to care of her. I guess they proved how well that plan worked!

So why don't they know what to say to the kids? I have some suggestions. Here is a list. Pick one. Pick several:

We're selling the house.
You have to move out.
We're moving to a Wrinkle Ranch, and you're on your own.

Now of course not everyone has as much money as Fred and Jennifer, and not everyone is supporting their adult kids and the grands in fine style in a big house. Seniors who are not in that situation still seem to be afraid to stand up and do what they know is best for themselves, especially when it involves spending money, their own money, money they earned and saved. These people have given their children fine educations and all the good advice they could ever need. Enough already!

These "kids" are in their 40s, 50s, and even 60s. When it comes to selecting the life style best for themselves, Seniors need to give their kids one more thing. They need to give them the *Word*, "We're taking care of ourselves so that you won't ever have to. It's the best gift we can give you!" Nonetheless we hear the refrain again and again. It's just "Life at the Wrinkle Ranch: But What will I Say to the Kids?"

Life at the Wrinkle Ranch: Not Good Prospects

We have discovered that many people embark on the search for Senior Living Communities without having any real notion about what is available or what to expect.

I suppose it is possible to learn and to sort out the information as one goes along, but surely it would be more efficient to start by doing a little Internet or Yellow Pages research and by touring some places close to home.

One day we were asked by Ranch Marketing to meet with prospective new residents, the Milsons, who had done none of that preliminary research. They had driven across the state to visit our Wrinkle Ranch as their initial foray into the investigation of CCRCs without first learning anything at all about the subject.

We are frequently asked to meet with new and prospective residents because we "show well," are representative of the military presence here, and are an example of the more active folks at the Ranch. Besides, having been in marketing myself for years, I am a very dependable source of feedback to the Ranch Marketing Department.

We had invited the Milsons to come to our apartment for a drink before taking them down for dinner in the dining room, and it very quickly became apparent to me that this particular couple had some serious problems.

First of all when they came in, we realized that although the husband, Rick, is tall, handsome, and very young by Ranch standards – only sixty – he is totally blind and uses a white cane as he walks. It seems he lost his sight when as a young Naval officer he was in a gun turret explosion. Frankly he is lucky to be alive! And of course he is not a candidate for Independent Living without a full-time companion.

The wife, Emily, is almost fifteen years older than he and at first seemed quite sophisticated and charming. While My Hero entertained Rick in the living room, I took Emily on a little tour of our apartment, which we find quite spacious at almost 1,400 square feet.

After touring the apartment and winding up in the master bedroom, all the while cooing the requisite "oohs" and "ahs" and a few "love what you've done with the place" comments, Emily asked, "Do they have larger apartments?" I assured her that there are indeed larger apartments here. To which she responded, "Good, because I have to get away from him. I can't stand the sight of him. He is repulsive to me, and I can't bear to get in bed beside him at night!"

TMI! TMI! My TMI light was flashing rapidly! I met this woman three minutes ago, and now she is telling me her most intimate feelings. How am I supposed to be the gracious hostess, the enthusiastic tour guide, when all the while my TMI light is flashing like crazy? She went on to say that she would not have told me those things, but she realized as soon as she met me that we were, "sympatica."

I wasn't feeling *sympatica*; I was feeling scared. The outburst in the bedroom was my first clue that despite the home in the mountains of North Carolina, the one on the private island in the Bahamas, and the elegant condo on the East Coast, all described in the first two minutes of their visit, there was trouble in the Milson paradise.

Emily was also quick to share that she had the "assets" and Rick had "income." Again something I did not need to know. And there was more: in a former life, Emily and a previous husband were very wealthy business people and even owned Emily Airlines in South Florida with a "fleet" of executive jets. I did not ask how many planes constitute a "fleet", but I presumed it was more than one.

Emily also told us that she and that husband had been in the jewelry business, their best customers were the Mafia, and she herself had many expensive pieces of jewelry. I managed to purr, "How lovely for you," and I didn't bother to tell her that jewelry was not a hot topic at the Ranch.

Learning that my husband had been a Naval aviator, she inquired if he could still fly. "Yes, with an updated physical," My Hero responded. "Oh good, then you can come to visit us at our beautiful home on our private island in The Bahamas. It has an airstrip. You can get a plane, and we can fly in with you," Emily announced! "Once you have had your own airplane, it is so annoying not to be able to fly wherever you want to go." At this point Emily looked deprived; Rick looked pained. She continued "I've tried to explain that to Rick, but he just doesn't understand."

I understood. I understood that we did not want to be on a "private" island with those two. I could just see the headlines, "Wrinkle Ranch residents on vacation witness mayhem and murder on private island in The Bahamas!"

We went to the dining room and had dinner, which could have been pleasant if only Emily had not spent most of the meal whispering negative comments to me about Rick, acting resentful about helping her husband find and cut up his food, and making ugly faces as he told his little stories.

Tuesday night we saw them in the Tavern, having dinner with another fairly new couple here – a retired USAF officer and his wife. Emily quickly jumped up from her table, abandoning her current hosts to show me her charm bracelet, which was huge, heavy, and sported diamond encrusted charms in the shape of little purses, which opened and closed. "Lovely," I murmured again in what I hoped was a sincere sounding voice.

Thursday night we ran into them yet again as they came into the Tavern alone and sat at the table where we planned to have dinner after we migrated from the drinking table at which we were singing the "oldies" with the rest of the Thursday night Tavern crew.

This time Emily's main complaint was that they just wanted a drink, not dinner, and that she was unhappy that the Tavern also served food. This should not have been news since she had eaten dinner in the Tavern both Tuesday and Wednesday nights, and why should it matter that they also serve food? They did not have to order any, and besides, it was all free – provided compliments of Ranch Marketing.

Rick was not a happy camper because he was convinced that his Scotch and water had coke in it. Now I could see the color of his drink and it didn't look as if it had coke in it. But he insisted that there must have been some coke left in the nozzle of the dispenser at the bar. We refrained from telling him that we do not have a multi-product dispenser in our Tavern and that the bar tender had taken a clean glass and added water, Scotch, and ice and brought it to his table. The obliging bartender just came over and took his drink away and brought him another drink, which looked a lot like the first one. Rick seemed to be mollified. Next, much to my surprise, these two who did not want dinner ordered a lot of food and stayed to eat it. Go figure.

Over his meal, Rick did some story telling. One was about Emily's former husband, who had been killed in the Viet Nam conflict. It started, "Emily has been married more times than she can count...." Should we conclude that Rick is just a teeny bit on the passive aggressive side? Needless to say, we had to eat and run!

The last time I saw Rick and Emily, she was pushing a luggage cart over flowing with luggage and clothes on hangers. Emily was complaining that when she called down and asked the Front Desk to send someone up for their luggage, she was told there was no bellman. Well Big Surprise! This is not a hotel. This is Independent Living. People either push their own luggage carts or arrange in advance to pay someone to do such chores for them, just as they did when they lived in their own homes.

My very last view of them was as they climbed into their brand new, S class Mercedes and drove away, presumably to impress the folks at the next Wrinkle Ranch on their list.

Somehow I doubt they will be back. I have informed Marketing that based on my assessment of the Milson's expectations, I think they would have better luck at a Wrinkle Ranch in, say, Palm Beach Gardens – something with the look and the services of a Ritz Carlton. Clearly between the shortcomings of our bartender and the lack of a proper bellman, Emily and Rick (thank goodness) are probably not Prospective Residents at this Wrinkle Ranch. In other words, it's just "Life at the Wrinkle Ranch: Not Good Prospects."

Life at the Wrinkle Ranch: Fear of Aging

Many people who come to the Marketing Office at the Wrinkle Ranch do not really want to move to a Life Care Community. They protest vociferously: They are not old enough, not ready to live around so many old people; besides it is depressing to see people in wheel chairs, and with all those walkers and canes.

Why, then, did they come to our Marketing Office, you might ask? Good question. Some have a spouse who wants to adopt our carefree lifestyle. Others have a partner who requires the services available at a Senior Living Community. I believe many of these people are in denial about the human condition. A reality of human life is people age and bodies fail. Seeing people who need assistance to ambulate is viewing normal people in a normal phase of life. If we live long enough, the most active and healthy of us may need some sort of assistance. Accept the thought. To paraphrase the Borg's admonition to Captain Picard, "Denial is futile."

This is a story about a woman who came to the Marketing Office at the Ranch reluctantly, a woman who is in denial about her own potential for frailty, a woman who fears aging.

Doris came with her husband Joe, a heart attack survivor and recovering alcoholic, clean and sober for almost thirty-five years. They were both physically fit and exercised regularly. Doris exercised obsessively. On a daily basis she walked six miles a day, lifted weights, and then rode her bike for thirty miles. She was quite slender; in fact she was so slender, she might have been anorexic. Joe seemed to have a more balanced approach to life. He was really excited about the varied and lengthy list of organized activities available for the residents of the Ranch. Doris just wanted to keep moving strenuously for hours a day.

Since we too are physically active, we were asked to be Ranch Ambassadors, to have dinner with Doris and Joe, to answer their questions, and to share our impressions of our new home.

We had an excellent dinner, and I was doing my best job of soliciting the prospects concerns, their preferences and attitudes, making an effort to answer their questions and to counter objections. As we were waiting for our coffee, My Hero suddenly leapt to his feet. Simultaneously I heard a thud. One of our fellow residents had decided to stand up, the brake on his walker had failed, and he fell flat on his back. These things happen. They happen in Life Care Communities, and they happen in bridge clubs, restaurants, malls, and anywhere else where people with walkers move from sitting to standing.

But what happened next amazed me: Doris burst into tears! People rushed to the fallen fellow and cautioned him to lie still until the damage could be assessed. My Hero backed off seeing the situation was well in hand. But now it was my turn to leap from my chair. Doris, the prospect whom I was tasked with shepherding, was crying! I put my arm around her and assured her that the gentleman would be fine.

But her next words, punctuated by sobs were, "I can't live in a place where this kind of thing happens!" She was not a bit worried about the man lying on the floor. Her concern was for herself. She was cringing from a slap of reality. It was not about him; it was all about her – her fear of aging, of losing the ability to walk six miles at a fast pace and then ride her bike for thirty more.

During dinner Doris had stated that next to her favorite activity, aerobic exercise, she liked the shooting range, with shopping at the mall a close third. Seized with a flash of inspiration, I hugged her and said, "That could happen anywhere, even at the mall!" I doubt that remark soothed what were obviously deep seated neuroses about aging, but My Hero picked up the standard and started an engaging and distracting conversation, and soon her tears, if not her fears, were stemmed.

The downed resident lay on the floor long enough for the emergency care givers to ascertain that he was just fine. It was his walker, not he, that needed repair. He got to his feet, but before he could depart, I went to him and said softly, "The woman at the table with me is a prospective resident. She was very distressed by your fall. Would you speak to her on your way out and assure her that you are fine?" I thought a vertical resident would be less traumatic to Doris than one horizontal on the dining room floor. He graciously agreed to assist me in my damage control plan and spoke to Doris in a firm voice before leaving the room, balky walker and all.

Doris had told us that a beautiful view was, for her, the most important attribute of her home. For me it's closets, but to each her own. So afterward we showed her and Joe the lovely view from our apartment, and she asked if we had good sunsets. We are on the east side of the building, so....

I suggested for good sunsets, a unit on the west side was the right option, but she objects to the afternoon sun. Let me see: You want sunsets, but please hold the afternoon sun. Marketing at the Ranch is very obliging, but somehow I don't think even they can suspend the laws of physics for Doris. Sunsets = west facing = afternoon sun. The west and sunsets, human life and aging – they share a certain commonality, an inexorable connection in which one follows the other.

Doris's real objection was not to afternoon sun but to the thought of growing older, of becoming less ambulatory, of being human and living through all the natural phases of life. I hope she will be able to overcome her unrealistic attitudes, but for now it's just "Life at the Wrinkle Ranch: Fear of Aging."

CHAPTER
2

Finding My Way

Any move is traumatic. The older you are, the tougher the job of packing and unpacking, and more than anything else, the more difficult it is to find your way in a new environment and to find your place in a new community. I was a veteran of over fifty moves, most of which were from one community to another, many from one state to another. I have moved from single family homes into apartments, from apartments into rented rooms, then into dormitories, high rises, condos, town houses, and back to single family homes. I am a pro at finding my way in new environments. All that said, the immediate impact of moving into a Wrinkle Ranch, even one I chose myself, was dramatic.

Since I was one of the youngest, most active residents, I seemed to arouse suspicion and distrust among the other Ranchers. I was unused to dealing with an elderly population. I mistook deafness for standoffishness and dementia for rudeness; however, I correctly diagnosed meanness for what it was. One thing I have come to understand: It is not that some people just get mean as they get older. It is that some mean people just live too long!

My Hero knows me well. I am an assertive woman, and that can lead to problems. He is an expert at getting along with others, and he warned me to keep a low profile in the first few months at our new home. He advised me to feel my way and "not make waves." The stories in this section describe how that went.

The first one is entitled "Acceptance" and explains how I gained complete, if sadly only transitory, acceptance from my fellow residents. It is followed by "Culture Shock," which lists in detail how life here is so very different from my previous existence. It took some adjustments.

In "Scented Peacocks" read about my aversion to the "art objects" in our elevator lobby, while "Getting Kicked Around" describes the reaction I prompted while not meaning to offend anyone and explores my growing frustration with the attitude I was getting from some residents.

"Saying Hello" is an actual message I sent to another resident in a last ditch effort to understand exactly how many times around here one spoke politely to another resident and was totally rebuffed before one ceased to speak to the recalcitrant neighbor. Talk about frustration!

"The Gotchas" is a recounting of some of the many times one of the hundreds of people we had met here and in the surrounding community reacted as if I were remiss for not remembering them or their names. I was starting to think that society burned books in Florida and had started with all the writings of Amy Vanderbilt and Miss Manners – another shock to my sensibilities.

Then there was the difficulty I had adjusting to the fact that the couple across the hall were not Independent Living candidates in my view. "The Runaway Bunny" is a story which reveals how I dealt with that discomfort.

The next story, "Washin' and Dryin'," explains how I corrected a serious miscalculation with the mere expenditure of thousands of dollars and the tossing of a few things that didn't belong to me anyway.

The last story, "The VIPs," written two years after our move to the Ranch, demonstrates that it can take a long time to learn all the ins and outs of life at the Wrinkle Ranch.

Life at the Wrinkle Ranch: Acceptance

Needless to say, as a "newbie" and one of the youngest and most stylish women at the Ranch, I was not universally welcomed into the community. As a matter of fact I was greeted with a mix of suspicion and dismissal. I was crushed. Here I was in my new "Forever Home," and hardly any of the other residents even spoke to me, much less welcomed me. A month or two of this went by and then I sprained my foot.

How did it happen? That is unclear. When we got home from the airport after a two-week trip to the West Coast, my left foot hurt. I figured I just had those fashionable Cole Hahn leopard print shoes laced up too tightly during the long flight, my feet had swollen, and that was that.

Well that was not that. When I took off the shoes, the left foot was not only swollen, it was very red and had a purple line across the top of the arch. It was sore to the touch, and I found it very painful to walk.

We waited a few days, and when the foot did not improve, we went to the convenient emergency room at the convenient hospital around the corner – literally in walking distance, given two healthy feet.

They saw me immediately and brought in the portable X-ray machine. I was concerned that I might have had a stress fracture. But the X-rays showed there was no fracture. The doctor ruled it a sprain and told me to stay off the foot.

He then prescribed a walker. Who in his right mind suggests using a walker all the while insisting you stay off one foot? A moment's visualization - hopping behind the walker while travelling down the very long halls at the Ranch - and I ruled out the walker and requested crutches.

Next he queried if I was over sixty-five. Duh? He was looking at my chart, which contained more information than anyone should ever know about me. Then he admitted crutches would work better, but "we don't give crutches to people over sixty-five." It took a little convincing, but he gave me the crutches. I can be very persuasive, and with My Hero right there, the doc didn't stand a chance.

For the next three days I crutched up and down and all around the Ranch. All the nasty old ambulation bigots who had always treated me with an attitude somewhere between distaste and disdain suddenly found me acceptable since I was clearly now among the damaged and decrepit. In other words, I was one of them. One day after multiple trips up and down the hall I declared my arms were tired. My Hero borrowed one of the many wheel chairs stored off the front entry way, and then he wheeled me to dinner.

Well that did it! I was soooo acceptable. You cannot imagine. I was almost popular. People who had never smiled or spoken to me before now greeted me most warmly. Of course it did not last. After a few days as the foot improved, I decided to tough it out and to go about my business on both feet, just icing the swollen one at night.

My acceptability went back to its original state. Once again I was *residenta non grata* among the youth and ambulation bigots at the Ranch. But what a learning experience! At least now we know what it takes. It's just "Life at the Wrinkle Ranch: Acceptance."

Life at the Wrinkle Ranch: Culture Shock

We had been at our new home for only a couple of weeks when all my old friends wrote and asked how it was going. This was my answer.

There are so many things to get used to when one moves. Especially when one moves from one lifestyle to another!

Many people I know have commented that when they moved to a Senior Life Care Community, they had trouble with eating an early dinner or seeing so many people using walkers. Those things created no problem from my perspective. What follows are the things that have *presented culture shock and not a small amount of frustration for me.*

Badges: Here we all have plastic badges with our names in large letters. They have a magnet. Some of the more creative people use them to fasten their napkins bib-style at dinner! I had to get a metal wallet to protect my credit cards when I put this badge in my purse.

It's not as if I dislike having a badge; I wore one to work every day of the thirty-five years of my career, and I liked the feeling of belonging it gave me, but since I retired, I have never worn a badge, and if I remember to wear mine, I frequently forget to remove it when I go into the outside world and so go about advertising that I live at the Ranch. It just seems to be one more thing to remember here in my new life at the Wrinkle Ranch.

Keys: Apartment keys are presented to the residents on a curly plastic bracelet, like a phone cord. That is actually terrifically convenient, but sometimes I forget that I'm wearing my blue plastic curly key bracelet, and if you think a bangle bracelet makes a clinking noise, you ought to hear it when it joins the multiple key noise on the same wrist. Not to mention the damage to a crystal wine glass that swinging keys can do!

To make sure we don't lock ourselves out, we must actually lock the door from the outside with the key. Thank goodness for that protection. I have been known to lock myself out in my past, and after years and years of driving up and just pressing the garage door opener to get into my house, who knows what I might forget.

Parking: For forty years I ran out the back door and hopped into the car in the attached garage; now I have to go down an elevator or multiple flights of stairs, out the front door, and walk seventy-five yards to a car port where my car is parked. Add five minutes at a minimum to getting anywhere. And if it's raining....

Also forget leaving things like sun glasses, cell phones, your purse, etc. in the car if you could possibly need them before your next auto trip because it's very inconvenient to retrieve them.

Now if we had chosen to live in the Villas – really condo-like units – we could have had our own single car garage. Why didn't we choose that? Many active residents do. On this campus the Villas are a quarter mile from the Tower building, and the residents there seem to exude an attitude of superiority about living down the road. They see themselves as the 'young crowd,' physically active, and mentally sharp, different from the Tower residents in that regard. Several Villa folk voiced disappointment that we had chosen not to join them; however, I see many of them as cliquish and not very inclusive, and I am happy with our decision to live in the Tower.

We chose the high rise because of the following reasons:

1. Closets! I must have lots of closets. The outlying condo two bedroom units do not meet my closet requirements.

2. My Hair! Do you know what happens when I have to go out in high humidity after I fix my hair? Imagine putting up with that every night of your life in order to get to your dinner. Fix the hair, go outside, watch the hair flop. No thank you! And what about rain? There is a tram that runs at dinner time. It is open with "isinglass curtains y' can roll right down in case there's a change in the weather." I knew that would just not work for me.

3. Action! All the activities at the Ranch are in the Tower. I love to be where the action is!

4. The Future! In twenty years we may not be among the most active residents here. And we don't want to move again. We chose what we thought we could live with as long as we could be independent, even if that level of independence changed. Moving here is all about planning ahead, and we did just that.

But back to the things I had to learn to accept:

Shopping: It takes two. One to drop off the other at the door with all the packages, grocery bags, etc. and then to go and park the car while the other locates a luggage cart and loads up for the trip to the apartment. Of course grocery shopping doesn't take on the same weight when dinner is not a requirement. We keep breakfast ingredients, sandwich makings, and cheese, tomatoes, and fruit here; however, we get busy, and it turns out we have skipped lunch most days. After all, dinner time comes so soon. Can you say, "Spoiled tomatoes," Boys and Girls?

Given that our local town is a shopping wasteland, bordered at one end by Home Depot and a few miles away by Walmart with a strip mall anchored by two dollar stores between, I decided that UPS will deliver most of my shopping which will be done via the Internet! UPS comes right to my door. Amazon.com, I love you!

19

TV: *After twenty years of DIRECTV and the associated remote control, now we must use Bright House cable. The good news: The Ranch pays all the basic charges; the bad news: it's cable, and the remote control is totally different. The guide and all the features involved with recording, finding channels, etc. are totally different. For a veteran surfer such as I, it has been frustrating and at times infuriating just trying to fast forward, or record, or find my Dodger games! I'm getting there, but would you believe this remote has labels for the functions above the function keys. I am familiar with finding those labels under the keys – talk about going nuts for a day or two!*

Hallways: *Being fully ambulatory, I have no problem with covering the distances in the hallways. In fact I welcome the exercise. But the 'art' hanging in the halls presents another problem. Apparently some management team in the past made a deal with a schlocky art supplier, which produced hundreds of bad prints for the hallways. The best ones look like photographs of still life, but there are not nearly enough of those. The worst ones…well, they are just awful and are mostly pastel pink and blue. I try not to look. It seems they started to run short of "art" when they got to the higher floors and since we are on a higher floor, we are fortunate to have fewer 'works of art' on our hall.*

Another hallway issue is the color of the walls in the halls, and I am very grateful that we live on a green hall instead of a pink one. The pink halls are very, very pink. Think Pepto-Bismol! I like pink golf balls, and I have a very lovely pink silk blouse; however, in my book, pink is not for hallways. Especially not for hallways that extend seventy yards in each direction from the center of the building. Thank goodness for my green hall!

Laundry: *Housekeeping washes our sheets and towels, and we chose not to have a washer/dryer in our unit. Why ever would we make such a choice? After all, there is other laundry besides linens. It seems having your own washer/dryer takes a large, ugly chunk out of the lanai, and My Hero said, "Don't worry about walking down the hall for the laundry; I'll do the laundry." The really dumb part is, I believed him.*

The laundry room is only thirty yards from our front door. It is spotless and features two large washers and matching dryers. They are available almost all the time; however, they take forever. It took me two hours yesterday to wash and dry a large load that I foolishly set for a second rinse cycle. I haven't been without my own laundry since 1964. This will definitely take some getting used to!!

Exercise: *There are a variety of exercise classes offered here at the Ranch. There is an executive golf course, par 63. There is also water aerobics three times a week. I went Monday. I showed up with my flotation cuffs, webbed gloves, and hand buoys. There is a very nice indoor pool so* *there was definitely water. What was missing was any hint of "aerobics." Mostly this self-led resident group stands in the water and raises their collective arms over their heads. At one point they chanted the nursery rhyme, "Jack and Jill," in unison as they raised and lowered their arms. The class is really more like wet yoga for the hands and arms. My concept of water aerobics is to work suspended, moving constantly. Guess I will be doing my own water exercise.*

There is also a weekly yoga class. I showed up for that also. Dressed in proper yoga attire, I took my two yoga mats, a large towel as a prop and my kitty cat eye pad for the relaxation period. When I arrived the instructor informed me that this was "chair" yoga. I asked if I was required to sit in the chair, and he had to admit I was not. Then as I spread my well-used mat with my name in big black letters on both ends, he asked, 'Have you ever done yoga before?'

"I have shown up with my props and my well-used mats, with my name in large letters, and you are asking me if I have ever done yoga before?" He had to admit that the question didn't make much sense. So all the other participants sat on their chairs, and I sat cross legged on my mat. There were even a few standing poses, although 'tree pose' for the class is done holding on to the chair with no suggestion of actually balancing unassisted.

Now before you all write to tell me what a bad decision we made in moving here or to sympathize with my "pain," let me tell you that our apartment is starting to look fabulous, we are getting settled and soon will have a new plan for golf, which will get us out into the community and playing on a full-length course with a real women's golf association.

The people who work here are professional and caring. The food is wonderful, varied, and tasty. There are some very nice people who live here, and we are meeting them.

This week we attended a private dance and were invited to join that dinner dance club mostly populated by people from outside the Ranch. One of the ladies who attended the dance was even wearing a Chanel suit! There was live music, a good dinner, and the location is a quarter of a mile from the front door. There may actually be life before and after 7 P.M. in the environs of the Ranch, and you can be sure we are going to find it, and we will enjoy it.

Nonetheless, so far these are my experiences. It's just "Life at the Wrinkle Ranch: Culture Shock. "

Life at the Wrinkle Ranch: Scented Peacocks

It is not my intent to sound arrogant or elitist, but I do appreciate good art, and although we have never been wealthy enough to be collectors of fine art, I have to admit to having reached this point in my life with certain ideas, even prejudices, about what constitutes good art.

Sentimental art is one thing. I have not one, but two chipped and badly made ceramic handprints in my kitchen and more than one child's messy water color in my collection of most prized possessions; however, when it comes to décor and art in public places, I have certain expectations. These expectations were not met when we first moved to the Ranch.

Let me hasten to say that a couple of years after we moved here, our Corporate owners spent millions of dollars on renovations and upgraded décor, and although not every piece of art on the campus is to my personal taste, it is all quite acceptable; therefore, the story I am about to tell you about the decorations in the elevator lobby is a story from the past, one that has been overcome by events – including the acquisition of a gorgeous and expensive credenza, a beautiful mirror, and some splendid "decorator items" to adorn that credenza on every elevator lobby in the building.

This is the story of my reaction to what I found in our elevator lobby when I first arrived:

Being a keen observer of my surroundings, I was immediately aware of the two seven-inch plastic and glass peacocks that adorned the top of the curio cabinet in the elevator lobby on our wing.

I had no idea who put them there. All I knew was that the two birds flanking the silk flower arrangement on "our" curio cabinet were terminally tacky, and I wished they were gone so I did not have to look at them multiple times a day as I came and went.

Finally in frustration, I called Sylvia, our administrative assistant, an adorable young woman who seems to know everything about the Ranch, and I cautiously inquired if that particular pair of elevator lobby peacocks belonged to a resident or had been chosen by some House Committee or other.

She quickly replied that they were the property of a resident who had generously offered up her peacocks to the hall decor for our viewing pleasure, and she added that since her grandma had been an Avon representative, she had recognized them as Avon perfume bottles!

"Trust but verify," Ronnie said. Well, verify I did, and I can attest to the fact that Sylvia knows her Avon. After she told me of their origin, on my next trip down the hall, I surreptitiously turned the peacocks up, viewed their little bird bellies, and checked her statement. The label on the underside of each peacock plainly read "Avon." Upon further investigation I discovered that each peacock held four ounces of Avon scent. I did not have the heart, the gall, or the nose to open the tail section and sniff. A quick search of e-Bay revealed that there are dozens of them out there. They are available for $13.95 each, just in case I have piqued your desire to own one or two. I have included a non-photoshopped image so you do not have to take my word for this. There they are: two, gold plastic headed, blue glass-bodied, peacock statuettes filled with Avon scent and adorning the top of the curio cabinet in the elevator lobby on my floor in my new home. This was our hallway décor.

It's just "Life at the Wrinkle Ranch: Scented Peacocks."

Life at the Wrinkle Ranch: Getting Kicked Around

Because I am a very assertive person with lots of management experience, we decided that when we moved here we would both be better served if I kept a low profile and did not make waves, at least in the beginning. In restraining my natural proclivities, I set myself up for stress and the symptoms associated with that nasty syndrome. Others may get headaches in stressful situations; not me, I get stomach aches.

These are two incidents that made my stomach hurt:

After golf one Sunday we rolled up to the front door at 12:50. Knowing brunch was over at 1 P.M., My Hero dropped me off to find out if we could eat in our golf clothes. I knew shorts are forbidden at dinner, but I did not know about Sunday brunch.

The young man at the entry desk at the dining room said it was OK and sent me to a small table in the Tavern. As I walked in I noticed that the room was empty except for a table with two nicely dressed couples who were almost done with their meal.

As I walked to my table, one of the women said in a voice loud enough to be heard anywhere in the room, "What is *she* doing in *here* dressed like *that*?"

You should realize I was beautifully dressed in an expensive outfit: purple shorts with a coordinated shirt, white hat with purple flowers and purple socks and white shoes, but I was wearing *golf* shorts.

I walked toward their table and said, "We are new. We just came from the golf course, and I asked permission before I came in. If my dress offends you, I'll ask to be seated in another dining room." I thought that was a polite response, both sensitive and cooperative.

A man at the table said to the rude women, "She heard you!" Duh, of course I heard her, and him too because I have perfect hearing. They are all deaf and speak loudly and so expect that everyone else is in the same boat.

The rude woman failed to respond to my polite offer to leave the room and said churlishly, "Well at least you asked." Unwilling to let her off the hook, I said again, "If my dress offends you, I'll leave the room." She did not respond, but the man (her husband?) obviously embarrassed, said, "No, no. Please sit down and eat."

That was Sunday. I did not enjoy my brunch because my stomach hurt.

Monday afternoon My Hero wanted a bridge warm-up before he ventured into the local unit game, and I agreed to play with him at the less than prime time duplicate game here at the Ranch. At one table we played against a woman who seemed to know what she was doing and her partner, a woman I did not recall ever seeing before, who clearly did not know the first thing about bidding. They had an auction in which the second woman bid very badly. After the hand the partner gently suggested what the clueless one should have done. That suggestion produced a blast from her partner. Then I opened my mouth. I should not have. It is inappropriate to comment on the opponents' play, and I know that, but the clueless one was making excuses to her partner and said, "I took the easy way out." I made the mistake of saying, "It wasn't the easy way for your partner." She glared at me. Realizing I had overstepped, I said, "Oh, I'm sorry if I offended you; I shouldn't have said that."

Obviously angry, she said, "You didn't offend me. But you have offended me before!" Now did I just say, I don't remember ever seeing this woman previously? Whatever I had done to offend her "before," if there had been a "before," was lost on me.

But it seems to me that some women here are out to get me. It seems as if I have a "kick me" sign on my back. Frankly I think that among our female population is a group of old, wrinkled up, and less than functional bitter biddies who are envious as all get out, and apparently they think they can say anything they want to me and get away with it. Well, I am done with the polite apologies for breathing and for opening my mouth. From now on I am taking no prisoners. My Hero says I can't win and I should just keep ducking, but if I can't win, at least I will go down swinging!

There will be no more spending the day in bed with a stomach ache. From now on I am going to demand the courtesy and respect I deserve because I am done with this abuse. It's just "Life at the Wrinkle Ranch: Getting Kicked Around."

Life at the Wrinkle Ranch: Saying Hello

What follows is a note I sent to a new Ranch friend, Barbara, in an effort to figure out how to respond to a difficult social situation.

Dear Barbara,

Since you have been here longer than I and seem to know how things work at the Ranch, I thought I would ask you: Is Sara Walters very deaf, or have I come up against another issue?

After our initial meeting, we have seen her many mornings coming back from her walk as we set out on ours. I always speak to her and address her by name. She never responds. Yesterday she passed me in the Lobby by the coffee pots. My Hero was there too. I said, "Good morning, Sara," in a clear voice. She strode by and did not speak – again. My Hero was stunned. "What's up with that?" he asked. Frankly, that's what I want to know.

A couple of weeks ago I spent an hour in the pool with Sara. We were exercising – just the two of us. We talked. Actually she did most of the talking; after all they are from Sarasota and before that her husband was the Deputy Chief of Police for Montgomery County and therefore important! Of course she never asked what my husband did and certainly did not inquire into my background, and she did not seem very deaf in the pool.

What is the Ranch SOP? How many times do you greet someone here by name and gracefully accept being totally ignored before it is correct never to speak again – ever? Ten times? Twenty times? More?

As you and I discussed the other night, people from Sarasota are superior to those of us who came from other places. They are more cultured than the rest of us, more self-assured of their higher social strata, and they only moved here to this lesser area under protest (and because Sarasota doesn't have a Senior Community that can hold a candle to this Wrinkle Ranch). I'm sure of those facts because everyone I have met here from Sarasota has explained them to me, repeatedly.

The problem is I am not clear on all the privileges that stem from this Sarasota Superiority. Do people from Sarasota have some special permit to ignore someone's greeting more times than people from other places?

I'm still trying to learn the rules, but I'm starting to wish we had detoured to drive through Sarasota on our way here. I'm sure if I could have said we came to the Ranch via Sarasota, it would have elevated our social status at least a little, and then perhaps Sarasota Sara would deign to speak to me. It's just "Life at the Wrinkle Ranch: Saying Hello."

Life at the Wrinkle Ranch: The Gotchas

I was taught as a child that having good manners is simply a matter of making the other person feel comfortable. As a new resident at the Ranch I discovered how few people have learned that simple lesson.

For example: There are many employees and approximately 500 residents at the Ranch. There are hundreds of members of the local bridge unit, and when you add the members of the various dance clubs we joined, there were over 1000 new people for us to meet, people whose names we needed to learn and remember.

That daunting task notwithstanding, early on in our residence here people would approach me with this opening salvo: "You don't remember me do you?" Way to put the other guy on the defensive! Way to go one up with your first remark! Way to be rude!

The first time I was assaulted that way, a little blond woman approached me on the dance floor of the Big Band Dance and hit me with it. Slightly off balance, I tried a polite duck: I stuck out my right hand in a traditional handshake motion and announced my name. Undeterred in her efforts to make me feel like a rude, uncaring, and mentally challenged idiot, she ignored my hand and continued, "I'm Ann, for the *third* time!" So I fell on my sword and said through gritted teeth, "I'm so sorry that I didn't remember your name." Only slightly mollified, she danced away, looking self-satisfied.

My next experience with a Gotcha happened when a man I didn't recognize came up to me at duplicate bridge. "You don't know me, do you?" he said accusingly. "I'm afraid I don't," I said apologetically. "Aren't you a member of the Summerset Dance Club?" he demanded. "Yes," I admitted hesitantly.

"I'm the President. I'm the one who stands up and talks," he continued proudly. At this, verbally dancing on the balls of my feet, I replied, "Ah, but you're out of uniform! I've never seen you when you weren't wearing a coat and a tie." (I looked around to see if the judges were going to applaud that fancy step, but sadly no one seemed to have noticed.) Then he continued his bullying tone. "Doesn't your husband play this game?" he accused. "Why yes, he's a bronze life master," I replied with what I hoped was a tone of great respect in my voice for My Hero's accomplishments in the world of duplicate bridge.

This seemed to set him back a bit, but he charged ahead and demanded to know why I did not play with my husband. I responded that I did not wish to make him "play up." At this revelation, he turned tail and retreated. But later in the round the standard rotation brought him and his partner to our table.

I opened three Hearts and his partner overcalled one No Trump! I called the director who explained his options after his insufficient bid. He bid three No Trump. We set them four tricks, vulnerable, for a top score. The taste of revenge is sweet.

However, when the next rude person comes at me with the "You don't remember me" local Gotcha ploy, I intend to take an offensive position. I will look that person straight in the eye and say, in what I assure you will be a gleeful and defiant tone, "*No!* I don't!" Let's see how that works out in dealing with my fellow Seniors. It's just "Life at the Wrinkle Ranch: The Gotchas."

Life at the Wrinkle Ranch: The Runaway Bunny

Early on in our Wrinkle Ranch lives I was amazed at the situation across the hall from me. A couple lived there. He was very much overweight and had breathing problems. She, I learned later, had advanced Parkinson's, and when they moved in, she was not given a life care contract. Therefore, if she were ruled no longer suitable for Independent Living, other arrangements would have to be made, and those arrangements were bound to be expensive. For that and other reasons he was in denial about the severity of her condition and more than once knocked on our door to ask us to help him pick her up off the floor after a fall, even though we have 24/7 EMTs who would have rushed up to assist her, but then they would have reported the problem. Since we were new, I didn't know what to do or to whom to report the health and safety issues I saw. Except for the SOS calls to our apartment I only saw these neighbors in the hall. My poor female neighbor could barely walk and was unable to talk clearly, so I probably could not have communicated with her even if I felt the urge.

We moved in on the first of April, and *no*, I did not think it was an April Fool's joke! I was determined that we would love living in our "Forever Home," and yet...the people across the hall.

Finally, in July I had had it with the Easter decorations facing me every time I opened the door.

So not knowing what else to do in those days, I wrote to Sylvia, the all-knowing Executive Assistant. After she received my message, a wonderful thing happened - the bunny disappeared! I wrote the following thank you to Sylvia:

Subj: Missing Easter Bunny
Dear Sylvia,
Are you to thank for the sudden and mysterious disappearance of the large, floppy-eared bunny and her three-legged stool that, since April, sat in front of my neighbor's door staring at me every day I opened my door and stepped out into our hallway?

Apparently in the same manner that the famous dish ran away with the spoon, so did the three kittens on the rug who sat on the floor beside the bunny because they too are nowhere to be seen.

I could have sworn they were all at their regular post when I last came in Tuesday night, but when I opened my door to pick up the Wednesday morning paper, I was greeted by an almost bare doorway opposite me. The difference hit me immediately. I let out a deep sigh of relief!

The disappearance of this collection of animals is a relief to me for several reasons:

1. They were crowding the doorway, and one of the residents in that apartment uses a walker. I was concerned that she needs that doorway space to maneuver.

2. The kittens were always jumbled up and therefore to my way of thinking a menace for an unsteady person using a walker – a real risk of tripping.

3. Memorial Day and the Fourth of July have come and gone, and I could have sworn that the bunny was getting a little long in the tooth and that she looked at me reproachfully from her perch on the stool. That's fully understandable since I think almost anybunny would have developed a sore cotton tail from sitting for so many months on that hard stool. And surely those cute kittens were tired of being stepped on!

Please don't misunderstand, I am all for seasonal celebratory items on our doors and in our hallways, but just as every dog has his day, I think everybunny has her Easter. Time moves on, and so – at long last – have my neighbor's Easter decorations.

Thank you for any part you may have played in this welcome change to my hallway. And just in case you are not responsible, please don't feel the need to put out an APB for a three foot, flop-eared bunny in a dress and traveling in the company of three small, downtrodden kittens. Frankly I am rooting for them and hope they have finally made a clean getaway!

I signed the message, "A grateful resident."

It's just "Life at the Wrinkle Ranch: The Runaway Bunny."

Life at the Wrinkle Ranch: Washin' and Dryin'

Life at the Wrinkle Ranch has some situations that require special planning and handling. For example:

When we moved to the Wrinkle Ranch, I was reluctant to get an apartment without a washer/dryer – even the half-sized stack version that is standard in most of our apartments but My Hero did not want the bump out in the lanai or the noise in the bedroom that the standard, apartment laundry offering entailed.

Since there is a community laundry room on every floor, right down the hall, he promised me that *he* would do the laundry and I would not have to go up and down the hall carrying clothes and laundry products to the community laundry room.

Interestingly enough, even though his memory is very clear on most accounts, My Hero did not recall that promise after we moved in. Needless to say, after a short period of time, this laundry thing was not working out to my satisfaction.

One day I noted that my soon-to-be neighbor across the hall was getting a stack washer/dryer in her hall walk-in closet as part of the remodeling of her apartment, which is incidentally, just like mine. Being fed up with the weekly treks down the hall and the necessity to set aside enough time to complete laundry cycles – about a three-hour commitment – I announced to My Hero that I too wanted a washer dryer in our hall walk-in closet. Of course I wanted a full sized Bosch, top-of-the-line version and not that little mini thing that she was getting.

He actually laughed at the idea, pointing at our hall walk-in, which was stuffed to the gunnels with, well – with Stuff – *his* stuff. Then he went off to play golf.

He should have known better. His wife, the Hurricane, threw out, reorganized, and shifted all the Stuff. In a matter of three hours there was plenty of room for anything I wanted in there, this side of a baby elephant! And I wanted a washer and a dryer – oh yes – and custom, built-in cabinets to go with them, and maybe even a fold-down ironing board.

There were a few minor issues that I knew we would have to pay to overcome, like putting a drain through twelve inches of concrete floor and running plumbing to a closet that was never intended to go aquatic. I had heard that venting might not be a problem since new technology dryers are self-venting, but those were minor technical, engineering issues that clearly could be overcome by the application of cash to the problem, and about which I did not intend to worry my pretty little female head. He should not have laughed. It's just "Life at the Wrinkle Ranch: Washin' and Dryin'."

Life at the Wrinkle Ranch: The VIPS

I have to admit it. I have always been a badge lover. My love affair with badges started right after college graduation. I was hired in the defense industry to work on the Apollo project and received a badge that showed by its color that I was degreed, and therefore salaried, and no longer an hourly employee as I had been before my graduation. This put me on the same professional footing as my friends, and I felt good about it. This badge romance continued as I changed jobs and worked in the high tech computer industry. At that point I had a picture badge, which I loved – I was always photogenic. Later when I became a defense contractor, my badge showed the level of my security clearance and allowed me to walk in and out of the Pentagon without an escort, another mark of distinction. Badges make me feel as if I belong. To me, a badge is a symbol that one is a valued part of the organization.

Now, of course, we received badges as soon as we moved to the Wrinkle Ranch, and because I was eager to take a leadership role in my new home, I admired the resident badges I saw that had additional titles – badges that showed the wearer was a Wrinkle Ranch VIP.

In addition to a title line, many of these badges sported a raised orange button, which I assumed meant the person was at the top of the Wrinkle Ranch food chain, since none other than the Resident Council president had an orange button, and so did many other residents whom I came to understand were highly regarded here.

I even inquired as to the meaning of the orange button and was told that those with the orange button were members of our VIPs. What addition data did I need on that subject? I wanted one.

So after a year at the Ranch, when I was chosen to be a Floor Leader and a member of the Residents' Council, and my new badge was presented to me at the Council meeting, I was disappointed to see I had no orange button. Disappointed that is, until I learned that the button is indeed only for our most special VIPs. The orange button designates the resident as a member of a well-organized VIP group here - our Vision Impaired Persons!

My mama always told me, "Be careful what you ask for, you just might get it!" Believe me, I no longer covet that particular symbol. It's just "Life at the Wrinkle Ranch: The VIPs!"

CHAPTER
3

The Intersection of Life and Death

Since I moved to the Wrinkle Ranch I have learned a lot about Senior attitudes concerning living and dying. I have also learned you might consider the address of every Wrinkle Ranch to be, "The Intersection of Life and Death."

This chapter explores some attitudes I have discovered among our residents towards the subject of "turning the corner" at that fateful intersection.

At the Wrinkle Ranch most of us celebrate life every day. Ranchers believe life is something to be cherished, and most of our residents fight to stay alive. Even when they are quite old and seriously ill, they fight; they exercise every medical treatment available and muster every ounce of determination they can just to have one more day.

There are a few situations in which that is not the case, especially when a terminal illness is involved and the quality of life is so severely diminished that hospice care is requested, and the fight is abandoned. In that case Death frequently comes as a blessing, bringing peace to the patient and to those loved ones left behind.

Since living here I have learned that sometimes a resident will decide that is it "time," and even in the case of a non-life threatening condition the body's critical systems shut down. The first story in this chapter, "A Time to Say Good-Bye," is about Leah, who was such a resident.

The next story discusses the surprising feelings of a loving husband about the fact that his wife turned at the Intersection before he did. It is called, "After You, My Dear."

A third story in this section deals with "Ranch House Humor" and describes one Rancher's attitude when he is told by his doctor that he is on borrowed time. It is an actual recounting of what I inadvertently overheard as he shared that information with his best buddy. As it turns out he was indeed on borrowed time, time that supported fewer and fewer of his favorite activities as it ticked away. He was my friend, a golf buddy, and after he died some years later, I spoke at his memorial service.

Of course Death with all his trappings comes calling frequently here, and my dealing with that aspect of Wrinkle Ranch life is addressed in "Dropping Left and Right" and "My Dwindling Fan Club." Since I had little experience with losing people to Death before I moved here, I had to adjust. It was hard.

The last story in this section is more upbeat. "Birthday Big Deal!" describes how every resident birthday, an event typically minimized and all-but-forgotten in the world outside these communities, is a major opportunity for celebration and rejoicing at the Wrinkle Ranch.

Life at the Wrinkle Ranch: A Time to Say Good-Bye

One day we had a celebration to honor the life of Leah Rosen. Leah, a Jewish woman, was born in Germany in 1919. Her father was a man of status, a WWI Veteran who had served with honor in the German Army. After the war he had amassed substantial wealth and respect in the community. By the time Leah was thirteen, she had it all – a beautiful home, two loving parents, a comfortable life, and many friends. Two years later she had practically nothing.

Leah's father was a realist. He saw what was happening in Germany, and in 1934 he moved the family to Prague to live with his in-laws, abandoning their large home, his business, and their friends because he saw what was coming and because he believed Czechoslovakia was safe from the Nazis! Of course that was not the case. Again the wisdom and military connections of Leah's father guided them to safety, finding airline passage out of Europe to England in 1939.

So Leah, now a young woman, and no longer one of wealth, privilege, and social position, was safe in England and working as a maid in the home of a British family. As she was fond of saying, "When a door closes, God opens a window." That particular window provided Leah with a view of a young American serviceman named Gerald. Romance, love, marriage, and a move to the USA followed.

In this new phase of her life Leah was a married woman with young children in a small walk-up in New York City. She said those were the best years of her life. When you came to know Leah,

33

she identified many times as "the best years of her life." Many meals and vacations were "the best of her life."

Leah had a survivor's attitude and mentality. Life was good. She was fortunate. Leah believed that all one needed to do to succeed was to "hang in there, don't quit, see it through." She not only believed in this approach to life, she also stressed it to her children.

Regardless of what opportunities were shut off in life, others – better ones – appeared. The Rosen family moved to upstate New York and prospered, enjoying a summer cottage on a lake, golf, tennis, and working together to build a happy life, one the children would never forget. Her husband was a successful pharmacist. Leah had a rewarding life in which she participated in the community and raised their children as her husband built his business and served as president of the local school board.

When Gerald died in 1981 after a number of years of devoted care by Leah for a serious medical condition, she moved to Boca Raton. Her loving sons and their families visited often. Every visit was the "best time" ever.

During this period, Leah was diagnosed, treated for, and defeated cancer twice. Our Leah was a survivor in the truest sense of the word.

In 2005, Leah then eighty-seven, knowing only one person at our Wrinkle Ranch, decided that this was to be her "Forever Home" and moved herself from the East Coast to the West Coast of Florida, becoming a resident in a comfortable and spacious apartment home on an upper floor in the Tower.

She immediately made friends, reaching out, telling stories as she loved to do – over and over – until her friends knew them all by heart. She bragged about her three sons and their families. She recounted events from her life, and every word was true. She and her friends went to the symphony, the ballet, and the opera. She loved music. She went out to eat. Leah loved to cook and to eat! Her family came to visit her regularly, and when they did, she cooked for them. "They love my cooking," she would say, and it was true. The family sent flowers for all occasions; they knew she loved flowers. Leah was not a temple goer, but she believed in the goodness of God. She had experienced His protection, and she never forgot His love and His grace.

Life went on. When I moved to the Leah's floor and inherited the floor leadership position, the people from Leah's end of the hall, older and longer-term residents, were not happy about the new young woman floor leader and her assertive ways, but Leah was the voice of calm and reason, pointing out my accomplishments and the things I did to make all our lives better. I admired and respected Leah, but I was very sad about one thing: Leah could not hear me. Over the years, despite trip after trip to well-qualified audiologists, Leah's hearing deteriorated badly. She became unable to hear the music she loved because the distortion was terrible, and along with that issue, a voice in the range and pitch of mine was almost unintelligible to her. At first I tried speaking more loudly, but that made it even worse. When the volume went up, so did the pitch, and it became even more difficult for her to hear me. I gave up and just smiled and hugged her when we met. There is so much more to communication than words.

For four years after I moved here, Leah was a ray of sunshine on our hall. She befriended her next door neighbor, Lydia, a brilliant and talented woman, also over ninety, who had some challenges in life. To complicate things, Lydia was almost blind. Leah was the bright spot in Lydia's life. Together they would venture out with their walkers and walk the Circle around our building and then sit together to have breakfast and coffee in the Bistro. They would joke that with Leah's deafness and Lydia's blindness, together they made one fully functional woman. Intelligence and a sense of humor were hallmarks of their relationship.

Then one day on their trip around the building, they fell. First Lydia, and then Leah, who lost her balance in an effort to stop her friend's fall. Lydia survived, bruised but otherwise unscathed; Leah broke her elbow.

Falls and broken bones are the bane of Senior existence, but a broken elbow is not the same as a broken hip. Major surgery is not involved. Mobility is not impacted. We all breathed a sigh of relief and waited for Leah to come home from our skilled nursing facility. But she did not.

First it was the pain. Somehow the doctor had not left the right prescription for pain medication. Our strong, enduring Leah spent the first night in the nursing facility in screaming agony. Then the pain migrated. Other body parts became part of the problem. There was a constant stream of visitors – a son and daughter-in-law, our floor "sunshine lady," the appointed resident visitors, and the many, many friends and caring neighbors from our floor, our building, the rest of the campus, and the community at large. Leah was a joiner and a doer. There were many people whose lives she had touched, and they came because they cared.

But the bounce back we expected did not happen. Rehab did not seem to work. It only seemed to make things worse. Her son, the doctor, came. She told him she was tired, tired of the pain, and she wanted to "go." Everyone who heard that had the same reaction. "No!" we cried out. Not our Leah! It was just an elbow. "Come home, Leah. Don't leave us!"

Leah was her own woman. She had met life on her terms for ninety-seven years, and she had decided that enough was enough. She requested hospice. Our Executive Director went to see her. She told him she was tired. She was clearly of sound mind, and that sound mind was made up.

Leah went to hospice. She stopped eating, and her body shut down. After a few days Leah got her wish. She died. The rest of us were left to deal with our feelings and our reactions to her death. Leah died as she had lived – on her own terms. She did not want to linger and be a burden, a "vegetable," as she put it – someone her friends and family did not know. Our Director wisely told us we must respect the desires and dignity of a person of sound mind. A local gerontologist weighed in and told us that it was very common for someone in their 90s who had seemed perfectly healthy and happy to have a sudden health issue and to decide that it was "time."

An elbow! It was just an elbow. But apparently it is not "just an elbow." It is a 90-something-year-old system, and with any apparently small jolt to that system, the 90-something-year-old "systems manager" can determine that "the time has come." The message goes out system wide, and the system shuts down. Those of us who live in a community like this one with trained professionals and hospice care are fortunate.

We were blessed to have known Leah. She was a woman of grace, dignity, character, and intelligence. She knew her own mind. She knew when to stand up, and when to sit down, when to tell a story, and she knew when it's just "Life at the Wrinkle Ranch: A Time to Say Good-Bye."

Life at the Wrinkle Ranch: After You, My Dear

You might be surprised to learn that at the Wrinkle Ranch a devoted husband or wife will frequently express the hope that he or she will be the *last* of the two to die. I think of it as a special case of the common courtesy we extend when we hold a door for another person, a Wrinkle Ranch version of "After You, My Dear." "What?" you say! "They actually hope that their spouse will die first! What kind of devotion is that?"

The concern seems to be that the one who is left behind is really getting the short end of the stick. The surviving one will have to go on living a life without the other who made his life wonderful for so many years. Such an existence is fearful for the resident to contemplate; therefore, in a true posture of unselfishness, he wants to take this odious task upon himself and spare his spouse the pain of loneliness.

Take for example the story of Tony and Maria. Tony told us about their lives one day at brunch. They were happily married for sixty-eight years! Then Maria died. She was ninety-six!

Typical of the times in the '40s and '50s, Tony was the breadwinner in their family and supported Maria and the children nicely with the income from the small business he started and ran for over thirty years. Maria was his partner in everything they did. A stay-at-home mom, she kept the books for the business. Tony explained it, "In those days if a business paid its bills by the 10th of the month, it received a 2% discount. Maria never missed a discount in thirty years, and that added up to a lot of money for us."

He also told us that she cooked his every meal, paid all the bills for the household, and catered to him for their entire marriage. She was his "best friend." He clearly adored her, and said he misses her very much.

He talked about how beautiful she was, looking a mere seventy-five when she was in her mid-90s. He said she loved asking people to guess her age. They never could. She had no medical issues even at ninety-six and did not use a cane or a walker. She didn't need one.

Then one day she developed a pain in her shoulder, and her doctor prescribed pain pills, pills that were clearly too strong for her! She became dizzy and fell. She shattered her hip in the fall and died after the surgery to repair it. Her 96-year-old mind and body could not recover from the trauma of the procedure and the anesthesia.

"I'm glad she went first," he told me. "She wouldn't have liked living without me, even with all the friends we have here. Life is just not the same. I wouldn't wish that on her. I'm glad I'm the one who's left. I can handle it better than she could."

I am not a psychologist, and I do not pretend to know if this is just a case of transference or if it is true, unadulterated devotion.

As a rule, the women at the Ranch seem to fare far better after the death of a spouse than the men. All the other widows gather around them, and they eat their meals in groups of four, five, six, or more. They go on the Ranch outings together and support each other in sharing memories and stories about their departed loves.

The surviving men, as Tony readily admitted, struggle to learn life skills necessary to accomplish tasks that their wives performed for them their whole lives. Skills like operating the washing machine and preparing simple meals are not in their repertoire, and they are so very lonely.

Yes, their friends are caring and supportive; however, male bonding and female bonding are different. This topic has been the subject of many dissertations, scholarly reviews, and even books on the Best Seller List. Who could forget *Men Are from Mars, Women Are from Venus*? Men, apart from the beer drinking that goes on after a round at the golf course, do not "hang out together" very much. Most men have spent their lives viewing other men as competitors, not as supportive friends. The development of real friendships with other men is just not a skill most of them have, even if they live to be ninety-five.

So in the case of Tony and Maria, is Tony right? Is he handling this life without his beloved spouse better than Maria would have? Who knows? But I do know that I have heard other Ranchers wish that they would be last to go in order to protect a spouse from the trauma of being the one left behind.

It's just "Life at the Wrinkle Ranch: After You, My Dear."

Life at the Wrinkle Ranch: Ranch House Humor

Surely there is a distinction between gallows humor and Wrinkle Ranch humor, but at times that distinction seems blurred to me. After all, here at the Ranch we live close to the edge – the edge where life and death meet regularly.

Let me tell you about Marv, a handsome 80-something fellow who was single and advertised himself to anyone who would listen as a career ladies' man.

He looked much younger than his years and frequently lied about his age, if he thought he could get away with it. When we met him, he had "settled down" and seemed to be going steady with a lovely lady from town, Colleen. She was an attractive, active Senior, rumored to "have money." She lived in a nice home and took him to Europe for vacation regularly while he continued to live frugally and loquaciously at the Ranch in a studio apartment.

He loved to tell stories to his fellow Ranchers about his exploits with the ladies B.C. (Before Colleen). And then one night I overheard him deep in conversation with a friend at dinner, bemoaning the results of his latest visit with his cardiologist.

He began, *I had a heart valve replaced a couple of years ago. Six months ago my echocardiogram showed that my heart was functioning at 50%. I was OK with that because I felt fine, but last week I had another checkup and the cardiologist said, "Your heart is functioning at 15%. You'd better start giving your money away because you're not going to live much longer! "*

He went on to his rapt audience, eavesdroppers included:

I still feel fine. I swim twenty laps a day – every day. I play golf four times a week, I go dancing with Colleen regularly, and I screw like a mule. But this doc says I don't have much time left.

I lie in bed every night and listen to my own breathing. I never paid any attention to my own breathing before. But now I'm afraid I'll hear it stop.

I'm thinking of going to a hypnotist to see if he can hypnotize me into getting rid of all the anxiety I'm feeling about my heart stopping any minute. I'm afraid the anxiety will kill me before my heart does!

What should the audience have made of this? Marv was a great raconteur and had been known to make a good story better. Should we have felt concern? Sympathy? Should we have let on that our excellent hearing allowed us to eavesdrop on what may have been intended as a private dining room conversation? Perhaps we should have pretended we did not hear a thing, or....

Since I knew Colleen, maybe I could have called her and inquired about the mulish attributes to which Marv referred, or maybe I should have given her my condolences that those services are now on the endangered list. What is the appropriate Wrinkle Ranch etiquette in such a situation?

I have to admit that although I hoped Marv had many, many more years to swim twenty laps a day – every day – and that he could continue to play golf four times a week and go dancing with Colleen and indulge in all the rest of his strenuous activities, I found some amusing aspects of his self-announced death sentence.

Since we are all on the Reaper's "short list" here, I guess this proclamation constitutes yet another example of that situation. It's just "Life at the Wrinkle Ranch: Ranch House Humor!"

Life at the Wrinkle Ranch: Dropping Left and Right

Up to now, very few of my close associates have died. Well yes, my grandmother and my parents died, and I had an ex-husband or two who are no longer on this side of the grass, but by then they had already acrimoniously disappeared from my life, and I did not miss them. I even had a couple of high school girl friends who died, but by that time I had moved far way, and I seldom saw them anymore.

Moving to a Wrinkle Ranch meant that not only would I have to become accustomed to living in an environment where many people are deaf, use a walker or a scooter for ambulation, are legally blind, and may suffer from various forms of diminished capacity, I would also have to get used to the regularity of death. From now on I will repeatedly lose people with whom I previously interacted on a daily basis.

At first the pictures, and obits, and flowers on the Lobby "Departure" table meant nothing to me personally. I was new and knew hardly anyone here. Most of the faces pictured were already in the nursing facility, or Assisted Living, or the memory unit when I arrived. And then....

I had not lived here long before we lost a 96-year-old man who played against me at my duplicate bridge club multiple times a week. Next, the gentleman who was the subject of "Action City" died shortly afterward, and I recognized his picture on the table.

The truth of the matter is that by the time they move here most of our residents have already lived beyond their actuarial life expectancy projections. We have several very active residents who are over 100, and many more who are still dancing and going to exercise classes in their mid-90s.

I really should not be surprised when my neighbors die. Most of them are very old. After all even Methuselah died, and eventually so will we all. It is a normal part of life and is to be expected. I will have to become accustomed to this frequent occurrence. It's just "Life at the Wrinkle Ranch: They're Dropping Left and Right."

Life at the Wrinkle Ranch: My Dwindling Fan Club

My Hero and I worked diligently to be good members of the Wrinkle Ranch community, to be helpful to other residents, to participate in activities, and to support the Ranch charities.

By doing so I finally developed a modest fan club. My Hero just naturally garners a big fan club wherever he goes so it is no surprise that he is well liked by everyone here. But given the negative reaction I had from so many of the old folks when we first moved in – I thought of them as "youth bigots" – I am pleased that many of our fellow residents now express admiration for my approach to issues and seem to appreciate my efforts around the Ranch, my attention to fashion (especially my hat collection), and my participation in such activities as the Thursday night Tavern singing and the regular Trivial Pursuit game – even though our team usually wins.

But one of the downsides of Wrinkle Ranch life, that is to say, one of the downsides of living at The Intersection of Life and Death, is that people with whom you have an investment, people you know and like, keep dying.

Take for example Elias Jones. Elias and I did not move in the same circles at the Ranch. He was in his early 90s and did not play golf, or bridge, or hang out in the Tavern, nor was he part of the resident governing body or on any committees, but when I was assigned as part of my job on the Residents' Council to review the 20-year-old dining room dress code, he wrote to me.

Elias wrote to me on a yellow lined tablet, and he used a pencil. He wrote two full pages. In this letter he expressed his joy of dressing up and going into the dining room for his evening meal. He waxed rhapsodic over the sight of the beautiful ladies in their finery, wearing their "jewels" to dinner. And he cautioned against doing anything that would detract from that environment.

Now I must confide that much of this view of our Ranch House dining experience existed only in Elias' fantasies since finery and jewels are in short supply at the regular evening meal although some of our ladies crank it up a notch or two for holidays and special events. As for the "beautiful ladies," mostly that is an "eye of the beholder" thing. Remember our average age here is eighty-seven, so many of the popular notions about what constitutes beauty in a woman – smooth skin, white teeth, long silken hair, and a toned, curvaceous body – are not in evidence here.

His letter was polite and nicely worded, and I certainly got his message. He was old school, and he did not want his dining rooms populated by a collection of old people sloppily dressed in tie-dyed tee shirts and ragged jeans. Well, of course, neither did I, and I spent quite some time writing an appropriate reply to his letter and reassuring him that I had no intention of taking away the elegance of our "fine dining" experience.

Apparently I quelled his fears because shortly thereafter I ran into him at a social, and he thanked me profusely for my response and my approach to the issue. And every time after that when I encountered Elias, I got a hug and a kind word and a compliment on what I was wearing.

I saw him one day across the Lobby, and we exchanged waves. I was stunned to learn that he died three days later. His picture and bio appeared on the "Departure" table by the mail boxes. He was a charming gentleman who always wore a coat and tie. I miss him.

Keeping ones' fan club in robust condition is clearly a difficult task around here. One no sooner wins over the approval and support of a fellow resident than he up and departs for "higher ground." It's just "Life at the Wrinkle Ranch: My Dwindling Fan Club."

Life at the Wrinkle Ranch: Birthday Big Deal!

Perhaps because I was an only child, my mother always made a "big deal" out of my birthday, and since I became an adult, my birthday has not been a big deal to anyone but me. Nobody had planned a party or made me a cake to commemorate the anniversary of my birth for many years.

Most people I know just seem to overlook adult birthdays except for the usual trite jokes about gray hair, wrinkles, and failing memory.

Given my childhood experiences, it was a little difficult to realize that nobody was going to make a fuss over my birthday any more, and eventually I decided that most adults try to ignore birthdays because they do not want to focus on getting older. The only ones they seem to recognize are the Big Birthdays, ones with numbers that end in zero or sometimes, five. Turning thirty or forty, or fifty still gets lots of attention. Major greeting card manufacturers even offer cards specifically designed to note these hallmark birthdays so they must be important to the general public.

At the country club where we spent so many years, the members frequently held lavish bashes at the Club for "her 60th" or "his 65th," but other than that everyone seemed to prefer to forget about birthdays – theirs and everyone else's.

We had to move to a Wrinkle Ranch before my birthday became a big deal again! At every event we attend here the person in charge always asks if anyone has a birthday that month. Then we all sing Happy Birthday, and immediately turn around and repeat the ritual for anniversaries. The message is clear. When it comes to birthdays and anniversaries, as far as the Ranchers are concerned, the more, the better – savor every one!

The Wrinkle Ranch monthly newsletter lists the birthdays and anniversaries of residents in that month. People take note. This attitude seems be prevalent in the surrounding community as well. Even my local esthetician sent me a birthday greeting complete with a half-off coupon for a facial. Was this a greeting, a gift, a warning, or just a commentary? Who's to say? But I used it.

Here at the Ranch, residents plan birthday parties for each other and gather in small groups in the private dining rooms for dinner with a cake and champagne and lots of cards. No gifts, just cards - the more elaborate and the funnier, the better. Cards today come complete with electronic sound effects and cost more than real gifts used to.

On my first Wrinkle Ranch birthday I received over twenty cards from neighbors on my hall, some from folks I hardly knew except to say "good morning," and from friends I had made here, and from the president of the Residents' Council, and even from staff members. Two of the cards "sang" to me. I was very surprised at the outpouring of birthday greetings I received from my fellow Ranchers.

This in stark contrast to the three cards I received from my life-long friends and my family, none of whom has entered the Wrinkle Ranch environment and so are still living in the BDP (birthday denial phase).

Why do these old people delight in birthdays while the younger crowd tries to ignore them? Apparently, in our youth-oriented society, which is full of baby boomers spending millions on face lifts, boob jobs, hair transplants, cosmetic dentistry, and spandex bulge smoothers all in an effort to deny that aging is taking place, there is some point at which the slope of the birthday attitude curve changes. What was a negative is suddenly a positive – "A year older? That's terrific!"

At which birthday does this attitude change take place? Is turning 70-something to be non-confronted, but reaching eighty or more is somehow an event to celebrate? Or since seventy is the new fifty, and eighty the new sixty, does one have to get even older before we all toast the anniversary of a birth openly and happily?

I do not know the magic number; perhaps it depends on the group. But I do know that the 90+ year old people at our Wrinkle Ranch get lots of respect, and the few who are over 100 are genuine celebrities. Every birthday they mark is a happy, well-chronicled Ranch event celebrated by all with champagne and cake!

Based on my observations, we must surmise that indeed there is a magic day when the joy of surviving for another year outweighs the sorrow over one's ebbing youth. I know it is true because nothing is a greater cause for celebration at the Wrinkle Ranch than another birthday. Outsmarting the Reaper for another year seems to make everyone here happy. I think I have discovered an important aspect of attitudes here. It's just "Life at the Wrinkle Ranch: Birthday Big Deal!"

CHAPTER
4

Going, Going, Gone!

One of the most surprising aspects of our new life at the Wrinkle Ranch was the large number of Independent Living residents who have some form of dementia. Of course dementia comes in various manifestations. Not all dementia is Alzheimer's. Sometimes it is a by-product of Parkinson's; other times it's caused by a brain injury or is medication related; unfortunately, however, too many times in today's world, Alzheimer's is the disease we encounter when people seem to be losing themselves and their grasp on the world.

When we moved to the Ranch, we were not prepared to deal with the number of residents we encountered who were somewhere on that road between their normal, fully-functional life in Independent Living and the point at which they would need to turn the corner to a higher level of care because of dementia. In many cases these residents live with a fully-functional partner, and the partner fights to keep his loved one by their side, sometimes from fear and sometimes from denial. Residents here never know if the residents in other apartment homes have full coverage in the Life Care Program. If a resident with dementia does not have that valuable coverage, the family may fight to keep the resident in Independent Living to avoid the higher costs of Memory Care.

At any rate, when we first moved to the Ranch, we ran into case after case of strange behavior for which we had no understanding until we finally came to appreciate the extent and the devastation of that terrible disease, Alzheimer's.

Stories I would have grouped under a different heading before I gained that understanding rightly belong here in this section, which is titled for what we see happening to our friends and neighbors as they progress through the stages of this hateful affliction. They seem to be traveling down a long road that takes them farther and farther away from us. We watch them travel, and as they recede from our view, there is a finality about their journey. We see them "Going, Going, Gone!"

The first story in this section is a recounting of our first night in the dining room as residents in our new home. It is entitled, "Action City." Shortly afterward we observed the events I recorded in "The Round Spoon." Another early-on event found us eating in the dining room with a couple who was "Engaged for Life."

A little later I was involved with the action described in "Retrieving the Keys," and years afterward there was the near disaster recounted in "On the Brink."

One of the most dangerous aspects of dementia among the elderly is that many Seniors with diminished cognitive abilities still drive! "The Run Down" describes the events associated with a couple who visited here regularly but were not residents. Had they been Ranchers, I think our alert Management would have "retrieved *their* keys!"

Our Executive Director was always striving to improve process and services here. He frequently referred to those improvements as "Getting to the Next Level." My story of the same name proposes another meaning for that phrase.

In the next story we explore the apparent compulsion to walk incessantly by people who now can't remember why they are walking or where they are going. It's called "The Land of the Wandering Wandas."

"Dining Misery" takes on a whole new light once you understand that Joan who is causing our "misery" is very ill with dementia and eventually moved to a higher level of care. At the time, I was not aware of her condition; although it was clear that Bob, who did everything he could to accommodate Joan's desires and to smooth her path that evening, recognized the situation. In retrospect, I wish I had been more understanding.

One of the early signs of a cognitive issue is the erratic driving of a fellow Rancher. Read about how exciting this can get in "Righting a Wrong on a One-Way Street."

On the lighter side, I have included "Smoke Gets in Your Eyes." This story points out that some loving couples can live together very happily, and with a few good laughs to boot, even when one of them has a moderate form of dementia.

The very last story in this section is "Silver Alert," which also reminds us that life at the Wrinkle Ranch has some very funny moments. Perhaps you should be forewarned that the Silver Alert in this instance was resolved when the "Senior" in question was found lying in the grass very near the last place he had been seen, and after a few apologies by some previously apoplectic residents, everything was restored to normal. Saints be praised!

Life at the Wrinkle Ranch: Action City

On our very first night as full-fledged residents at the Wrinkle Ranch, we went to the dining room for dinner. We stopped at the desk of the maître d' – if that is what one calls the teenager who sits behind the podium and directs the Ranchers to a table in one of the lovely dining rooms. The youngster, clearly making an effort to look the part, had grown a mustache, and in his deepest voice he ordered the – also teenage – waiter to seat us at table 14 in the Blue Room. And off we went.

I was delighted to see that we were at a table set for four, and eager to meet our fellow residents, I told the waiter that we would be pleased to share our table. My Hero sat down long enough to muss his napkin and take a sip of the coffee he ordered and then made a bee line for the salad bar. No sooner had he departed than the waiter reappeared with a very pleasant looking older couple who sat down with me.

Just then a distinguished looking gentleman walked up and declared, "I'm supposed to be at table 14." Not knowing if the waiter had misdirected my two new companions or if the newcomer was in the wrong place – and wanting to make a good, if perhaps erroneous, impression – I momentarily hesitated to take charge. And then the new arrival began a descent into My Hero's chair!

Well, I have been around the block a few times, and I recognized this for what it was – a very bold pick-up maneuver. After all I appeared to be a lone female, and moreover probably the youngest, best-dressed lone female in the room. Of course this sly dog was making a move. I had seen this movie before!

My mind was racing! I projected that at any minute now, My Hero would return with his salad, and in his best Naval aviator style would shout, "You SOB, trying to make a high side run on my stuff, get out of that chair!" What a scene! I was a little unsure about what would happen next because actually, it has been years since men fought over me.

But ere the newcomer could get his not-so-spry body into the chair, a lovely young lady came and gently led him away. "You're supposed to be at Table 11," she said softly.

47

"That's his great-granddaughter," my new dining companion whispered. "She is a server here. He forgets where they tell him to sit, but she looks after him."

Well, I guess for a minute there I forgot too; I thought I had moved to Action City! And I have to admit I was a teeny bit disappointed. Not that I would swap My Hero for anyone else, but it did seem exciting that on my first trip to the dining room some guy would hit on me right away. Then I realized that the "sly dog" was just a confused old man. Alas after a few more days in residence here, I am learning that at the Ranch inattentiveness and failure to respond are probably symptoms of deafness, not disdain, and what in another environment would be a bold pick up move is, sadly and more likely, confusion, disorientation, and dementia.

In fact, if there is any action here at the Ranch, I have not found it yet; however, I have not stopped looking, just in case it's "Life at the Wrinkle Ranch: Action City."

Life at the Wrinkle Ranch: The Round Spoon

One night we decided to eat in the Aloha dining room, which had a splendid buffet that evening.

We were sitting alone and were almost done with our meal when a couple I had never seen before walked in hesitantly. "Where are we supposed to sit? Nobody told us where to sit," kvetched the woman. I could have told her tables are not assigned in the Aloha, but she wasn't asking me.

Next she fretted about whether or not to sit at a four-top where two places had clearly been used. "What if those two come back?" she queried to no one in particular, "Which seats do you think we should take at that table?" she asked her companion. I would have suggested the two with the clean napkins and the fully intact place settings if she had asked me, but then what do I know?

Then she began a rant about the soup. Two soups were featured on the buffet and the names were listed above the general area of the tureens. One was Italian wedding soup and the other was minestrone. "There are two soups, but I don't know which is which," she complained. I could have told her the wedding soup was the green one, but frankly by this point I was too busy watching the scene unfold.

They helped themselves to soup, and on the way to the table, the man lifted his small, handle-less soup cup, saucer and all, to his mouth and took a sip. I didn't think that was too untoward. Sometimes spurred by raging hunger and the tantalizing aroma of the wonderful homemade soups here, I feel like doing the same thing, except since I am possessed of an overactive superego that was stoked by my very proper Southern mother, I don't.

When they both sat down, the woman picked up her soup spoon and brandishing it in the air instructed her dinner companion in a most didactic voice, "The round spoon is for the soup!" she declared.

Frankly between her New York accent and her attitude I had already pigeon-holed her as the stereotypical Jewish mother. But then something happened that changed my mind. She took the man's hand, closed her eyes and began to pray in a clear voice, "Lord, make us thankful for these and all our other blessings, pardon our sins, and save us in Heaven for Christ's sake. Amen." Then she crossed herself. I was forced to remind myself, not all "Jewish mothers" are actually Jewish!

Now thoroughly sanctified, they both addressed their soup. Again she picked up her soup spoon, and this time she beat a tattoo on the table cloth, and in cadence with her beat she once again insisted, "The round spoon is for the soup." As far as I could tell, no one was disputing that fact. I left the dining room shaking my head.

The next day another resident told me that the husband of this new couple has been diagnosed with Alzheimer's. I am learning not to be surprised at the type of behavior displayed by this couple. It has taken me a while, and I am learning that not everyone here at the Ranch who seems rude, or bossy, or who exhibits strange behavior is actually rude, or bossy, or eccentric. Many of them are in the early stages of dementia or are desperately making an effort to cope with a loved one who has that affliction. Perhaps rather than wondering why these people are acting so strangely, my real question is, "Why are these people in Independent Living?"

Nonetheless, I don't think I will ever look at our soup spoons again without intoning, at least silently, her mantra because it's just "Life at the Wrinkle Ranch: The Round Spoon is for the Soup!"

Life at the Wrinkle Ranch: Engaged for Life!

On day two of our Life at the Wrinkle Ranch My Hero and I were joined at dinner in the Rose Room by a charming couple, June and Barrington. June introduced them both, and holding up her left hand which sported a perfect one caret, Tiffany-set diamond she announced, "We're engaged – for life!"

49

I knew that romance bloomed at the Ranch, especially among those folks who were happily married for years and years and lost a spouse late in life. Many people who have been content for fifty years or so with a partner are just not comfortable alone, and here at the Ranch, it seems they find each other.

I had a resident directory with me and was busy checking off the names of people we met, making notations, and doing my personal Ranch orientation thing. June took the book from me and found her name. She carefully crossed off the apartment and phone numbers by her name and wrote in her name and phone number after Barrington's name. "We moved in together in November," she confided, "but we're never getting married!" she declared with a firm shake of her white ringlets.

"Barrington is 106 years old! Doesn't he look wonderful? He still plays golf," she exclaimed enthusiastically. And indeed he didn't look much older than My Hero, and I too thought he looked unbelievably vigorous to be over 100! My Hero and I both expressed our admiration and amazement.

"How long have you lived here?" I asked the centenarian. "I moved here nineteen years ago from a neighboring town when I was just seventy-five," he replied. The adding machine in my head flashed "Error!" No wonder he looks so good. He's a mere ninety-four! Barrington never said a word when she misstated his age! I immediately recognized, analyzed, and incorporated one of the cardinal Ranch rules of these "last chance" Ranch romances: "Do not correct Partner's statements." I've decided that there are some good reasons for this rule.

1. Probably no one else present was actually able to hear the statement.
2. Anyone who could hear likely is not analytical enough to question the statement.
3. The partner making the statement has his or her own view of reality, and it is bad form – and pointless – to challenge it.

Barrington, except for his poor hearing, seemed to be fully in synch with ambient reality. June has a more ephemeral grasp on the current space/time continuum. Her conversation was rather like a merry-go-round. There were only a few horses on her carousel, and they passed by us repeatedly during our dinner. I could almost hear the calliope music playing in her head. I know I could see the horses.

First there was the golf horse. June is no longer able to play golf after thirty-four years of swinging a club. She blames her second, and still healing, pacemaker surgery for holding her back. Although she played golf in the Washington, D.C., area for years before moving here, she no longer recalls the names of the courses she played. She does recall that all her golf trophies are now in Barrington's apartment. The golf horse passed us multiple times. It is white, with an arched neck and a flying mane.

One of the horses belongs to her son. His horse circled by us several times during dinner, in fixed order with the others. He lives in a nearby city; he lives in a friend's house; he lives there for free because he is good at taking care of the yard. Well actually he oversees the yard maintenance. She hopes he will come for Easter dinner. Did I mention he lives nearby? His horse is black and doesn't look very spirited. As a matter of fact, it looks positively "down at the mouth."

And of course there is the engagement ring horse: When it went by it moved up and down joyously. "We're never getting married," she warned me more than once as she gazed lovingly at the bling on her left hand. It was easy to recognize the gold horse with the beautiful jeweled saddle. It was clearly her favorite. It was my favorite too.

She seemed so very happy, and although Barrington did not say much, I think he is happy also.

Ranch Rules are different from the rules at your usual private club, but I am learning to appreciate them. After all, where else but at the Ranch can a woman announce that she is "engaged for life," and no one is surprised? It even makes perfect sense to me, and I am a newbie here. It's just "Life at the Wrinkle Ranch: Engaged for Life!"

Life at the Wrinkle Ranch: Retrieving the Keys

I was sitting in the Wrinkle Ranch Lobby chatting with my friends, Barbara and Dennis, when Lettie, a fairly new resident, joined us.

I had been told Lettie was a Ph.D., a well-known mycologist, who at one time lectured in her field internationally. It was also reported that she walks constantly inside and outside the building and acts strangely – in a variety of ways.

Lettie was holding her pocketbook. It was open, apparently empty, and the lining was turned to the outside. She asked us if we

51

had scissors. Her nose was running badly, and she was sniffing repeated in order to keep pace with a thick yellow mucus drip.

We did not have scissors, but Dennis, always the helpful engineer, hopped up, declared he had a knife, and produced his pocket knife before I could stop him. There are just some people around whom I do not feel comfortable unsheathing sharp objects, and I was sure Lettie was one of them.

"They're in there. I can feel them," she repeated over and over. "We'll just have to cut them out," she persisted. From the jingling sound of the hidden item, she had clearly lost her keys in the lining of her purse.

I positioned myself between Dennis and Lettie and explained that if her keys were inside the lining there must be an opening in it, and I would find the opening and retrieve the keys – no cutting was necessary. Dennis quickly evaluated the situation as a "woman thing," and put his knife back in his pocket. Much to my dismay Lettie's nose continued to run.

In an instant I had unzipped the pocket in the lining and presented her keys to the amazed Lettie.

"How did you do that?" she kept asking, while sniffing back the mucus that was dripping visibly from her nose. "I should pay you for that," she went on.

Of course, since she is profoundly deaf she could not hear my explanation, so she never understood how I performed my magic. My guess is her vision is so poor that she never saw the zipper. Furthermore, given what seemed to be the state of her cognitive abilities, figuring out how to solve the "lost key" problem was beyond her.

I ducked into the rest room and brought her some tissues. "Blow!" I commanded. And blow she did. Then to my surprise, she retorted sardonically, "Thank you, Mother." On second thought, maybe she has not totally lost it after all. It's just "Life at the Wrinkle Ranch: Retrieving the Keys."

Life at the Wrinkle Ranch: On the Brink!

You have already learned that in Independent Living environments, we have people who are not capable of living independently. Remember if they have a partner who is able to provide care and who is independent, special arrangements can be made.

Such a couple are Mike and Judy. Judy earned a Ph.D. in mathematics and taught math in a university. Mike was an engineer. I saw them on a visit early in their decision process and went over to introduce myself. I looked at her carefully, and when he stepped between us to field my, "Hi, where are you from?" question, I recognized the situation at once. Judy had dementia.

So they moved in. I never saw them eating in the dining room. I never knew why, but I surmised it was because he had to dress her and was only able to manage to get her into shorts. Shorts are not allowed in the dining rooms at dinner. Speculating about other residents' lives is a popular, if inaccurate and frequently inappropriate pastime. I discovered later that Mike and Judy had chosen not have a meal plan; not all contracts are identical. So much for my surmising.

Mike and Judy kept to themselves, and I was given to understand that he had been directed by Management never to leave her alone. You will soon learn why!

Moving from the role of a partner in a lifetime relationship – a team of equals who have raised a family together, had responsible careers, and shared ideas and activities – to that of a caregiver for a dementia sufferer is not an easy transition.

Mike was coached repeatedly that he could not let Judy out of his sight. He could not even take her to meetings in the auditorium and then let her go alone to get her own cup of coffee and snack in the back of the room, because Judy could not manage the simplest task. Time after time I have seen our watchful and caring associates, and even some of our residents, rush to Judy's rescue when she spilled her coffee and dropped her cookies while Mike was busy with his own concerns and was inattentive to her.

One day as I pulled into my parking space I noted Mike and Judy were driving to their space down the aisle from me. Probably they had been out to the store I thought as I hurried into the building, running late for my dinner date as usual. I zipped upstairs, regrouped, and ran down again, not giving another thought to Mike and Judy whom I never saw in the evening.

When I reached our communal "great room," the Lobby, I found our dinner dates and was informed that since one of our larger dining rooms was still under renovation, we were on a short wait, so I settled myself on a comfortable couch across from my dining companions, and we began to visit. My seat afforded me a view of the lovely curved staircase with the elegant spindles that ascends to the second floor open balcony. As a matter of fact, my seat was the closest seat to the foot of the staircase. We had an animated conversation going on about the water exercise classes when a crash riveted my eyes on the stairs.

A walker was careening down the stairs at a great rate, preceded by some onions in a mesh bag and a few other small items, including parts of the walker that were breaking off during the fall. Before the walker negotiated the last curve near the bottom of the stairs, I was on my feet, praying that the walker would hit the marble floor before I reached the staircase. I was praying hard because at the top of the stairs I could see tiny Judy in her shorts standing on the brink of the staircase, looking indecisive and confused.

The walker hit the marble and veered out of my way. I raced up the stairs faster than I ever thought I could move, dodging a falling wallet and some onions, just in time to embrace Judy who had apparently hesitated at the top of the stairs after seeing the fate of her walker just long enough for me to reach her before she, like Jill, "came tumbling after." I grabbed her and pulled her back from the brink of disaster.

"I want to go downstairs," she said.

"Let's walk around the corner and take the elevator," was my firm response.

By this time several Directors and other associates had joined me on the second-floor balcony. I still held Judy's arm, which I had grabbed at the top of the stairs, and our Director of Services took her other arm. Together the three of us walked, oh so slowly, to the elevator while Sylvia, our administrative assistant, ran to find Mike. By the time our elevator opened on the first floor, Mike was there.

"I told her to wait for me while I parked the car," said the distressed and clearly overwhelmed husband. Another resident produced the dented walker complete with the onions which were probably bruised, but better the onions than Judy! Mike marched her off, and I went back to couch sitting.

In reviewing what had happened, those of us who had seen the entire event decided that Judy, left alone, somehow found her way to the second floor in the elevator, became disoriented, and decided to walk down the stairs behind her walker. God only knows what caused her to turn loose the handles of the walker once it went over the edge and started its wild descent down the stairs. My original plan was to grab the spindles of the banister with one hand holding either side, brace myself, and break Judy's fall. I never thought for a moment that she would hesitate long enough for me to reach the top of the stairs. I guess The Big Guy Upstairs realized that even though Judy does not weigh ninety pounds, my plan was more likely to take us both down in a disastrous tumble than to break her fall. My Hero pointed out that would not have been the first time I have leaped into action without a well-thought-out plan. I am very grateful we had such a favorable outcome, with only a chipped and dented walker and a few bruised onions to show for Judy's adventure. It's just "Life at the Wrinkle Ranch: On the Brink!"

Life at the Wrinkle Ranch: The Run Down

It was a Saturday morning. My Hero and I set out from the Tower for our morning walk, staying well inside the golf cart lane that lines both sides of our private entrance road, when all at once a bright red, late model Mercedes coupe came flying down the tree lined, divided boulevard – posted speed limit: 25 mph – and headed right toward us.

We gave the universal hand signal for a slow-down, which the driver, a very sweet looking little old lady with white curls, totally ignored.

As she neared our position, she veered into the cart path lane more and more until she was aimed directly at us. In short succession, My Hero issued a number of four letter orders using command voice, and at the last minute as we jumped backward, she swerved away. Seconds later we heard the brakes squeal as she screeched into a "residents only" short term parking space in front of our building.

My adrenalin was pumping, my heart was racing, and I was furious. I know that no one here owns such a vehicle, and so not only is someone trying to kill me in front of my own home, she is a trespasser as well!

Later I investigated at the Front Desk and discovered that this couple – yes there was a little old man in the passenger seat – comes to our campus every Saturday morning to have breakfast in our Bistro where the breakfast menu is not only delicious and varied, but also the most cost-effective in town, relegating Mickey D's, Burger King, et al. to the high-priced column.

I also learned that "someday" this couple may move here. "Great," I thought, "then she can aim at me the other six days of the week too!" But somehow nobody knew their names. I think staff believed they might have been preventing a homicide by not supplying those names; I was that angry.

A few days went by, and although I still was resentful of the callous attempt on my life, I consoled myself by constructing a game plan for what I would say to this little old lady, if ever the opportunity presented itself. And then it did.

The very next Saturday as I set out on my walk, I saw the red Mercedes parked in the "residents only" spot right by the front door. I turned on my heel and headed for the Bistro. "Which is the couple with the red Mercedes Benz?" I asked the manager, who promptly pointed to an innocuous looking pair at the front table.

I approached with my best marketing smile and started my strike out routine with a slow, easy pitch. "Good morning," I said mentally referring to my well-rehearsed game plan. "We are so pleased that you enjoy having breakfast here. It is the best bargain in town, isn't it?"

You see my plan: Start by throwing the batter off stride with an easy pitch.

Then I went on, "We only ask that you respect our speed limits and lane markings when you drive on our property." Again the little old lady smiled in agreement. Then, following my well-scripted plan of attack, I laid a strike right across the plate, "so that you never again try to kill me on your Saturday morning visits!"

At this point she furrowed her brow in puzzlement, and the man with whom she sat, her passenger, never said a word nor gave any indication that he heard anything I said, which in this Senior environment was probably the case and not very surprising.

"Don't you recall last Saturday morning," I asked, readying my second strike. "You came barreling down our boulevard far in excess of our 25mile an hour speed limit. My husband, a retired naval aviator, gave you the universal slow down signal, which you ignored...."

At this point the pretty face under the white curls broke into a huge smile, "My late husband was a naval aviator too!" she confided happily. The passenger, like de Tar Baby, "ain't sayin' nuthin'."

It seemed that some invisible ump had just called "time out." So I stuck out my hand and introduced myself. Thanks to the local newspaper, My Hero is pretty famous here in this Senior "ball park" so I thought I would name drop – if indeed you can name drop with your own husband's name – but she didn't seem to react except to shake my hand, smiling all the while.

Then with time "in" again, I went on with my plan to strike her out. It was time to retire this batter. I hurled my fast ball down the middle of the plate....

"Then you proceeded to drive into the cart path lane where we were walking, and my husband yelled at you. Didn't you hear him?"

"No," she said reapplying the puzzled look to her sweet face. But suddenly the clouds seemed to clear. Again she smiled, "I remember now, you jumped out of the way. I'm really sorry. I'll be more careful." And all the while the passenger kept staring quietly into space.

This was a bit of a letdown. I had struck her out! and she was still standing at the plate, smiling. I had expected an angry denial, a counter attack, maybe even a rush at the mound, bat in hand, Johnny Roseboro style. After all, I had just accused this woman of trying to kill me! I was ready to handle it all. I had a script, and I had scripted the dialog for all the parts. This was the part where the ump was supposed to throw her out of the game.

Yet there she was, still standing at the plate. No denial. No anger. No bravado – just a simple apology.

Should I, like George, declare, "Mission accomplished," and just go back to the dugout? After all I had chastised the transgressor, and she had repented. I won, didn't I?

So why am I not feeling safer, as another Saturday morning approaches? Could it be that I do not think she will remember a thing about our conversation? Could it be that I think she will drive just as dangerously next Saturday and every Saturday thereafter until someone finally takes the car keys away from this charming, and potentially homicidal, little old lady with the pretty white curls? Oh well, it's just "Life at the Wrinkle Ranch: The Run Down."

Life at the Wrinkle Ranch: Getting to the Next Level

In business we frequently refer to the process of improvement or upping our game as "getting to the next level." It is viewed as a positive achievement and certainly something a good organization would strive to do.

At the Ranch however, for a resident in Independent Living, "getting to the next level" means moving to a higher level of care and no longer residing independently. This is viewed very differently from "getting to the next level" in the business world.

In this book we have explored the attitudes and the fears of prospective residents as they contemplate moving to an Independent Living Senior Residence. See "Are You Ready?" They tell their friends they would not want to live in "a place like that" whatever "that" means. They say they are "not ready" and seem to confuse "ready" for Independent Living with "requiring a nursing home."

Fully ambulatory visiting Seniors see the assistive devices in our community, and instead of realizing that savvy Seniors are practicing "fall avoidance," they see "pathetic old people." They are in denial that they may ever need such assistance and react as if assistive devices are contagious.

Once such feelings are allayed and fears of living in a Continuing Care Community like ours are overcome, most new residents quickly decide that moving to the Ranch was the smartest thing they ever did. After all, they have full independence without all the annoyances of home maintenance, yard work, housekeeping, and cooking. They come and go as they please. Wonderful meals and transportation are provided along with in-house entertainment, companionship, and a myriad of activities. What's not to like?

And then one day people begin to realize that they have done exactly what they moved into Continuing Care to do: they have "aged in place." Perhaps they now use an assistive device and need help to accomplish things they easily did on their own in the past. Memory issues may be – well – an "issue." And putting out their pills every day is a chore that requires assistance. They no longer want to cook an occasional meal and do not feel comfortable doing every day chores. Well, how fortunate they are! Isn't that why they moved here in the first place? The first "C" in CCRC is "Continuing." There are various levels of care available in the community to accommodate a resident's needs. Management, family, and the resident's physician work with him to determine the proper place for him to live in the community, and when agreement is reached, he may decide it is time to move to "Assisted Living." It sounds so logical – so neat and tidy.

Well hold on to your seat belts because frequently the ride to Assisted Living is bumpy! Our old friend, Denial, is still with us. The same Denial who insisted we were not "ready" for Independent Living some years ago is now actively fighting the logical conclusion that given the circumstances, Assisted Living, and in some cases, Memory or Nursing Care, is our appropriate destination. Despite the urgings of a caring Management team, a loving family, and a dedicated physician many IL residents fight false tooth and acrylic nail to stay where they are because – Surprise! – people fear change, and old people fear it fiercely!

Take, for example, a bright woman named Franny. She had been a social worker in her professional life, and when I moved to the Ranch, she was spry and involved. She ran a regularly scheduled evening activity called Timely Topics where residents discussed specific, and frequently controversial, subjects, and she volunteered on several committees. She had lots of friends, and always had dinner dates with other residents in the community. Franny had Parkinson's, and the effects of the disease were beginning to be a problem in her daily life. She was in and out of our Skilled Nursing Facility and frequently had to be rushed to the hospital in the middle of doing everyday activities. More than once she forgot her laundry in the communal laundry room on her floor between the washer and the dryer cycles as she was taken out on a gurney. Her floor leader became a regular when it came to finishing Franny's laundry, and still Franny fought the idea of moving to Assisted Living. Of course eventually she did move, but only after a lot of work on the part of others who wanted the best solution for her and only after a lot of upset on Franny's part. Once she was comfortably ensconced in her new digs, she discovered that she was much happier and had much less stress because of the additional services now easily available to her.

Sometimes residents who need, but are resisting, a "higher level of care" claim to their friends that Management is pressuring them to move to Assisted Living. They even claim Management is moving them against their will.

The truth is that cannot, and will not, happen. There are laws governing such situations. Unless a resident is a danger to himself or others, Management cannot arbitrarily move a resident from Independent Living to Assisted Living. Besides, do the math. At our community under the terms of our contract, we can move to Assisted Living and under some conditions pay the same fee we do in Independent Living, yet the ratio of associates to residents is much higher in AL, three meals a day are provided, and the cost of keeping a resident there far exceeds the cost of maintaining him in Independent Living. No management team in its right financial mind is eager to move IL residents to AL unless it is truly necessary and in the resident's best interest.

A couple who had been at the Ranch for ten years when we came here planned their move to AL two years in advance. They had a been very active during their lives at the Ranch. For many years he put his expertise, gained working in financial management for a major auto manufacturer, to good use as chairman of the residents' Finance Committee. They loved living in their spacious apartment, and they were realists and planners. Two years before they intended to move to AL they began to plan with Management. They were both in their 90s, her memory was failing, and he walked unsteadily. They knew they needed more support, and they embraced that move with the same good attitude with which they moved to the Ranch in the first place. No trauma, no fighting with Management and the family.

Speaking of the family – families can have a wide range of attitudes about Life at the Wrinkle Ranch. Some family members who see themselves as rightful heirs of whatever the Senior leaves behind, fight any expenditure the Senior makes. They fight their parent's moving to a Senior Community, and they fight the idea of new cars or cruises for them once they have made that move. We have discovered there are some very greedy, selfish "kids" out there.

Others are in denial about the failing ability of their Senior to care for himself and to make good decisions. One gentleman here was in a severe accident years ago. He dressed beautifully and was very handsome and trim. He was absolutely charming, and he had brain damage from the accident. When he first moved here he parked his cars, yes "cars," – he had two – in the one-hour zone for days on end. At night he wandered in the halls, and someone had to check on him and "tuck him in." Although he always smiled and was genial, he had no friends because, as one lady said to me, "I know he's nice, but he creeps me out!" He should have been in a higher level of care, and Management had explained the facts of the man's life and his abilities to his two self-proclaimed wealthy sons who lived in the area. They rarely came to visit, and when they did they denied the reports about the wandering and other odd behavior and refused to allow "dad" to be moved to a higher level of care. Their attitude put Management in an awkward position and left dad at risk for situations he would not have encountered in a more controlled and watchful environment.

Another resident, Joan, who had always been a power to be reckoned with in her family, became increasingly less able to function on her own. See "The Changing of the Guard." After having to give up her automobile, she took to terrorizing pedestrians on our property as she drove her golf cart full throttle without regard for those of us who walked around the campus. She was a sight to behold in her plastic shower cap – saving her hairdo from the wind she created – as she bore down on us. Her behavior became more and more bizarre, and her children were kept fully informed, but she did not want to move to AL. Although they were in their 60s, and despite Management's urging, the "children" had never opposed Mama and were not going to start now. If she did not want to move, they were not going to try to convince her. It took a number of well documented incidents and the threat of legal action to get the "children," who were clearly intimidated-for-life, to agree that Mama should move to a higher level of care, and even then they demurred until Nature intervened. Mama became ill, had to go to the nursing facility, and never recovered. Otherwise she might still be here, raising hell and getting her own way.

Granted some of our senior Seniors pass the centennial mark and stay right here in Independent Living with a little assistance from the extended services available at an additional cost. Some have companions, and other just farm out the ironing and the dusting; however, most of us, if we live long enough, will eventually move across the street to our beautifully decorated, specially designed home where assistance is part of everyday life. Residents would avoid a lot of trauma and ease their lives if they set aside Denial and embraced moving to a higher level of care when the time is right. After all, it's just "Life at the Wrinkle Ranch: Getting to the Next Level."

Life at the Wrinkle Ranch: Land of Wandering Wandas

A compulsion to walk is a symptom of Alzheimer's that appears in some sufferers as their illness progresses. It seems they feel compelled to go somewhere, sometimes to a specific location, and other times just to walk, to keep moving, as if they could get away and escape the tangles in their own brains.

The subject of "Retrieving the Keys" was one of these wanderers. One day a Driver from our Transportation Department encountered Lettie stopping traffic by walking in the middle of the highway in our local town. He stood by to protect her and called the Ranch for additional assistance. She insisted that she had to "go home" but had no idea which home she was seeking. The event gave Management the impetus they needed to have a doctor remand Lettie for a hospital stay, and based on the results of examinations during that stay, Management was able to secure her in a higher level of care where she would no longer be a danger to herself or others.

In a Wrinkle Ranch there are lots of Wandering Wandas. All of them demonstrate some level of confusion, their wanderings can take various forms, and many wander with determined purpose. Some are indoor wanderers, and others head for the wide open spaces!

If ever we are missing anything from our common areas – a vase, a small plant or anything portable – staff knows just where they can find it. They go to an apartment that houses a lady who has lived here since the doors opened over twenty years ago. It seems she wanders around the building and just can't help picking up portable items.

She was permanently banned from the local Walgreens and Walmart years ago; however, until she winds up in a higher level of care, staff will just have to drop by her apartment and retrieve whatever goes missing from our common spaces.

When we first moved here, my neighbor across the hall suffered from a variety of ailments, and some days were better for her than others. Although she usually moved very slowly, if her husband were distracted momentarily, she was likely to turn her walker in a tight 180 and head in the opposite direction at an amazing speed! Other times he made the mistake of entering their apartment ahead of her, and she would just keep going down the hall. Fortunately her walker usually ran into a wall before she went too far, and even with his bad knees, COPD, and the impediment of his immense abdomen, he could still catch up to her.

Occasionally when his tendency to incontinence overwhelmed him, he had to duck unexpectedly into one of the strategically located hallway rest rooms. Then, despite his admonition to "stay right there," she was off like a shot.

One night they had guests for dinner in the dining room. They were about to give the guests a post dinner tour of the building when the husband's "urge" became urgent. He left her to conduct the tour, apparently thinking the guests would keep her in check. When he reappeared, neither his wife nor his guests were anywhere to be seen. We came across him, sprawled disconsolately in one of the big chairs by the elevator, just hoping she would reappear and too afraid he would miss her in passing if he took the elevator down to look for her. Of course, he was too afraid to call the Front Desk and get help because if Management could document her wandering, he feared he would be pressured to send her to a higher level of care.

One day I encountered a new Wandering Wanda. I was returning from my exercise walk, headed toward the Tower and walking in the golf cart lane of our divided main entrance road when a very old woman with a walker approached from the opposite direction on the other side of the center divider. At first she was in her golf cart lane, but she quickly made a hard left turn and walked out as if to cross the street to my side.

The problem was that she did not make this move in a cross walk, and I was sure she could not negotiate the curb, the grass, and the crepe myrtles that make up the center divider. As far as I could tell, her walker was not mil-spec and did not come equipped with tank treads – just the standard, commercial-issue walker wheels. So I quickly moved to intercept her and gently suggested that she go back into the cart lane where she would be safe from oncoming cars.

"I'll remember that for another time," she said politely. Finally, I realized that she wanted to cross the street to reach the parking lot. I did not know if she had a car there, but I hoped not. Fortunately, a staff member came by at that moment, and I turned "Wanda" over to him. Later he told me he had protected her while she crossed the street but did not know who she was or what to do after that. I hope he called for reinforcements or they may have had to issue a Silver Alert. If they needed help describing the woman or the walker, I could have assisted. I have learned how important it is to be observant when you live here. It's just "Life at the Wrinkle Ranch: The Land of the Wandering Wandas."

Life at the Wrinkle Ranch: Dining Misery

My Hero was at a dinner meeting so I went to the dining room alone. I was joined at a table in the Colonial Dining Room by a nice lady, Paula, with whom I frequently speak, and Bob, a pleasant gentleman and long-time resident I had not met before. Our fourth was Joan, who arrived after the rest of us were seated.

I had never had a conversation with Joan, but as I have already described, I have jumped out of her way on our boulevard as she bore down on me in her golf cart without so much as a honk and raced by wearing her plastic shower cap to protect her hair-do from the stiff wind raised by her excessive speed. Just a heads up: You will read about Joan again when you arrive at Chapter Six, discover her in "Defending One's Turf," and again at Chapter Nine in the episode entitled, "The Changing of the Guard."

Joan clearly had some "issues," and this particular night she was in "Dining Misery." Shortly after she arrived at our table, so was I.

She complained about every aspect of the meal. The only words out of her mouth were complaints. When she was not complaining, she was looking dour and not speaking at all, which I have to admit was preferable. She was curt with the young dining associates and could not frame a polite request. Every word to an associate was an order delivered in a harsh tone of voice.

Just to let you know how deplorable things are in our dining rooms and to help you to appreciate how "reasonable" her attitude was, here are some of the intolerable conditions to which she was subjected by our miserable dining system:

Her water had ice in it! Bob removed the ice for her. She then complained that she preferred water that had *never* had ice in it. Nothing on the menu "appealed" to her. After confirming that indeed tilapia is a fish, she reluctantly ordered it, bypassing the two alternative featured entrees and the ten or so others, but complained that there were no vegetables on the menu. So what are carrots, fennel, and broccoli? Chopped liver? She ordered half a sweet potato, and when her meal was delivered, she had a dreadful surprise! The server delivered a whole sweet potato! Granted it was split down the middle, but Joan awarded no credit for that. You would have thought the young man had just committed the unpardonable sin. Perhaps she has not read Oliver Twist.

After ordering, she complained to us that she had not asked for butter for her potato. Apparently when one is in total complaint mode, complaining about oneself fits right into the pattern.

She went to the salad bar – where there is butter – but came back without it. Then she stopped every associate who passed our table, complaining and demanding they bring her butter. All the associates were busy taking orders at other tables and doing their jobs. Somehow no one brought her butter. Bob offered her what was left of his butter and instead of a simple, "No thanks," she acted miffed and rejected it, tossing the wrapper and morsel of butter back at him. Paula had two pats of butter, still wrapped, but didn't offer to share. After all the grousing we had endured, I could not blame her. By that time, I was not feeling very charitable either; therefore, I did not volunteer to get up and get her any. When one associate approached the table with little margarine cups, a more experienced server who obviously knew Joan well intercepted her and advised her to get "the real thing." Would you believe, when the butter finally arrived, it was pronounced "too cold!"

Her next complaint: It was cold in the dining room. According to her, it is always cold in the dining room. She complained that she should have brought a sweater. She always brings her sweater. She has to because it is always so cold in the dining room.

The coffee did not come fast enough; the crackers were too difficult to open. It took too long to take our dessert orders. Since she had eaten only a small portion of her dinner, Joan must have still been hungry because for dessert she ordered the orange cake. When the cake arrived – are you ready for this? – the piece was too big, and it came with *pink* icing!

Well that was, to coin a phrase, the icing on the cake! She demanded to know if it were really orange cake. She took a few bites and declared that it did not look like orange cake. Another surprise: she did not like it. Besides, she said, "We don't make good cake here." And she ordered it because?

To add to our miserable dining experience with Mrs. Negativity, she blew her nose on her napkin repeatedly throughout the meal. And I mean *blew*! not dabbed, not sniffed – and then used her fingers to stick parts of the napkin into her nasal cavity to get any residue left behind by her hearty blow. The ratio of complaints to "blows" was about four to one. Once you caught on to the rhythm of the thing, you could pretty well project the timing of the next blow, but that did not make it any easier to endure.

I make it a point not to eat dessert and was finished and ready to leave before the others; however, I just did not feel right about leaving two very pleasant people alone with the Queen of Complaints. Finally to my great relief she asked if we would mind if she left the table because she was so cold. Just to show you what a charming dinner companion I am, I stifled my, "Hallelujah!" and smiling politely, I said, "Don't worry about us. Please go right ahead."

Surely this is not appropriate behavior in an Independent Living environment. Rudeness to associates, bringing everyone's mood down, and then leaving germ laden napkins for associates to handle does not sound like the actions of an Independent Living resident to me. It's just "Life at the Wrinkle Ranch: Dining Misery."

Life at the Wrinkle Ranch: Righting a Wrong on a One-Way Street

A resident was backing out of his covered parking space here on campus one Sunday morning and observed another resident in his parking row also backing out her large white Pontiac SUV. The Pontiac just missed the car in the next space as the driver inexpertly backed out and turned to exit her space.

Our "reporter" then followed the Pontiac, which was traveling in excess of our posted speed limit, down the Boulevard. He was expecting that vehicle to turn onto the public street at the end of our Boulevard. Suddenly the Pontiac turned left as if to enter the Golf Club parking lot; however, that left turn was followed by an immediate right turn. After this last maneuver the Pontiac was traveling outbound in the inbound lane of the divided Boulevard!

To complicate matters an unsuspecting driver had turned into the Boulevard from the public street and was now faced with a potential head-on collision with the Pontiac SUV, and he had nowhere to turn!

The Pontiac driver solved this impasse by making a diagonal right turn *across* the curb, and the Boulevard divider, through the flowers, dodging a palm tree, over the other curb, and finally repositioning her SUV in front of our thoroughly stunned reporting resident, who had slowed the progress of his vehicle to observe these events. The erratic driver then turned right onto the public street and whizzed off.

It happens that My Hero is the Chair of our Transportation Committee and has created a complete database of resident vehicle descriptions and parking space numbers; therefore, I was able to relate, with conviction, the name of the owner and probably driver of the white Pontiac to our Management. She owns the only Pontiac in the data base, and indeed it is an SUV; it is white, and she parks two spaces down from our reporter. I know that would be called "circumstantial evidence" in a criminal court, but we at the Ranch take a more pragmatic approach to such things.

I have suggested to our splendid Management leader that he may want to "investigate the matter and meet with" the lady driver. That is "Leaderspeak" for, "OMG, take the car keys away from her before she kills somebody."

I am happy to report that Management was able to accomplish that task, but not without additional time and effort. It's just "Life at the Wrinkle Ranch: Righting a Wrong on a One-Way Street."

Life at the Wrinkle Ranch: Smoke Gets in Your Eyes

As we have discussed before, there are a number of Ranchers who have moved into Independent Living in our community although they had previously been diagnosed as having signs of dementia.

Especially if the affected resident has a spouse or partner who is devoted to keeping the loved one in Independent Living as long as possible and if the medications prescribed are doing their job, he or she may live here for some time among those of us who still believe we are fully functional "upstairs."

There are times when the interactions with a Rancher who is stricken with the early signs of Alzheimer's or some other form of dementia are upsetting and sadden us. Who can forget "The Round Spoon" or "Retrieving the Keys," but sometimes the effects of moderate cognitive disorder can lead to situations that are just hysterically funny. Take for example the visit of one of my good friends, Karen, to the urologist.

After struggling for months with a Urinary Tract Infection that refused to respond to several courses of very strong antibiotics, my friend went to see a well-recommended urologist in the area and took her husband, Donald, along. Donald is a happy person, easy going, and quite conversational. Although he has some cognitive issues, he is certainly not at the point that he needs constant supervision. There were several errands planned for the trip, and his presence at some of them was required so along he came.

The meeting with the urologist went well, with Donald sitting through all the discussions in the exam room. Finally the doctor decided that he should do a pelvic examination. Donald and Karen have been married for well over fifty years, but having Donald present for Karen's pelvic exams had not been among the experiences they had shared.

After some poking and probing, typical of such a procedure, the doctor raised his head from his work and announced, "You never smoked!" Karen confirmed this analysis, but Donald, still rather overwhelmed by the entire event, asked, "If she had, would smoke come out there?"

I was told that it took some time for Karen, the nurse, and the doctor to recover their composure and complete their business.

Donald never did understand why his question rendered them all weak with laughter. But I understand. On this particular day, this particular urologist got a glimpse of what we experience regularly. It's just "Life at the Wrinkle Ranch: Smoke Gets in Your Eyes."

Life at the Wrinkle Ranch: Silver Alert

For those of you who are not familiar with the terminology, the "Silver Alert" is a special type of public announcement – commonplace in Florida – that indicates that a Senior is missing. Usually the Senior is someone with dementia of some sort, or one who lacks the ability to care for himself. Sometimes it is a Senior who still has access to a vehicle and has driven off to parts unknown; other times it is one who has just walked away. Silver Alerts are flashed on electronic signs along the highway and posted around the neighborhood.

One day our Wrinkle Ranch Director of Maintenance came to me, in my official capacity as the Resident Association President, and in the spirit of full disclosure shared that the statue of St. Francis of Assis that had been ensconced in a flower garden on the west side of our main building had been reported missing. Our St. Francis was surrounded, not only by beautiful flowers and plants but also by statues of small animals and birds. Residents who walked around the building always enjoyed the garden, as did those who viewed it from their windows and balconies every day.

I was concerned and asked a number of questions, learning that the absence was reported by residents whose homes look out on the garden. I also learned that the resident who years ago had established the garden, St. Francis and all, had just died. Was grief involved in this disappearance? And if so, whose?

So now there were a number of possible explanations. Perhaps the family of the deceased had collected St. Francis and taken him to a family home or even to the burial plot of the deceased. Maybe an entrepreneurial resident, knowing that the Saint's sponsor had departed for the Big Garden in the Sky, had relocated the Saint to watch over and bless another of our gardens. Perhaps the grounds maintenance staff had inadvertently bumped into St. Francis and broken his heart, or some other body part, and had buried the evidence – so many possibilities and no definitive answers.

And still there was a chance that St. Francis had just become tired of hanging out with such a young crowd as the one that inhabits our community. After all he is 843, and our oldest resident is only 105, so he may have been looking for people his own age. It's understandable.

Since I was able to assess the situation from a number of standpoints, I decided that the best way to assist our Management in finding St. Francis was to issue a Silver Alert. My Hero and I rushed to our computer, and we created the following poster, which we placed in key locations around the campus.

SILVER ALERT!

NAME: St. Francis   AGE: 843

ADDRESS: Wrinkle Ranch
                          Door 5 West Garden
                          Ranch City, Florida

Last seen in the company of small animals & birds

Report all sightings to Florida Highway Patrol *347

We then stood by to see if the State Police and local authorities in cooperation with our own security force could locate the Saint before he came to harm. After all, at age 843 who knows what situations might pose a threat to a Senior, and in this modern era it is possible that a nature loving Senior in a cassock might prove a target for any number of evil doers. All we could do was hope and pray that, God willing, our Saint would be returned intact to his rightful position in his garden. It's just "Life at the Wrinkle Ranch: Silver Alert."

CHAPTER
5

Love and Marriage

The subject of love, marriage, and romantic relationships at the Wrinkle Ranch is fascinating and provides a rich area of study for sociologists and gerontologists focusing on the many issues of aging.

Most of the residents at the Ranch have been married for years. Although a few have had more than one spouse, most were married early in life and have lived with that spouse for a very long time; however, by the time people reach their 70s and 80s, the sad truth is that illness steals many lives, and Seniors lose their long-term partners. Cancer claims a large number of them, and Alzheimer's draws others away into the darkness, slowly but surely.

We know a number of Ranch residents who have spent years caring for a terminally ill spouse, men and women who have patiently nursed and tended a loved one, and sat by their bedside at Hospice until finally, it was over. Death had taken their partner and left them alone.

One of the wonderful advantages of living at a Wrinkle Ranch is that one is never really alone – except by choice. When a spouse dies, the other residents gather in support. They dine with the grieving one, escort him to exercise class, accompany him on field trips, and bring him along to the Saturday night movie. They sit and talk over coffee in the Lobby. The Ranch family is there for the long haul, not just for the few days or weeks immediately following the funeral as is so often the case outside Life Care Communities.

For many, a Senior Community is a life-saving environment. Depression is a frequent companion of the bereaved, and depression among the elderly can hasten death. Instead of being faced with the loneliness of an empty house where every simple task seems onerous, eating holds no interest, and just getting out of bed and getting dressed in the morning seems pointless, people who live in a well-run Wrinkle Ranch will be surrounded by friends and plenty of things to do. They will be supported by caring people who provide pleasant activities and fun outings and who will make sure a well-balanced dinner is ready on time.

Despite the friendship and community support at the Ranch, it seems apparent that people who have been happily married for most of their adult years usually prefer being in a committed relationship. It is not surprising that many people at the Ranch who become single, subsequently become attached again; however, the logistics and the legalities of this attachment can take varying forms depending on the personalities, the values, and the pressures on those involved.

No matter how true Frank Sinatra's words were in 1955, at the Wrinkle Ranch "Love and Marriage" do not always "go together like a horse and carriage." When faced with the reality of losing an excellent medical insurance policy or a substantial chunk of monthly income, many women who would never had dreamed of "living in sin" in their younger years couldn't care less about all those old rules from the past.

Of course given the number of men here who have had prostate cancer and considering the age of both parties in such a union, there may not actually be much "sin" left in the "living."

There are men and women who have coffee together in the morning at the Bistro, cocktails together each afternoon, dinner together every night and consider themselves couples but continue to live separately and have no plan to do otherwise. Far be it from me to judge that they are less committed than those who actually marry.

Some couples, like the one "Engaged for Life," know that time is not on their side and are happy to choose the "eternal engagement" avenue until one or the other goes to a higher level of care.

One beautiful 90-something woman here, having lost two husbands during her time at the Ranch, has a special friend who would like to marry her, but she prefers to keep the ties looser. No more "knots" for her. It might be significant that she has excellent military dependent's benefits that she would lose if she ever remarried! Now there is an example of "the tie that binds!"

Her situation is an example of a coupling decision based on financial considerations. After all, if one has a spousal-based pension plan or other lifetime financial benefits that evaporate upon the next marriage, is a next marriage a good financial decision? It depends.

We have met people, usually women, who have given up military and corporate pensions, social security, and other benefits for a new love and for their sense of propriety; however, more practical, and less traditional, people consult an accountant, go for the financially-based best deal, and ignore that "old time religion." None of these approaches is right or wrong. It is a matter of what feels right for the Seniors involved. Or perhaps it depends on what feels right for their children? Yes, the children. They do get involved as you will see!

It seems that many of these people have families – including children in their 50s or 60s – who have planned their whole lives around inheriting the parents' estate. These people do not want the distributions muddled! It is true that some of these offspring unselfishly want to ensure that a grieving parent is not entering into a poor financial or emotional situation by way of a potentially transitory relationship; however, the bottom line is many "children" just want to make sure their parent is not out spending *their* inheritance.

Still and all, marriage is a frequent choice of our single Seniors, especially ones who were happily married before and cannot imagine living alone.

In this chapter I have included two stories, "The Bundling Board" and "Sticking to Her Guns," both of which are about couples for whom the old-fashioned code held sway.

"The Package Saga" explores the sensitive nature of relationships that spring up when one spouse is left alone in Independent Living while his beloved wastes away from a fatal disease in another part of the campus. The heartbroken spouse will visit daily and sit and gaze at the shell of a person who is no longer the same person who travelled through life with him or her. Then when some caring resident down the hall offers a supporting hand and a shoulder to cry on, the guilt of the grieving spouse can be overwhelming. Even after the death of the terminally ill spouse sometimes there seems to be an urge to hide the new relationship. Note: Hiding *anything* is not easy at the Ranch!

"I Promised My Mom..." deals with the problem of "the children" – actually fully grown adults – who for many different reasons fought their parent's remarriage.

The last story in this chapter treats a frequent Ranch House problem: the issue of the over-anxious male. He's suddenly alone. He does not know how to deal with grief, cannot operate the washing machine, does not know how long to microwave his oatmeal, hates to wash the dishes, and is soooo lonesome. To make matters worse, the sound of his life clock ticking away his remaining days is deafening! He casts about for a likely-looking single woman, and he pounces. His courting skills – if they ever existed – are long since rusted as you will see in "Working Fast." Fortunately, Ranch women have developed some excellent defensive moves!

I hope, after reading this chapter, you will see that love at the Wrinkle Ranch is a "many splendored" and multi-faceted thing.

Life at the Wrinkle Ranch: The Bundling Board

We know that some Seniors feel that marriage is the only legitimate and allowable vehicle for sharing a roof and a bed. For them it is a matter of morals. These people were raised with these codes, and they are ingrained. Never mind that the cultural reason for those codes was to protect inheritance and ancestral lands and to make sure that any offspring from the union be legitimate in order to ensure the line of succession. Never mind that none of these people has been fertile for years! One's values are one's values!

One Rancher, a man in his 90s, was about to marry his fifth wife. The first four died of cancer. He was a founder of this establishment, a caring husband to every wife, a devoted mate, and a well-respected member of the Ranch community. In order to live together, the fiancée, also a Ranch resident, planned to give up her apartment and pay the additional fee required to move into his residence – one larger and more elegant than hers. Upgrades in one's life come in various forms, and some require cash deposits.

Her children were so worried about her future – and theirs – that they hired an attorney to draft a prenuptial agreement, that type of deal the movie magazines call a "prenup." This is not unusual here at the Ranch; after all many people want to render unto their offspring the things they are expecting, regardless of new alliances, and many offspring are dedicated to seeing that happen.

The sad fact is that in this case the prospective wife was so worried about what her children – 50+ adults – thought about all of this that she would not marry without the prenup they are having drafted and would not sleep together with her prospective groom without first marrying him. In the meantime, based on circumstances, she needed to move out of her apartment immediately. What to do? What to do? How were these very ethical, moral, and traditional people to handle this situation?

The prospective groom seriously confided to friends that he did not know what people would think of them, living together without benefit of clergy. He jokingly suggested to some of his buddies that he thought he and his fiancée needed a "bundling board."

Lest you think old age implies a lost sense of humor, one resident wag commissioned a "bundling board" from the Ranch woodshop!

I immediately researched the original specifications employed by the Puritans in the hope that extensive ornamental carvings were not involved. The project required a quick turn-around, and carvings take time!

One thing bothered me about that creative gift: What, if in a moment of enthusiastic passion, our Senior lover made an effort to bridge the bundling board, failed to make the requisite height in his leap and broke a hip??!! Imagine the headlines, "Bundling Board Breaks Up Courtship!"

So among the other challenges to the path of true love here, we have pinpointed another potential hurdle in Ranch romances. It's just "Life at the Wrinkle Ranch: The Bundling Board."

Life at the Wrinkle Ranch: Sticking by Her Guns

Jim was my friend and bridge partner and was ninety years young. He was a West Point graduate and had worked on the Manhattan Project. He was very handsome with a full head of white hair and twinkling, bright blue eyes.

He moved into the Wrinkle Ranch when he could no longer supply all the services at home required to support his beloved wife, suffering from advancing Alzheimer's. After almost destroying his own health with the burden of care giving, he relented and brought them to a place she could receive the care she needed. After a year at the Ranch, only a few months before we met, she died, and Jim, a devoted husband, was consumed with grief.

We began to be bridge partners almost immediately. He was a good bridge player, and he needed something to occupy his time and to stimulate his substantial intellect. We played quite a bit at first, and then one day about three months later he told me he was going to have cut back on his bridge. Concerned for his health, I asked the reason. "I've met someone!" was his happy response.

During the summer and early fall we attended a few events with Jim and Jerri, as charming and beautiful an 80-something woman as you could ever meet. We entertained each other with funny stories at dinner, and we went to the theatre. She was a true Southern belle from southeastern Virginia, with a soft Southern accent. My Hero and I fell in love with her too.

Throughout this time Jim continued to tell us that Jerri insisted that he "take it slow." And that she refused to allow him to be as "close" as he would like, gay blade that he was.

Then in December Jim told us shyly that they were engaged. They were married shortly thereafter at the local Catholic Church. Both sets of off-spring were there, all handsome, accomplished grown-ups, some with grands of their own and all obviously delighted that their parents had another chance to love and be loved. Not a one was reported to have misgivings or be worried about his inheritance. Attached is the poem chronicling their courtship, which a friend produced for the happy occasion:

> The Ballad of Jim and Jerri
> Jim is a handsome, charming guy
> And lived in wedded bliss.
> But then one day he lost his love.
> His life had gone amiss.
> He was so down, his friends remarked,
> "He just is way too sad."
> For Jim looked like the picture of a man
> Whose life's gone bad.
> And then one night he chanced to sit
> With some nice folks at dinner,
> And met a gal both tall and smart –
> A model is no thinner.
> This pretty girl looked up and smiled
> And gave Jim quite a fright
> Because he feared he fell in love
> and that was at first sight.
>
> But Jerri knew these Army types,
> And she said "take it slow."
> She set the rules and made them stick
> Though Jim was set to go!
> No hanky panky for Miss Jer.
> She knew he was a winner,
> But still she set the pace,
> And ran the show from that first dinner.
> When Jerri broke her wrist last fall,

Jim offered to assist.
His eyes were on the button holes.
Her standards said, "Resist"
Today this couple married,
And I know they both are glad,
The next time Jerri breaks a wrist,
For buttons, Jim's her lad.

It's just "Life at the Wrinkle Ranch: Sticking by Her Guns."

Life at the Wrinkle Ranch: The Package Saga

I came home one day to find a package at my door. Actually there were two packages, one of which I was expecting – containing a fine pair of Puma hot pink and purple plaid golf shoes I had ordered the day before – and another one I was not expecting. I opened the door and slid them into my apartment with a practiced shove of my foot and rushed off to open my new golf shoes with never another glance at package #2.

The next day I asked My Hero what he had ordered that still sat unopened on the front hall floor and he said, "I didn't order anything. I figured it was another pair of those God-awful golf shoes you like so much."

At that point we looked at the address label, and that was when we discovered the package was not even addressed to us. It was addressed to another resident of our building, a man who lives in the other wing with a similar apartment number. Once we knew it was not our package, we did not look to see who sent it, a fact which is germane to the rest of the story, as you will see. And thus the Package Saga began in earnest.

When I went out the next day I moved the package to the alcove in the hall and told the Front Desk that a misdelivered package was outside our apartment. They promised to come right up and take it to the appropriate resident.

However, in the meantime, My Hero, in one of those typical male, take-action moves decided to deliver the package to the apartment of Susan, a nearby neighbor and a good friend of the package addressee. Why? Why do men do anything? No thinking woman would have ever done such a thing. Who knows what was in the package? Maybe a gift for someone – not Susan! Maybe something from an "adult" toy store that he didn't want her to see. Maybe a surprise? Who knows? But certainly, taking the package to the door of a lady who is "a friend" of the addressee breaks every rule pertaining to male/female protocol. Not only is it a bad idea. It is just plain *wrong*!

But he did it; when the Front Desk came for the box at our door, it was gone, adding even more drama to the Package Saga.

Susan eventually opened her door and found the package. She was puzzled that it had been delivered to her apartment. She checked the sender and noted that it was from the Cremation Association of North America! Her friend had recently lost his beloved wife, his soul mate, who had spent the last five years in a higher level of care on our campus. Apparently this package was the urn for her ashes!

When Susan noted the sender, *she* was unwilling to deliver such a package to her friend, especially when she had no idea how to explain why she had it. What could she say, "I found your wife's urn at my door and thought you might like to have it"? Or how about, "Now that your wife died, does the fact that packages addressed to you come to my door have any special significance? And if so, why did we have to start with her urn?"

No! No! Susan was not having any of that! She immediately carried the package downstairs to the Front Desk, alerted them to the importance of the contents, and asked *them* to deliver the package.

The next day, while My Hero and I were still blissfully unaware of the contents of the mystery package, I saw Susan leaving the tennis courts. I took advantage of our chance meeting to explain that My Hero had, all by himself, decided to take the package to her door and asked if she had given it to her friend yet.

That was when I discovered the rest of the story. Imagine my embarrassment and consternation when I learned that we had been shoving such special cargo around with the same respect I showed plaid golf shoes.

How such a package came to be left outside our door will probably always remain a mystery. Surely a container for human ashes, especially those of a beloved spouse, a soul mate, deserves to be handled with greater care. But strange things happen here where we live at the Intersection of Life and Death. It's just "Life at the Wrinkle Ranch, The Package Saga."

Life at the Wrinkle Ranch: I Promised My Mom...

Doug had always been a winner. A good looking young man from a fine family, he graduated from a prestigious service academy, had two successful careers, a wonderful wife, and three great kids.

He retired when he was still young enough to enjoy it all. He played golf, was active in the community, president of his country club, and in general enjoyed the epitome of the "good life."

As Doug approached his eighth decade, there was only one serious problem in what was otherwise a very nearly perfect existence. His beloved wife was a smoker. Not just a casual smoker, a multiple pack-a-day smoker, an I-know-it's-not-good-for-me-but-I'll-never-quit smoker. Not surprisingly, after years of respiratory problems, she developed lung cancer and died a lingering and painful death.

Doug was devastated. The daughter who lived nearest, swarmed to support him. For company, she bought him a little dog, a companion to share his life. After all she loved her father and so did everything she could think of to help him through the crisis of her mom's death. Unfortunately, by this point Doug had some health problems of his own, and these were exacerbated by the emotional distress of his grief. Things were not going well for Doug. Keeping up his house had become impossible, and not surprisingly he wasn't eating properly.

So with the blessing of all three of his children Doug sold his home of oh-so-many years, and he moved to our Wrinkle Ranch, bringing much of the furniture and many of the lovely things he and his wife had collected over their long marriage. Even after he had settled in here, Doug appeared to be a broken man; his body was failing and so was his spirit.

He and My Hero were alumni of the same school and had similarities in their backgrounds. They knew many of the same people. We reached out to him; we had dinner together and tried to cheer him up, and it seemed hopeless...until...Marie, the pretty widow right upstairs, the one who had always been a great golfer and exerciser extraordinaire; Marie, who was a member of his church, looked his way and smiled.

Before we knew it, the light came back into Doug's eyes. Now he was on a mission. At eighty-one Marie's pretty blue eyes were as bright as ever and her smile just as fetching, but her body was no longer cooperating with her desire for an active life. She had some health issues and was not moving well.

Doug was always a man of action, and he was determined to assist her. He accompanied her to doctor's appointments; he advised her about investments; and he handled her automotive issues. In other words, he made himself indispensable. And Marie loved it!

A romance developed between them, and our two starry-eyed Seniors decided they wanted to get married. Marie's children, who had quickly become fond of Doug, were delighted, but his adoring and supportive daughter was not a bit pleased with Dad's plan.

She rallied her siblings, and they voted 2 to 1 that Dad could not get married again. Like it was their business! He was of sound mind, if not of body – besides everybody knows love heals both the soul and the body. They should have been pleased, but instead they were adamant: No wedding for Dad!

Everyone at the Ranch liked Marie. She was an exemplary individual, an established member of the community, and certainly had no nefarious plan to run off with Doug's money or to break his heart. Even when the third, more understanding sibling flew in from afar to run interference for Dad, the family battle raged on.

What makes grown children respond this way to a single parent's desire for coupling? Some are truly concerned about their parent's future and want to be protective, but there was no need for protection here. For some it's greed. They do not want Mom's or Dad's estate to be divided in more ways than they had anticipated. Was that the issue? Others attempt the control coup of the parent-child role reversal that seems to infect so many children about the time they reach fifty. Doug's kids fit that criterion. And some, in what seems to be a childish reaction, just do not want "another woman taking Mom's place."

At this point in Seniors' lives, how many years are left to enjoy a fulfilling relationship? Are these disapproving people really their loving children or an incarnation of the Grinch?

Amid all the furor, and despite the guilt trip Doug's children laid down, Doug and Marie got married. However, Doug continued to live downstairs with his little dog while Marie still resided above. You see, Ranch Rules said dogs were restricted to the first floor, and by now Dog was an integral part of Doug's life.

The logistics of this situation turned the lives of the newly-weds upside down. One night at dinner, I teased them, "Many people I know live together before they get married. You two do not live together even *after* you are married."

Clearly this situation had to change. Marie's apartment was too small to accommodate both their belongings, and besides she could not take in Dog. Doug's apartment was also too small, and his children refused to "allow" him to dispose of "Mom's things." Doug offered to give his kids any of the "things" they wanted, but they didn't want them; nonetheless, they were insistent: he had to keep them. It seems Doug and Marie were trapped in a maze, a regular catch-22.

As far as Doug's children were concerned, as long as their father had married – against their will – to "that woman" he could just keep on living downstairs with the dog they had bought him for companionship, and they would non-confront the entire situation and do their best to pretend Marie did not exist.

Although torn by love for his children, still Doug had made up his mind. He and Marie would live together as befitted a married couple, despite the objections of two-thirds of his offspring.

So…they traded in both apartments for a three-bedroom unit and moved everything they owned into the new space. All the while Doug's daughter was intoning, "We promised Mom on her death bed, no other woman would ever have her things…."

Is a death bed promise the real motivation of children who act this way? Are they truly conscience-bound to fight this battle based on that promise? Are the departed really so churlish? What about the happiness of the living?

Is it just unvarnished greed, ugly, selfish greed that causes adult offspring to act in an effort to control their parents' estates and maximize their own inheritance? Or is it just another twist in the complexities of Senior romances. In either case, it's just "Life at the Wrinkle Ranch: I Promised My Mom…."

Life at the Wrinkle Ranch: Working Fast

The single and widowed men who live at the Wrinkle Ranch frequently seem more interested in finding a lady friend than the other way around. Many of them operate from a sense of urgency spurred by loneliness and by the footsteps of Father Time echoing in their hearing aids. They know they need to work fast!

Take for example, the experience of my friend Jane who was a lovely, bright 80-something. Jane has been widowed for a number of years. She had a beautiful one-bedroom apartment, ate with friends every night in the Tavern, enjoyed a glass of wine at the bar most evenings with the Ranch drinking crowd, and drove herself wherever she wanted to go.

Jane was intelligent, wore pretty clothes, and despite some aches and pains and a lot of hearing loss, she brought a happy face and a good sense of humor to each new day. Her grown children, although living some distance away, were attentive. Jane had a good life.

One day Kathy, a physical therapist at the Ranch, who had been using massage to work with Jane's persistent neck pain had what she thought was a good idea. Aware that Jane had been a Monday night regular at a local piano bar a few years before, the therapist told Joe, a recent widower, that Jane would like to meet him and that she wanted him to invite her to go to the piano bar!

When Kathy mentioned this to Jane, Jane was surprised, but thought nothing would come of it and so did not make any fuss over this unwanted match-making.

Unfortunately Jane underestimated the mating urge of the Lone Rancher and had no appreciation for how fast such a man can work. Before the day was out she had a rose in her mailbox and a note from the gentleman in question, a note which announced that he was rather deaf and not good at chit chat, and so he had to decline *her* invitation to go to the piano bar!

It was unclear to Jane what chit chat and a trip to the piano bar had to do with each other. Most people go to a piano bar to hear the music, not chat; however, it is difficult to decide which surprised her most, the confusing content of his message, the speed with which he acted, or the fact that he acted at all. Nonetheless, she assumed his message declining *her* invitation was the end of the story.

Apparently Kathy had convinced Joe that Jane's interest in him was intense, and so after his opening move with the rose, the next day Joe escalated his campaign. He showed up unannounced at Jane's door, carrying a brown paper bag. Being a kind and well-mannered woman, Jane invited him in and was again surprised when Joe announced that the paper bag contained soup for *his* lunch.

There was an awkward moment while Jane contemplated the implications of this announcement. Fortunately Jane was a sharp lady. She quickly came to the conclusion that Joe expected her to heat his soup and serve him his lunch, and she knew that was not going to happen.

Jane was an independent woman with a full life. She had no interest in a new "friend" who expected her to heat his soup,

81

especially a new "friend" whose hearing was even worse than hers. After a few minutes, Joe announced that his soup was getting cold and he thought he should go. Jane agreed immediately and was about to usher him out when he asked could he "have a hug"? Before she could respond, he wrapped his arms around her and helped himself to an embrace!

Beyond surprise and bordering on astonishment, Jane disentangled herself and opened the door to the hall in an unmistakable gesture of dismissal. That was when Joe laid his next egg in what was rapidly becoming his fouled nest of premature, ill-considered, uninvited, and clumsy courtship. He asked for a kiss!

That was the last straw. Jane had already moved to a safe distance even before this last request. She told him she really was not interested in him, his hugs, his kisses, or his cold soup! Adroitly maneuvering her walker in front of her, she nudged him through the open door.

I hope she told Kathy about the mess she had made with her match making; however, being the sweet lady Jane is, she probably did not mention it. I do know that Jane had gained a new apprehension about the spastic mating moves of the Lone(ly) Rancher and in the future scrupulously avoided single men bearing a brown paper bag containing soup.

On the other hand, as an observer and not the indignant recipient of unwanted attention, I can afford to be philosophical about this sort of thing. It is obvious to me that given the slightest glimmer of encouragement, even second-hand encouragement, these lonely men, set adrift without a spouse so late in their lives, will leap into action. They will work fast! A rose today, a cooking opportunity tomorrow, followed rapidly by a quick thrust into the world of physical intimacy. Clearly these fellows feel the press of time. After all when you are eighty-seven, you realize there is no time to waste in lengthy courtships, and if you're going to strike out, don't bother standing around fouling off fast balls. Go ahead and take a few big cuts, and if you do strike out, move on to your next at bat. It's just "Life at the Wrinkle Ranch: Working Fast."

CHAPTER
6

Senior Attitudes and Actions

When I arrived at the front door of our Wrinkle Ranch, what I did not know about Seniors could have filled a book. Maybe that is why I felt compelled to write one. The stories in this chapter talk about some of the realities of Senior life in general and about my life here specifically. After I had lived at the Ranch for a year or so, I was of the opinion that falls were the greatest risk to Seniors' health; later I changed my mind. I now know that the greatest risk of all is *Denial*. It is Denial that causes most falls; Denial that keeps people isolated in their own homes when they could be in the physical and emotional comfort of a Senior Community. Denial ignores warning symptoms for heart attacks and other serious health problems that could be dealt with if the sufferer sought help in time. Yes, I now believe our fundamental human tendency to ignore and reject unpleasant truths like needing a walker or requiring assistance to complete basic tasks such as taking medication represents the biggest contributor to the accidents and health crises that plague our lives as Seniors. It is the Big D! *Denial* is the culprit! If you do not believe me, just ask Nettie. She now has moved from Independent Living to Assisted Living, and she could tell you all about it; so will "Off Balance."

"Feeling our Way" discusses sincere corporate efforts to follow the dictates of the Federal Americans with Disabilities Act (ADA) and points out the foolishness of some of provisions of the Act, which seem to have been overcome by events. "Eatin' and Drinkin'" discusses the importance of the food and beverage experience in Senior life and how at this particular community, at one point in time, this "E & D" experience was provided to us. For a new resident there was a lot to learn.

As long as we are discussing "Drinkin'," read on. "Public Enemy #1" will demonstrate just how small and self-righteous some people can be – regular disciples of Carrie Nation – if you ask me! And I thought the 21st Amendment cleared the air on that one. In the same vein I included "The Booze Budget" in which I make a splendid suggestion for an efficient use of "left overs." Next we explore what should be a sweet issue, as a matter of fact, "a piece of cake," but instead turns into an ugly public scene in, "I Can't Believe He Said That!"

"A Lifetime Supply" demonstrates how old habits die hard, especially shopping habits and asks insightful questions about the true shopping "economies of scale" for Seniors.

In "Defending One's Turf" we again meet Joan, a woman who holds on to her designated Ranch House role with all her might, and is she ever good at doing that! Over the years I have found her attitude to be widespread here, as if giving up even one little official responsibility represents another nail in the coffin. Maybe it does....

On the other hand, the Seniors who are "Creating Stuff" have found other ways to enjoy and enhance their lives. They don't need a Ranch job or a title to feel fulfilled; however, there are some other issues for them.

Of course pets play a major role in the lives of many Seniors, and "Poop, No Scoop" describes how attitudes and pressures can converge to cause... well, a problem. Following that stinky little story, I have fun with the memo put out by a former Executive Director of our community, a memo that reminds us of yet another reason he may no longer be with us. It's called "Pee, No Tree."

Shortly before the arrival of a new Executive Director, Corporate Management began to invest heavily in the facilities, décor, and technology at our 140-acre community. Such investments were not universally welcomed by our residents, some of whom are categorically opposed to change of any sort and react strongly and negatively to anything that involves technology. It was just such a reaction that inspired "Drop Off the Key, Lee...."

And finally, "National Enquirer Material" gets down and dirty with Wrinkle Ranch gossip. Strangely enough the gossipers are both the sources and the *subjects* of their stories! What kind of rumor mill is powered by the subjects themselves? See if you agree if the stories these people tell about themselves belong on the pages of that famous tabloid by the grocery store check-out counter.

Life at the Wrinkle Ranch: Off Balance

One of the major pitfalls of life at the Wrinkle Ranch is falling. Actually tumbling into a "pit" is not necessary for a fall to be catastrophic, even fatal. The truth of the matter is that many residents of Wrinkle Ranches live their lives off balance.

Take for example, my friend Barb, a lovely lady not yet eighty, but with balance problems. In her youth she studied ball room and tap dancing. But according to the scans, the part of her brain that controls balance has been shriveling up, and now she is not steady on her feet.

One morning she went into her walk-in closet to choose her clothes for the day. Her husband of a lifetime, Donald, took his coffee and the newspaper to their lanai to enjoy the view and the quiet.

Barb fell in the closet. We have very thick concrete walls, and although she called and called, Donald who is rather deaf, did not hear her. It was more than an hour before he began to wonder where she was and found her lying on the closet floor, scratched and bruised, and unable to get up without assistance.

Now Barb wears a pendant around her neck. It has a one button connection to the EMTs downstairs. Let us hope that the next time she falls, she does not lose consciousness, which would render her fail-safe device a fail-sure.

Fannie and Joe lived across the street in their own home for years. Fannie was an Army nurse. Now in her eighties she has macular degeneration and advanced diabetes. Although our marketing people had waged a strong campaign, Fannie never wanted to move to the Wrinkle Ranch and was intransigent on the subject. But one day she fell in her home. Fortunately, Joe was there, but he could not lift her. He had to call the rescue squad.

The next week they came to the Ranch Marketing Department with renewed interest. They now live just upstairs, right above us, and Fannie has a pendant she can press to call for help anytime she needs it. Joe can go to the golf course with impunity and not worry that she will be lying on the floor alone and injured when he returns. She is going to PT to strengthen her quads, and they are putting their lives back in balance.

Nettie was the most amazing ninety-four-year-old woman! At age ninety-three she jumped out of an airplane. On purpose! It was the wish of a lifetime for her, and she won a contest sponsored by Corporate Management, who generously granted her wish.

She was tall, elegant, and had the posture of a dancer. She was smart and beautiful with the most charming manners. She and I frequently discussed fashion, and she gave me a cloche that she used to wear in the 1940s. Seventy years later, I wore it with pride.

Nettie realized that she had some balance problems and was a regular at the Ranch yoga class for just that reason. She had a cane, but detested the idea of walking with assistance. I swear I have seen her brandish it defiantly in the manner of a drum major as she marched down the hall.

One day she came to brunch wearing dark glasses. She had two black eyes. She had fallen on her face and seemed more serious about using the cane as it was intended. Unfortunately, despite that warning experience, she did not bother to take the cane into the bathroom one night. She slipped, fell, and broke her hip. I was concerned about her because it is very difficult to recover from such an accident at her age. Sure enough, after some time in the hospital, then in Skilled Nursing, she moved to Assisted Living.

My neighbor Marnie fell, just reaching up in the kitchen to put something away in a cabinet. She hit her head, causing bleeding and multiple contusions.

Her husband Horace, like so many here, is rather deaf and so did not hear her calls for help. Unable to get up, she crawled into the next room, leaving a trail of blood on the white carpet as she went and wound up spending the next few hours in the hospital trauma center, where they treated her spiking blood pressure and her bleeding head.

When Bobby Burns wrote, "Ah, but a man's reach should exceed his grasp, or what's a heaven for?" he was not talking about kitchen cabinets at the Wrinkle Ranch and was not taking into account the impact of old age on balance. I am starting to think that this balance issue is a major cause of trauma for older people.

Senior balance problems are the reasons I am a fan of that ubiquitous Ranch assistive device, the walker. When I first came here, I hated walkers. The walker users were clogging the halls and seemed to delight in working together to trap their fully ambulatory neighbors by simultaneously passing in front and behind the unsuspecting "ambulator" who was very likely to trip over the unseen walker-wielding scamp behind him.

It seemed to me that walkers put the users' knees and hips out of alignment with their shoulders and were bad for posture. I also believed that doctors must be in cahoots with walker manufacturers and that was why they prescribed so many; however, now I see things differently.

Walkers keep at-risk folks from falling! If Nettie had set her vanity aside and used a walker, she might have avoided that fall that broke her hip. If Marnie had been using the walker her doctor had prescribed, maybe she would have had something to stabilize her and would have kept her balance as she reached up to put her glass in the cupboard.

When the Ranch first opened its doors, nobody using a walker was admitted to residency. Of course once you were in, you were here to stay, even when the time came that you had to use a walker. But today, thanks in part to the Americans with Disabilities Act (ADA), many walker-users move in with their wheeled devices. And if they really use them properly, maybe many of them will keep their feet on the floor and their hips intact for a long time!

It seems that the Book of Proverbs had it right when it taught "Pride goeth before...a fall." If more unsteady Seniors set aside their haughty spirit and false pride, maybe they would not be forced to experience this risk. It's just "Life at the Wrinkle Ranch: Off Balance."

Life at the Wrinkle Ranch: Feeling Our Way

According to the Internet, 20% of Americans over sixty-five years of age are vision impaired. The average age of our residents is in the mid-80s, and far more than 20% of us are vision impaired. At our Wrinkle Ranch we call our vision impaired folks, the VIPs, which stands for vision impaired persons. Other communities in our "corporate family" have similar groups with catchy names such as the "Visionaries," and the "NoSeeUms."

I was born vision impaired – terribly nearsighted – but totally correctable so before moving to the Ranch I did not know anything about the issues associated with this sad, and frequent, accompaniment of aging. After a few years here, I have learned there are many, many different degrees of vision impairment as well as a variety of symptoms and causes of this impairment.

One of our most severely vision impaired residents progressed from having some difficulty seeing as a result of wet macular degeneration – a frequent cause of vision loss among the elderly, especially diabetics – to being almost totally blind after experiencing several small strokes. I have learned: These things happen.

Some of our VIPs can read relatively small print as long as there is great contrast. We were able to create legible documents for one resident by using the computer to print white letters on a black background; ink intensive, but effective! Others can read when there is large print. Many of our residents have various types of electronic systems to assist them. Some have software that reads to them, and others have a voice recognition computer program that "hears" what they dictate and writes it for them.

A number of our VIPs read fonts as small as size twelve, others can drive – just not at night – and some cannot see the white dinner plate on the white table cloths and have trouble locating rice on their plates. Some must memorize their way around the building because they cannot see much of anything, and yet these people are still considered "independent," especially those with a sighted spouse. They live here in an Independent Living Community, and Management has a responsibility to support their needs.

Many of our VIPs are quite active in community life. When I was first elected to the Residents' Council, I received a new badge and was disappointed to see that it did not have a big orange dot like the Council President and many of the other Council members – disappointed that is, until I learned that the big orange dot identified members of the VIPs.

Since all our VIPs, even the most seriously impaired, were sighted through most of their adult lives, not a single one reads Braille, and given that electronic support systems are the most popular way to assist those with vision issues these days, nobody is offering Braille lessons at our community. Thanks however, to the Americans with Disabilities Act (ADA), all the signs in our community are required to have their message displayed in Braille as well as in English letters.

At one time, here at the Ranch, we were in the throes of redecorating all our halls. For the first twenty-two years of this community the old, non-ADA-compliant plastic signs, which were created in-house, displayed the room designations, residents' names, and room numbers throughout the building. These are now replaced by fancy signs with raised letters and little bumps that are Braille translations of the lettering, all advertised as fully ADA-compliant. As you might expect, procuring these signs was expensive, but they were designated by Corporate as the signs we were to use at each community, and the budget for the signs here ran in the tens of thousands of dollars – after all, every room, office, and apartment home had to have a sign, and we are a large community.

Well, except for the pain in the finance department, the signage project was going along swimmingly – until a fully-sighted resident, Bea, who has a certification from the Library of Congress as a Braille expert, decided to teach one of our most seriously vision impaired residents, the founder of our VIP group, how to read the Braille apartment numbers on the signs. The VIP founder did not really want to expend the effort to become proficient in Braille; however, she thought she could learn to feel the difference in the ten symbols for the digits and that could help her as she traveled around the building.

Our Braille expert made a chart of the Braille numbers and invited her student over for a lesson. After some practice with the chart they moved out to the hall to "read" some Braille numbers on the apartment home signs. Oops! The first number turned out not to be a number at all. Instead it was a series of punctuation marks. A quick check of the other signs on that hall proved that not a single one had the representation of any numbers – only punctuation symbols, almost like comic book profanity, #@&*%!$.

Miss Bea is thorough. She checked every sign on every room in this multi-story building. The signs are totally consistent. It seems that someone made an erroneous mapping from one line of the Braille chart to the next, i.e., from numbers to punctuation symbols.

Later Miss Bea told me there was one office identification sign with an incorrect Braille translation: A mechanical equipment room which has that same designation proclaimed in standard lettering, reads in Braille, "Executive Assistant." Sylvia was not amused.

Frankly I think someone at the signage company has a sick sense of humor, but regardless of the cause of our "blasphemous" bumps, I doubt the inspector from the ADA will be amused either. That official will probably not appreciate, as I do, that it's just "Life at the Wrinkle Ranch: Feeling Our Way."

Life at the Wrinkle Ranch: Eatin' and Drinkin'

In a Wrinkle Ranch "eatin' and drinkin'" are among the favorite resident pastimes. At our community meals are provided for the residents, and whether one is on the meal-a-day plan or has selected a plan with fewer meals per month, there are those who choose to have their main meal at lunch and those who elect to have it at dinner.

At our Wrinkle Ranch, generally the lunch bunch is made up of single ladies and members of the older crowd; however, since this particular establishment is over twenty years old, there is a nucleus of "Old Timers" – not to be confused with "old people" – who make up the perennial cocktails and dinner crowd.

For years these seasoned Ranchers gathered in the Tavern at 4:30 every day. They put their place markers at the six and eight-top dining tables, and then this group of a dozen or so proceed to sit around the long, rustic style "cocktail" table and to enjoy their cocktails for an hour, chatting away in the comfortable manner of people who have known each other for a very long time.

After the cocktail *hour* – a term they take literally – they split into smaller groups and migrated to the dinner tables in the Tavern where they had previously deposited their markers and ate their dinner.

Most of the members of this group were couples, and losing a spouse did not mean expulsion from the Tavern crowd. People who lost a loved one frequently just kept on coming to these daily gatherings, and if they found a new love, that person was readily accepted into the "club."

This entrenched group had caused some annoyance among the later arrivals to our establishment. The "newbies" viewed them as cliquish and exclusive. You can see how the "come early and reserve a seat for later" process might be off-putting to the newer residents. When these more recent move-ins showed up after 4:30 and saw there was no room in The Tavern at the "cocktail" table and that two or three of the six dinner tables were already filled with markers, they felt like interlopers if they entered the room.

The truth is that if you wanted to drink with Tavern crowd, join in with the group sing-along on Thursday, and wear a red jacket in support of the troops on Friday, the Old Timer Tavern folk would accept you with open arms; however, new people entering an unfamiliar and definitely different environment were not always bold enough to cross the threshold of The Tavern, preferring to be assigned to eat in this or that dining room with other people who also eschewed the particular camaraderie of the Tavern. Eventually renovations and redecorating and a new Dining Committee Chairman put an end to the "come early and reserve a seat for later" plan, but even that change, unpopular as it was with the Tavern goers, did not disrupt the camaraderie of the Tavern.

Now do not let all this discussion of the Tavern crowd and their cocktail hour lead you to believe that the lunch bunch does not drink. Many of those who prefer to take their main meal at midday rise very early and enjoy their morning activities before indulging in a martini – or two – at the table before lunch. Then they retire to their apartments and nap in the afternoon. An early bedtime usually follows on the heels of the 6:00 evening news.

But other lunchers include the set of ladies who never change out of their house dresses and comfy shoes and rarely venture out of the community. Another lunch group is made up of single women who firmly believe that dinner is for couples and are sure they would not be comfortable in the dining room in the evening. And perhaps they would not; however, if that were the case, it would be self-induced. Evening diners are very welcoming.

There are groups of single women who eat together regularly at dinner, and single women are regularly seated with couples. But old stereotypes live on. These women came from the world of couples, and it seems they just do not want to risk being alone or with "strangers" at dinner so they show up at the noon hour, Monday through Saturday, and have their main meal, but on Sunday....

...On Sunday the two groups, the lunchers and the dinner people, mix and mingle at that wonderful Wrinkle Ranch event, Sunday Brunch!

Everyone gets gussied up for Sunday brunch, even those who do not go to church, because Sunday Brunch is special.

The dress code on Sunday strongly recommends a jacket for gentlemen and forbids shorts for anyone. So those of us who are golfers and get an early tee time in order to be right on time for brunch have to wear long pants to the golf course and plan ahead by stashing a jacket, perhaps in the car or in an empty drawer in the Lobby. Planning ahead is crucial because you would not want to be late to Sunday Brunch. Sunday Brunch is a Main Event. It is Wrinkle Ranch Prime Time.

First of all, management sets out the booze in the Lobby right after 11 A.M. The dining room doors may not be open yet; however, the large punch bowl with the bloody Marys or Mimosas, or other cocktail of the day, is filled and placed on a "help yourself" table, along with glasses and ice and the rarely poured non-alcoholic wine. And "help themselves" the residents do. Some repeatedly!

There is a wonderful buffet in the Aloha, replete with ham and bacon and sausage and scrambled eggs and cheese grits. Not to mention chipped beef, hash browns, and the weekly surprises the chef has created. There are biscuits, English muffins, and bagels. The bagels are really important because there is always smoked salmon, cream cheese, chopped eggs, and capers...need I go on? And then there is the weekly chef's entree from the kitchen. It might be eggs Benedict or omelets or fresh blueberry pancakes, but it is always delicious and in high demand. Oh, and do not forget dessert. There are a number to choose from, and I have seen many a double-dip root beer float top off this sumptuous feast. Sunday Brunch is indeed a special event.

We had noticed that a group of regulars congregate in the Lobby every Sunday before 11:00 in expectation of the arrival of the punch bowl. We took note that these residents continued to sit in their conveniently arranged conversational grouping long after we grabbed our Sunday cocktail and went into brunch, and we could not help noticing that they were still there when we left the dining room after brunch.

Finally one Sunday I, tactful as ever, asked, "Are you planning to skip brunch, and just drink your midday meal?" The remaining half-dozen imbibing residents laughed and said, "Oh we don't take our meals here." Another revelation! Apparently early on in the history of the Ranch, people were allowed to move in with a contract that did not require a meal plan. Not anymore!

I have noticed that these same people partake of all the free coffee, hors d'oeuvres, and booze whenever those items are served. They hold a coffee klatch six mornings a week in the Lobby, sitting cozily on the sofas and easy chairs. They never fail to gather for the Sunday brunch punch bowl, Sip 'n Socials, and the generous spreads with adult beverages put out before all holiday meals. Of course they always show up to eat and drink at the no-cost, special event parties in the auditorium, and there are certainly plenty of those. Can you say, "Working the system," Boys and Girls?

Well I say, "More power to them!" Perhaps they deserve a Silver Alert of a different kind. All I know is they are a very real part of our community. It's just "Life at the Wrinkle Ranch: Eatin' and Drinkin'."

Life at the Wrinkle Ranch: Public Enemy #1

Management at the Ranch knows that many people here like their adult beverages. Every Tuesday from 6-7 P.M. there is a complimentary "Sip n' Social" in our Lobby.

Our generous Management provides at least one other opportunity to gather and imbibe on the house every week, not to mention a very reasonably priced bar in The Tavern, which is open from 4:30 to 7 P.M., Monday through Saturday.

Anytime there is a social event in the auditorium, alcoholic and alcohol-free beverages are available. At least that was the case for nineteen years.

Then a resident who does not drink – and does not approve of alcohol for others – discovered that the liquor license granted to this establishment by the State almost twenty years ago extended only to the first floor of the Tower! This whistle blowing disciple of Eliza Thompson summarily reported the discrepancy to the State Alcohol Beverage Control Board.

Well, what could the authorities do? The law is the law. They issued a "cease and desist" order for alcohol service except on the first floor here, and the Management at the Ranch responded by petitioning for a hearing to extend the license to the other common spaces on the campus.

The initial hearing was held, and a poem written by a resident was part of the Ranch presentation to the ABC Board. It is included here. After a series of public hearings the license modification did pass with flying colors. Oh yes, flying colors and a $15,000.00 fee, which doubtless was passed on, in part, to each of us.

I understand the attached verse was extremely effective in getting our license extended, although it may not be in line for inclusion in the Best American Poetry Series.

> *To the Liquor Board from Our Residents*
> *Our average age is 86,*
> *Some are half-blind and cannot hear,*
> *Many cling to canes and walkers,*
> *And night time driving is our fear.*
> *We enjoy our little parties*
> *Where we can take the hallways home*
> *And never brave the highway race.*
> *We hate to leave our building here*
> *To buy our alcoholic drink.*
> *It's best for us if we don't leave,*
> *At least that's what we think!*
> *We take a lot of medicines,*
> *And often are sort of spaced.*
> *If you folks want us on your roads,*
> *We'll be the worst nightmare you've faced.*

In the meantime, if the identity of the self-righteous, self-appointed, arrogant, egotistical busy body who finked to the State becomes known, my guess is that he or she will discover that Hell hath no fury like Senior sots denied. After all, even people here who do not drink were disgusted by the pettiness of the "narc," and I figure people who have lived as long as most of the residents here must be experts by now at getting even. If not, I can certainly make a few suggestions for dealing with those who ratted us out. It's just "Life at the Wrinkle Ranch: Public Enemy #1."

Life at the Wrinkle Ranch: The Booze Budget

It is obvious that adult beverages play a large part in the socialization process at the Wrinkle Ranch. That thread, or should I say "flood," runs through many of the stories I have recorded about living here.

In case you have forgotten, let me refer you to "Public Enemy #1" or the discussion about the Sip n' Socials and Sunday Brunch with the oh-so-popular bottomless punch bowl.

If we turn away from the considerations of resident health, morale, and socialization for a moment, we could consider this phenomenon from a Management/financial standpoint. Of course there has to be a booze budget. But I had not given it a thought until one evening after a Sip n' Social.

I had walked up to the portabar in the Lobby after dinner and asked the bartender, "What are we pouring tonight?"

"Oh, wine," he said rather unenthusiastically, pointing to the half empty collection of 1.5 liter, low-cost bottles of popular varietals on the bar. Being an old hand at these events by now, I inquired, "And what is the specialty drink tonight?"

There is always a specialty drink. Usually something sweet with an exotic name and of no interest to those of us who are serious drinkers, but sometimes there is vodka as yet unadulterated by the fruit punch they plan to add, and on Tuesdays some of us carry a few olives secreted away in a plastic bag for just such after-dinner opportunities.

"There isn't one," he shrugged. Not being part of the Management team, our bartenders frequently blurt out the truth of a situation, unfettered by the Corporate spin. "It's the end of the year, and our budget for this sort of thing is spent, and we have these cordials left over...so I could pour you some apple pucker or peppermint schnapps, or I could mix them," he offered gamely.

I discovered long ago that any expository lectures to the staff in an effort to educate them to the evils of mixing cordials willy-nilly or to explain such niceties as the difference between real Zinfandel and that icky sweet, pink abomination some Sutter Home marketing guy named "White Zinfandel" all those years ago, were a lost cause. So I smiled sweetly and said, "No, thank you." and went upstairs and made myself a real drink.

As I was sipping, I had an "Aha!" I took off my toper's topper and put on my management hat. Of course there has to be a budget for booze at the Ranch, and with New Year's Eve champagne still to come out of this year's pot of dollars, what could Management do to use the supply on hand and make the social more interesting? I love a good marketing problem, especially when a good marketing solution will satisfy both the bean counters and the resident drinkers!

In less time than it takes to mix a martini, I whipped out the following e-mail and sent it to the head of Dining Services: "Tonight in the Lobby I noticed that instead of a mixed drink of the evening, we were offering a wide selection of cordials and liquors, and there didn't seem to be a lot of takers. Perhaps if a little coffee and some whipped topping had been available, an 'exotic' coffee after-dinner drink would have been a 'hot' offering."

Much to my surprise I received a gracious and speedy response, "That's a good idea. Often we have odds and ends of liqueur to use up. 'International' coffee is a good idea. Thanks."

So there you have it, another link in the intricate chain that alcohol plays at the Ranch. It's just "Life at the Wrinkle Ranch: The Booze Budget."

Life at the Wrinkle Ranch: I Can't Believe He Said That!

We have lots of open meetings at the Ranch. We are nothing if not well informed about what is going on here. Management holds Town Hall Meetings and Coffees. Information is presented, and resident questions are asked and answered. The Resident governing body does likewise. In addition, there are numerous open meetings every month where the residents' favorite topics, the menu and our food service, are discussed in detail.

As in every group, there are a few Ranchers who come to these meeting and cannot wait to get their hands on the microphone and present their personal gripes in detail and without concern for generally accepted standards of courtesy and decorum.

For example, our Corporate Dining folks developed some new baked desserts and held training classes for local food service directors, after which they were ordered to "go forth, bake, and serve." Among the new items were individual cakes baked in a ring mold. This approach makes an efficient offering for our dining service environment. The cakes come out of the oven as individual servings, so no cutting is required. They look quite elegant, and they are always fresh.

So if one happened to order one of the new desserts and did not care for it, what could one do? Well, he *could* send it back to the kitchen and order one of the other four or five desserts on the menu that night, and if he wanted to express his opinion of the new offering as *constructive* criticism, he could fill out a "Comment" card, write a note, send an e-mail, or tell one of the dining services managers.

Or if he were a real jerk and totally bereft of class and breeding, he *could* stand up at the end of a Town Hall Meeting and berate the Dining Director for straying from her goal of providing "fine dining" by serving cake that did not measure up to the traditional piece of cake cut in a wedge. You know, like the one he described as "pictured on every box of Duncan Hines Cake Mix." Duncan Hines Cake Mix boxes: Now there is a pictorial example of "fine dining."

He *could* continue by telling the assemblage that the dessert looked just like "animal dropping," and did not taste much better. How does he know what animal droppings taste like? I wondered. And he *could*, at some point in his three-minute rant, describe the dessert as "phallic!" Now I didn't know what *his* looked like, but based on my limited experience, I certainly would not have come up with that description for our new cake. And to my amazement all of those comments are exact quotes from his statement! I know because I was there, and I took notes.

Later one of our staff asked me to explain what Mr. So and So meant when he referred to the new cake as "phallic" so I explained the meaning of the word. "Oh my," said the well-bred young woman, "I can't believe he said that in front of *everybody.*"

The really sad thing is that almost every time there is a meeting, someone who took his nasty pills that morning demands the microphone and says something we would all like to forget. Sometimes the references are scatological and sometimes even sexual or slanderous. They are certainly mean-spirited. It's just "Life at the Wrinkle Ranch: I Can't Believe He Said That!"

Life at the Wrinkle Ranch: A Lifetime Supply

I have never been a fan of shopping at discount warehouse stores like Sam's Club, or BJ's, or Costco. Sure, I like to get the "best price" on big ticket items, and if I can find a deal on things I use regularly, such as paper towels or ink cartridges, I always think of that as a good thing.

But for years there have only been two of us, and I have no intention of being in the warehouse business. Even before we moved to the Wrinkle Ranch, when we had much more storage space, I never bought in large quantities. For example, an eight-roll package of paper towels always seems like an adequate supply to me. When I get down to the last couple of rolls, I will just buy some more. We live in America, the land of plentiful paper products, and I have every confidence that the grocery store will still be there when I need more help from Brawny, Scott, or Viva.

I have always thought of that bargain box of 1000 Splenda packets as a "life time supply." In fact, that goes for any packaging of household consumables that will probably last the user for longer than a couple of months. That warehouse mentality is just not my thing.

So imagine my surprise when one day I saw one of my fellow Ranchers, a 90-something, loading her small order of groceries onto a luggage cart at the front door of the Ranch. Among the items was the biggest package of Charmin I have ever seen! There must have been at least twenty-four large rolls. I immediately said to myself, "Now there is a lifetime supply if I ever saw one." I was not using that expression in the literal sense, but just as I always have, as another way to say, "That's more that I would ever want in my house at one time."

To my dismay, the next week I saw that very Rancher's picture on the Departure Table along with her bio and the vase with the beautiful red rose – which is our way of announcing that she has moved on to the "Highest Level."

Good Grief! It suddenly dawned on me. There literally is such a thing as a "lifetime supply," and when it came to Charmin, our departed resident certainly had one, and lots left over besides.

Right now the actuarial tables show that I am statistically good for at least another thirteen years; and given that I am in perfect health, probably even longer. So I could realistically stuff every cabinet in my apartment full of twenty-four roll packages of Charmin and use it all before my picture winds up on the

Departure Table. But as the years go by, it is something to think about.

When I reach eighty-seven, do I really save money by buying a six-month supply of toilet tissue? Will my estate chastise me *in absentia* for my foolish "savings" when, after my "departure," my heirs discover sixteen rolls of Charmin remain in my linen closet? At what point in our lives is a half-price sale on a year's supply of Depends no longer a smart buy?

Those are just some of the considerations that are part of everyday life here. It's just "Life at the Wrinkle Ranch: A Lifetime Supply."

Life at the Wrinkle Ranch: Defending One's Turf

In the Big World of Working People, many folks define themselves by their job. The job becomes who they are. Ask a person on the street, "Who are you?" and most will respond, not with an insight into his human condition but with his job title!

It never occurred to me that residents in a Wrinkle Ranch would suffer from the same malady. After all, they are all retired. They no longer have "real jobs," and surely they have lived long enough to be able to define themselves with a broad brush and not with the fine point of a calligraphy pen dipped in the ink of some Wrinkle Ranch function.

Take for example the "job" of chairing the Ranch Movie Committee. When the Black History Month (BHM) Committee landed the Poet Laureate of a nearby major city for a reading of his works on a February Saturday night, the committee members wondered if some of the Ranchers would miss the Saturday night movie – if they would complain about a change in the seemingly immutable Saturday schedule that always includes beer cheese soup at dinner and a movie in the auditorium afterward.

But nobody on the BHM committee anticipated that the head of the Movie Committee would throw a fit worthy of Bobby Knight and go into a "full court press" in defense of her turf. After all, what is one Saturday night out of fifty-two? And nobody was interfering in the selection of movies or any other function of her committee. It is just that there is only one auditorium and Management assumed that "live" free entertainment by a well-known and talented local celebrity would trump Netflix. After all, you can run a canned movie anytime, right?

But it seemed that nobody from the Activities Department consulted with Madam Movie, nobody co-opted her into the process of celebrating Black History Month, and nobody found a way to make her part of the solution instead of the having her become The Problem. She was miffed to say the least.

When the time came to put up the weekly movie sign with the white plastic letters that wedge into the rows of black felt – an example of the finest 1950's communications technology – the sign merely said, "No movie this Saturday," although the designation "with subtitles" did remain on the bottom of the board. So when the unsuspecting BHM committee members requested that the alternate event be spelled out on the board, they were told the felt board "belonged" to the Movie Committee and could not be used for any other purpose.

That allegation was patently false, and silly, and was met by derision when reported to the Executive Director, who immediately decreed that the live event be posted on the "movie board."

But then, where were the white plastic letters? Not in the Activities office to be sure, but in the apartment of Madam Movie where she could be certain that nobody else but she could ever post a message on that board.

Of course the quick-reaction team from the Black History Month Committee just printed a full page sign, pinned it to the Movie Board, and went on with their lives, but it certainly pointed out a Wrinkle Ranch truth.

Be aware: People at the Ranch who take on a responsibility, who get a little local power in some small manner, will hold on to it with both hands. They will fight false tooth and gel nail to protect their little fiefdoms.

Madam Movie is just one example of such a Rancher. She had been head of the Movie Committee for nineteen years and doubtless intended to die in that capacity. The Movie Committee was her life, and heaven help the unsuspecting Rancher who stepped into her bailiwick. It's just "Life at the Wrinkle Ranch: Defending One's Turf."

Life at the Wrinkle Ranch: Creating "Stuff"

Active, productive people create things all their lives. During their careers, and depending on their line of work, they participate in the process of making consumer items, military equipment, and dinner. They make babies; they make deals. They produce athletes, plays, and ad campaigns. And then they "retire."

Some lucky people find that in their retirement lives, they still love producing whatever they did in their "work" lives, and they enjoy knowing that they are doing it for themselves, on their own schedule, and in their own way. Some even manage still to get paid for doing it.

Other retirees cannot wait to move to an over fifty-five retirement town or a Senior Community like our Wrinkle Ranch and take up a new creative hobby, something in the area of arts and crafts – you name it: ceramics, painting, beading, stained glass, wood work, cross stitch, or Bunka. Now it is true that some retirees spend their free time in activities such as golf, tennis, bridge, mahjong, and other games, and by doing so they are in a far different situation from those who choose arts and crafts.

Let me explain. People at our Ranch and in the neighboring over fifty-five communities who play games, read, and exercise in their spare time are not creating "stuff" that must then be given physical storage space. They are spending their time and perhaps their money, but producing nothing that must then be displayed or stored in their "downsized" retirement homes.

For those who cannot wait to take ceramics classes or learn to make stained glass creations, it is a different situation. At first the novice workers in clay or glass may produce a work of art that is not up to their artistic vision; however, given the sweat and in some cases, tears, not to mention the money expended in the creative process, most cannot bear to toss the final product, and so the problem of where to display the latest creation arises immediately.

I have retired friends who live in their own homes and who just love their ceramics classes. Their yards are full of ceramic frogs, bunnies, and alligators not to mention snails which sadly will never materialize on my plate as escargot.

LIFE AT THE WRINKLE RANCH

Inside these homes at every holiday, there is the seasonally appropriate ceramic pumpkin, Santa, Easter Bunny, or witch displayed on the dining room table. Just in case the ceramics aficionado has not yet produced the proper holiday item, there is a ceramics club store where the more accomplished retiree crafters sell their wares so that no table, yard, or curio cabinet need go without the correct seasonal ceramic.

When it comes to painting, the problem is more difficult. The problem is called "wall space." In our last house we had walls that begged for art work. We shopped for and bought framed prints and original works to fill those empty spaces. Then we moved to the Wrinkle Ranch and had to sell or give away all but our very favorite pieces because we now had far fewer linear feet of wall on which to hang works of art. Surely others here are in the same situation, and then they take up painting! Once their work is completed, it must be framed. That usually involves an expensive trip to a local crafts store or art shop. Then it dawns on the "artist!" – "Where do I hang this latest work of art?" Smaller works can be grouped, but depending on the productivity of this new artist, available spaces are soon taken, and then what? Gifts to friends and family? That outlet alas, too soon, runs dry.

Throughout the ages, in the ultimate art conservation move, artists who could not afford new canvases painted over failed art works, a habit that has led modern art scholars to "discover" works by Picasso and Van Gogh painted beneath something created later, sometimes by a lesser artist. But these days, the retiree is more likely to "save" all his creations and just start another, and soon there is no place in his abode to hang another piece of art.

When it comes to the stained-glass hobbyist, the artists seem to be torn between the desire to look out their windows at the beauty of nature and the urge to cover part of their natural view with one or more of their creations. If one has a number of windows, there are a number of opportunities to hang stained glass, but in our comfortably, roomy Ranch House apartment homes most of us have a maximum of two double windows! Of course we do have a large glassed-in lanai with floor-to-ceiling panes, which to some would seem to be begging for small pieces of colored glass set in a frames and suspended between the viewer and the great outdoors.

Here at our Wrinkle Ranch there was a first floor lanai almost totally blocked from outside view, not by blinds or draperies, but by a large number of small, framed works of stained glass depicting dogs, fish, flowers, and birds at various levels between the floor and the ceiling.

What will our stained-glass artist do when the view from the last of the available clear spaces on his lanai is finally filtered through red and blue glass? I don't have any idea. Will he bravely strike out into the unknown and take up another hobby, or instead will he suffer from some deep depression associated with stained glass withdrawal? Perhaps he will take up jigsaw puzzles. After all the two skills seem related, both having to do with linking small pieces together. The jigsaw hobby should lend itself to limited space because once solved, the puzzle can be broken apart, returned to the box, and donated to the Activities Department. Unless, God forbid, our frustrated stained glass artist is unable to fight off the desire to glue the puzzle pieces to a board and varnish the entire project, creating yet more "stuff" to store.

My take from these observations is that those Seniors who spend their retirement reading, playing bridge, or participating in sports are avoiding this serious retirement risk – the proliferation of Senior art works and the resultant problem of what to do with them.

So how can Seniors deal with the "productivity" of retirement? What hobby can a Senior embrace that allows creativity without creating tangible "stuff"? – "stuff" that needs to be hung, displayed, dusted, stored, and eventually taken away by his heirs to some "unwanted stuff" place?

I suggest writing. These days with a terabyte of storage available for a pittance and unlimited space just waiting to be filled in "the cloud," the wannabe author can write night and day and never produce a single paper book or even one piece of paper, much less bookshelves full of his original works. All his writings can be stored electronically, sent to his readers via e-mail, and even published and sold by Amazon.com over the Internet, and never take up an iota of space in his downsized Senior world.

So Seniors, before you leap into the world of creativity afforded by your newly earned leisure of retirement, think about what you plan to create, and where you plan to put it. Consider carefully because storage problems abound in our community. It's just "Life at the Wrinkle Ranch: Creating 'Stuff'."

Life at the Wrinkle Ranch: Poop, No Scoop

All of us who have lived in an urban environment where pets and people coexist are familiar with the "Poop, No Scoop" problem.

New Yorkers are probably the most experienced at dodging this particularly distasteful type of street litter, but even in the spacious environment of our former home in North Carolina, a demographically diverse, upscale, gated community, there was general consternation over the failure of dog walkers to use their scoopers and deposit the refuse in the many green boxes positioned around the property for just such a purpose.

Given my previous experience, it did not seem surprising that poop-no-scoop behavior was an issue in our new community, a community made up entirely of old people. Many residents of the Wrinkle Ranch have given up doing many things they did earlier in their lives – driving at night, dancing, playing golf – and apparently among those activities many have abandoned is cleaning up after their dogs.

Despite the multiple green stations around the beautiful grounds surrounding our Wrinkle Ranch where we are offered plastic bags and depositories for doggie droppings, when we first arrived, our Executive Director, Paul, found it necessary at our general resident meetings to admonish the resident dog owners to "pick it up."

Of course there are a lot of reasons Ranchers don't "pick it up." Some are suffering from lifelong arrogance exacerbated by age and feel the rules are for everyone but them; others are too blind, too feeble, or just not flexible enough to operate a scooper. And then there are the ones who are past caring about much of anything.

One of our residents, the subject of "The Round Spoon," perhaps overwhelmed by the impossible task of caring for her husband, Al, whose Alzheimer's was advancing rapidly, would walk their little dog, all the while glancing nervously around until she thought no one was looking, then allow the poor thing a quick squat, and move away from the scene of the crime as swiftly as possible to avoid having to deal with one more unpleasant task in a life now full of unpleasant tasks and daunting challenges and exacerbated by a painful back problem.

Her other problem was that I kept showing up. Really I was not on poop patrol, but repeatedly I would happen to appear at just the time she and her little dog were trying to make a surreptitious deposit.

Once I was on the ninth tee of our golf course when she was on a stealth mission. The dog had just assumed "the position" when My Hero hit a great drive, and it made that satisfying "crack" as the ball left the club. Startled by the noise, she whipped around and realizing they were caught in the act, jerked the poor thing up by the leash and dragged him away, still unrelieved.

Another time we were at a side entrance, unloading the results of a productive booze run to the nearest package store when the three of them wandered into view. The dog was providing fertilizer for various of our verdant bushes with unrestrained abandon, and she, scooperless, was making a concerted, but not very successful, effort to propel both the dog and her husband along before they could be found guilty by association. But she knew I saw her. Eventually whenever she and the dog saw me, she would pick him up and flee in the opposite direction.

Finally, Ranch management realized that given the pace of advancement of Al's disease, it was necessary for him to move to memory care where professionals could watch him 24/7. But I never gave up my vigilance as long as she and the dog were here. Old habits die hard. It's just "Life at the Wrinkle Ranch: Poop, No Scoop."

Life at the Wrinkle Ranch: Pee, No Tree

On the heels of the events that inspired me to write the preceding story, "Poop, No Scoop," our Executive Director, Paul, surpassed the shock value of his speech at the quarterly residents' meeting with a memo, hand-delivered to each apartment in our building. It seems that the assault on our landscaping has been eclipsed by a far greater crime. Somebody on the first floor was allowing a dog to piddle on the hall carpet! In other words, instead of "Poop, No Scoop," we were now faced with an indoor voiding issue completely a-voiding the use of every dog's favorite targets: shrubs and trees. You might say we were dealing with a case of "Pee, No Tree."

All the apartments on the first floor have a private exit to the outside. All dog owners must live on the first floor for just that reason. They can take their dogs outside without ever entering the hallway. Many first floor residents maintain lovely flower gardens outside their back doors, and they are all supposed to take Fido out the "garden" door and down the garden path.

Some residents contend a recent economic downturn seemed to have loosened entrance standards here at the Ranch, and of course the years can take their toll on residents who were perfectly competent to take their dogs out for relief in the past and may have lost that whole "walk the dog" concept on the way to growing older, and now we have wet carpet.

Paul has promised to sleuth out the peepeetrator and to give him one written notice. Upon further carpet abuse he will be subjected to contract cancellation and expulsion. If I were the E.D., I think I would first offer to impound the pooch, and allow the owners to continue as paying residents; however, Paul is clearly a man of direct action who intends to eighty-six the whole kit and kapoodle.

I am eagerly awaiting the next action in this battle between the recalcitrant resident who wants to seep this all under the rug, and Paul, who must be getting a huge volume of complaints from those residents on the first-floor hall who have not yet lost their sense of smell. I'll bet they are pretty pissed off.

People around here do not spend much time in the hallways. Under current practices, it might be years before anyone actually observes these urinary infractions. Perhaps there is a new surveillance camera in our future, or periodic foot patrols sent out from the Front Desk.

Better yet, maybe the first-floor residents will organize themselves in the manner of a Neighborhood Watch which would keep one of them on duty in the hall around the clock – at least until the carpet dries. On second thought there are many inherent problems with that solution. Since so many of our residents suffer from serious vision impairment, the number of Ranchers who would actually be able to see who was letting the dog into the hall may be so small as to make the available pool of watchers negligible. Besides none of them would be able to *stand* watch, and based on the number of residents I have spied napping in the lobby chairs, "sitting watch" is probably not a viable option either.

What will Paul do to nose out this miscreant? How will these residents respond to having their dirty linen, uh, I mean "carpet," exposed to the entire building? Will Paul's threats of expulsion cause the dog owner to give up on the daily habit of sneaking into the hall for canine bladder relief and instead to return to the more traditional methods of dealing with doggie elimination? Who knows? It's just "Life at the Wrinkle Ranch: Pee, No Tree."

Life at the Wrinkle Ranch: "Drop off the Key, Lee…"

…and set yourself free." This catchy line comes from a blockbuster hit by Paul Simon, and I am borrowing it to introduce and explore an aspect of life here at the Ranch. For the first twenty-four years the doors at our Ranch were locked and unlocked by keys – standard metal keys. Apartment homes and outside doors were accessible by turning one of two keys given to the Ranchers when they signed their contracts. Many of our residents wore little curly plastic bracelets from which dangled various keys, their apartment home keys among them.

Then one day the word came down from the Corporate heights, "Keyless Entry" was a line item in the capital budget for the year. Suddenly our residents were thrust into a technology insertion program in a very personal way.

"Big Deal," you say, "keyless entry has been around for years. Anyone who has been to a good hotel in the last ten years has used a programmable card to insert in the door or wave in front of a sensor to unlock his room." Unless of course, the programming failed or he managed to desensitize the card on his way to the room and now was stranded in the hall with all his luggage and no way to get in to his room. But based on personal experience, I digress.

As I was saying, Corporate leaders decreed, "Keyless Entry" was the watchword for the year, and so it began, a new chapter in "Technology Meets Wrinkle Ranch," and for such a simple application, there should have been nothing to it, right?

Wrong! First of all, it is a change. In every group there are always a few members who balk at change, any change – good, bad, or indifferent. To them change is at worst inherently evil and even at best, unnecessary. When you include the word "Seniors" in the statement about groups and change, the number of resistors goes up dramatically!

"Why are keyless entry locks a benefit?" recalcitrant Ranchers inquired. "Why did Corporate leaders mandate the change? Why can't they leave well enough alone?"

How about improved security and elimination of easily copied keys? Keyless entry reduces the weight of those heavy key rings management personnel carry. There is immediate reprogramming to deactivate access by terminated employees or to change lock settings. Cost is reduced. Management has the ability to track entry; we eliminate the risk of lost or stolen keys, and it is easy to grant and control temporary access. These are just a few of the reasons that a keyless entry system offers benefits to any organization, especially one populated by frequently forgetful Seniors.

And why would our Ranchers object? Consider this comment offered in an open meeting here, "My mother lived here before me for fourteen years. I have lived here for ten years. Keys were good enough for us all those years, and they should be good enough now. Management is purposely harassing us."

In the face of such flawless "Senior logic" how could Management possibly insist on going forward with the expensive replacement of every lock in the community and the installation of such a system? But insist they did.

So now that you know what the mandate was, "How," you might ask, "did this significant technology insertion project progress?"

Early on in the project we installed the new entry system at the multiple auxiliary doors to our main building. It took only a day before a fully sighted resident, frustrated that the door opening mechanism did not respond instantaneously when she hit the "Press Here to Open Door" pad, then pulled the next lever she saw – the red one – the one labeled, "Fire Alarm!"

Of course it was a weekend. Of course the new fire alarm system – destined to become the subject of another story – was unfamiliar to the weekend associates on duty. It took forty-five minutes, a trip to work by the Director of Maintenance, who drew the short straw since he lives closest to the Ranch, and a visit from the fire department to shut the incessantly honking thing off. By then we were all crazed since the emergency policy at our Wrinkle Ranch is to "defend in place." All I can say is it is difficult to feel positive about that approach while defending in place by covering one's head with a pillow.

It would have helped if we could have been informed that it was a false alarm. Unfortunately, the automatic dialing system with the prerecorded reassuring message had not yet been implemented, and the old loud speaker system did not really function anymore. So we added another pillow and prayed it would soon be over.

I am sorry to report that unlike any proper colonial American community, we have no pillory in front of our main building, and so it was impossible to administer a good old fashioned, and well-deserved, public humiliation to the idiot perpetrator whose name was assiduously protected by Management in an effort to avoid widespread retaliation. Not since the pair of self-righteous teetotalers turned us in to the State Alcoholic Beverage Control Board for not having covering our entire campus by our liquor license twenty-some years ago, an oversight resulting in the distressing cessation of alcohol sales in some areas of the campus for months and the payment of a sizeable fee, has the urge to punish another a fellow resident run so high among the majority at the Ranch.

But back to the massive project of installing keyless entry throughout our community. As you might expect, given the over 400 apartment homes and numerous other offices and doors at the Ranch, there were many more glitches that were part of this trek to the new world of keyless entry.

Take for example our very own apartment home door, which had the new lock installed along with all the other keyless locks on our hall. When we waved the "magic" card in front of the lock, the green light flickered right on cue, and we entered without a glitch. "Wonderful! Flawless," you might say. We were happy.

But My Hero and I are scientists, engineers, and questioners. One day, as a test, we did not wave the magic card. No green light flickered. We just turned the handle, and still the door opened! Upon further investigation it seems that in their haste to install over 400 apartment door lock sets, the installers from the outside contractor – pushed as they were by a time constraint – did not test their installations. Aha! Upon careful inspection, it seems the bolt on our door was not aligned with the hole in the door frame and so the bolt could not insert into the frame. The door was never locked. No wonder it opened without the wave of a card!

Once we reported this glitch, Management was forced to try every door in the community to ascertain if any others had the same discrepancy. Oops! You can certainly see why My Hero and I are popular with Management here at the Ranch.

Of course months later there were some outside doors not upgraded, so we still needed to carry the outside door key. Many apartment doors waited a long time for the required plug to close off a now-unnecessary hole in the frame, and there were other miscellaneous issues. Residents who never left their home in the old days without the bracelet or key ring with all their keys frequently went out forgetting their "magic" card and had to ask for assistance to open their door. Be aware, the technology insertion road, regardless of how beneficial in the long run, is a bumpy trail, especially at a Wrinkle Ranch.

There were the not-unexpected objections by residents who had always "left a spare key" with this friend, or that neighbor so someone could feed the cat or walk the dog when the resident was out and about. Others thought a non-resident relative or friend absolutely had to have access. Of course Management was forced to deal with the many requests to open a door for one person or another, and the issue of who should have access required new procedures and individual conferences; however, eventually the project was completed, and relative calm descended across our Ranch once again.

Management issued a call to all residents to "drop off their keys" so they could dispose of this useless glut of metal, and despite Paul Simon's admonition, we still have some residents who are not sure about this new technology. It's just "Life at the Wrinkle Ranch: Drop off the Key, Lee…."

Life at the Wrinkle Ranch: *National Enquirer* Material

If you were a reporter for the *National Enquirer*, what elements would you look for in a story? Just how would you determine that an event measured up to your salacious standards? If you were the editor would you select one of the following tales for the front page of your tabloid?

Following the death of a well-liked, ninety-eight-year-old man at the Ranch, his children came to dispose of his effects and were touched by the caring and support they received from his neighbors. In response they threw a little party for a few of them – cold cuts, cookies, beer, wine – the works. I guess you might call it a Wrinkle Ranch wake.

The gathering quickly broke into two groups: the four men sat at the dining table while the six ladies gathered on the sofa and in the big upholstered chairs. At first, while the wine flowed, all the talk centered on the recently departed gentleman. After a while Edna, one of our WWII war brides from across the pond, a former Senior beauty queen and still a diva, grew tired of the conversation since it was not about her. To relieve her boredom and aided by a second glass of wine, she told the following story:

A few months ago I received a phone call from a man who said he was an attorney in Spain, and he told me I had inherited money – a lot of money. Of course I had to prove my identity to collect it, and I sent several letters to the address he provided with the information he needed, and I paid a fee to cover the costs of all the legal paperwork. Finally, a couple of weeks ago they called me and said I had to fly to Madrid to collect my inheritance in person, and of course they warned me not to tell anyone, after all – you can't be too careful these days. I bought my round trip ticket, and scheduled a return flight to give myself a few days to enjoy Spain, once I had collected my inheritance.

When I arrived in Madrid, I retrieved my bags and waited at the airport as I had been instructed. And I waited, and I waited. No one came or called. After several hours, airport authorities came and inquired as to why I was sitting there so long. By that time, I was quite upset and told them I was waiting for the people to deliver my inheritance. They called the American Embassy and a couple of nice people from the Embassy came and took me with them, and I stayed at the Embassy until I could get a flight home. Once I was home I called our Management, and they called the sheriff. He came over to see me, and I had to talk to the detective in the fraud department.

Needless to say this "true confession" of naivety and reckless, foolish behavior had the desired result. Our fading beauty queen was immediately the center of attention. She was barraged by questions from her neighbors about the details of her exciting, if foolish, quest for free money. Some of them had seen the sheriff leaving Edna's apartment home and had been gossiping for the last week about the reason for his visit. Now at last they knew, and the truth was juicier than any of their speculations.

So if you were a reporter for the *National Enquirer*, would you choose to run with this story? What would your headline be? "Spanish Señor Suckers Silly Senior" or how about "Old Bag Abandoned! Madrid Airport on Alert!"

Well, except for reaffirming that old people are stupid, greedy, and eager to confess it, I frankly do not think this story rates coverage by the likes of the *National Enquirer*. It certainly does not seem to measure up to the *Enquirer's* Scale of Salaciousness – no alien encounters, interspecies sex, or supernatural events. In fact, no sex of any kind – just a foolish old lady, a victim of identity theft who was duped out of her money. Sad, but probably not exciting enough for the *National Enquirer*.

But wait! The party was not over. The wine was still flowing, and another little lady, Flora, was about to speak up. Flora was a very pretty 90-something widow, always nicely dressed with her blouses tight across her ample bosom and tucked in to show off the fact that she, unlike most of her neighbors, actually had a waist line. She wore her hair in a mass of tiny curls, and she never went out without her makeup done just so. Flora had lost interest in the current conversation since it was all about Edna and not a bit about her. It was bad enough when they all were discussing a man who was not around anymore, but now Edna was getting all the attention, and Edna was still annoyingly alive!

In a masterful move, Flora began the process of stealing the limelight. "I know that must have been a frightening and upsetting experience," she stated. "As Edna just told us, you really can't trust anyone these days. I too had something frightening happen to me, and it happened right in my own apartment." With this intriguing introduction, Flora began to tell her story to the audience, which was now expertly set up and eagerly awaiting her words.

The physical therapist had just left my apartment, but apparently she didn't close the door properly because I went into the bathroom, and when I came out a man was standing in the middle of my hall! At first I was startled, but not frightened, because he is resident here, a man I know. He teaches a history class here every year and he was Council President once.

The listeners leaned closer – this could be good! Flora continued:

But then he led me into the living room and pulled me down on the couch! He told me he had not had sex with his wife for fifteen years, and he started kissing me and caressing the top half of my body all over.

At this point Flora definitely had everyone's attention. Even Edna was listening intently.

I kept telling him, "No! No!" and finally after about fifteen minutes of wrestling with him and pushing him away, he gave up and left.

Unsatisfied by the abrupt ending of this tale of uninvited intruder and unfulfilled sexual desire, and wanting more, one after the other of the ladies asked, "Who was it, Flora?" Flora milked the moment for all it was worth, demurring with a coy, "I don't want to tell anyone his name." This, after having provided enough details at the beginning of her titillating tale to finger the suspect! Finally, one of the ladies asked, "Are you talking about Frank Smith?" And unable to tell a lie, Edna confirmed the I.D. And then immediately begged her neighbors "not to tell!"

Now this story is definitely *National Enquirer* material! It has all the requisite elements. First a lovely widow, put in jeopardy by a caregiver who was not careful to close her door, victimized by a neighbor, a fellow Rancher who apparently had been staking out her apartment, just waiting for an unlatched opportunity. This story has an innocent victim, sex, violence, and betrayal, and it raises the frightening specter of being attacked in one's own home.

Senior sex is always a hot topic. Remember the furor raised a few years ago when "60 Minutes" did the exposé of STDs at the Villages? The American Public is definitely curious about what goes on behind the closed doors of a Wrinkle Ranch. "Enquiring minds want to know."

I can see the headline now, "Horny Historian Invades Her Home! Feisty Flora Fights Back!"

Yes, when the reporter from the *National Enquirer* comes to my door for comments, I'm going to say, "It's just 'Life at the Wrinkle Ranch: *National Enquirer* Material.'"

CHAPTER
7

A Funny Thing Happened...

If you are contemplating where you are going to spend the rest of your life and you are wondering, "What is life really like at a Wrinkle Ranch?" I can tell you. Life here is like life everywhere. Life is sad, and life is happy. Life is easy, and life is hard. Life is depressing, and life is funny as all get out!

I had some stories that did not seem to fit into any of the other chapters. They have to do with the essence of Wrinkle Ranch Life because they are funny.

You can imagine my reaction in "A Little Excitement!" Would that experience have been different if I had lived in a high rise in any major city? Well maybe the workers would have had a better view, but let's not go there!

Before we installed the washer and dryer described in "Washin' and Dryin'," I had an experience involving a trip to our communal laundry room, which I have entitled, "The Pretty Good Housekeeping Seal of Approval."

These days we have a regularly scheduled Trivia Challenge night. Management buys questions and answers from a service, and we have organized teams that compete. We call our team, "Anchors Aweigh." We have really smart people on our team, and we win a lot! Many nights we go home with $2.00 apiece, after putting up only $1.00 each to play – a pretty good return on investment for less than two hours of effort! We meet in the Tavern after dinner, and residents run the entire activity. It is well organized and efficiently managed. The story in this chapter, "Trivial Pursuit," describes the first Trivia event ever held here and what happened that night. As you will learn, it was a very different experience....

Then comes "Evasive Maneuvers." Surely you have gone out of your way not to disappoint your friends. Well, that is just what we did. It could have happened anywhere, maybe....

113

The next story in this chapter introduces my experience with "The FU Grad School" followed by another, which describes some of my adventures when My Hero volunteered "us" to teach a computer class for our fellow residents. That story, like the class we taught, is called, "Loving Your E-Mail." If you are not familiar with e-mail, you may not find this story as entertaining as those readers who already "love" their e-mail.

In retrospect some of these stories could fit into any number of chapters, but I decided, for example, to put "Another Red Car" into this one. Later I discovered that the driver suffered from dementia and would soon be on his way to a higher level of care. Although I had a close escape, what transpired was funny in that wry manner shared by so many Wrinkle Ranch vignettes that are humorous to me, so it wound up here.

The Ranch dining rooms are always a good place to pick up a juicy steak or a juicy story. After all when you mix impatient, hungry Seniors with alcohol and complex social situations, anything can happen. Read about how I literally walked into one such situation in "Dining Debacle."

When I was a girl, I longed to be "la belle of the ball." Our next story tells about a male Rancher who was the center of attention at one of our Wrinkle Ranch "balls." It is entitled, "Le Beau of the Ball," and tells about some exciting night life at the Ranch and how, amazingly, our Rancher's assistive device required for him to navigate the halls became totally unnecessary on the dance floor – when provided with the right "inspiration."

Next comes "The Red Arrow," which might just as well be entitled, "When All Else Fails, Read the Directions."

"Talking Turkey" discusses the possible reasons and the actual solutions for a surprise problem with what might have been some Rancher's potential traditional Thanksgiving treat.

We end this chapter with another story about the rigors of getting older and encountering situations we could not have imagined in our younger days. Called, "Wardrobe Malfunction," I can guarantee the veracity of the details of this story because the wardrobe that malfunctioned was mine, and the laugh was definitely on me! This experience is a reminder that laughing at ourselves is the healthiest kind of laughter.

Life at the Wrinkle Ranch: A Little Excitement

One morning while still clad in my pajamas I raised the blind on my bedroom window and saw two men standing just outside, staring in at me! What could be a surprising sight becomes truly exciting when one lives on an upper floor and has no balcony! Apparently they were hanging in mid-air!

When I recovered from my surprise, I realized they were standing on a cherry picker and were on their way up to the roof to fix a gutter that had blown loose in a recent storm. It seems our usual splendid management communication system had overlooked the need to alert those of us who were on their route to the top.

That is the sort of omission that might give some residents quite a scare with disastrous results. On the other hand, there is always the potential that the workmen may get quite a fright also. I mean it is a good thing I was not in the process of shedding those pjs, or there might have been a lot of excitement on the part of both parties!

I reported this issue to the Executive Assistance who replied conspiratorially as follows:

We should have mentioned in the Weekly that the cherry picker was coming out to fix the gutters and would be traveling up by the set of apartments under the broken gutter this morning. We could have really given some old person a scare! I can only imagine the look on your face when you saw someone outside your window…. Sorry 'bout that…. Let's blame Maintenance.

Having been in Corporate America for years, I appreciated her attitude. By all means, we should blame someone else, certainly not ourselves! It's just "Life at the Wrinkle Ranch: A Little Excitement!"

Life at the Wrinkle Ranch: The Pretty Good Housekeeping Seal of Approval

There are a number of aspects of life at the Wrinkle Ranch that have given me difficulty. One is the laundry.

When we made the trade-off to forego having a mini stack washer/dryer in our apartment, which by the way would take a chunk of furniture space out of our lanai and was unacceptable to my interior design plan, we resigned ourselves to going three doors down the hall to use the large, commercial style washers and dryers that are there for the use of all the Ranchers on our floor.

These machines are there for our use at no cost, are always clean, and are usually available; so what's the big deal? After all it is just a slightly longer walk than it was in my house. But the big deal is that in my house, I did not have to be properly dressed to do the wash. We could walk in from the garage, pull off our sweaty golf clothes, and drop them in the washer, start it up, and head to the bathroom already clad in proper shower attire; we could leave the clothes in the washer until we were good and ready to dry them, or in the dryer until we were ready to take them out. If they were there too long, we could just reheat them and then remove them and fold, sans wrinkles. Everything was done at our convenience whenever it suited us.

Not so anymore. One must be prompt to remove clothes from the washer and the dryer and must complete the laundry in a timely manner, once begun, and naturally one must be clothed to walk down the halls. Furthermore, it takes almost two hours to do a wash load and then dry it, so one must remain dressed throughout the process and set a timer so that one can show up, appropriately attired, and put the wet things into the dryer, and then arrive again to carry the dry things back to the apartment. It is enough to make a Dutch woman wear dirty clothes!

So who is to blame me when the other day, I came in from exercising outside, hot and sweaty, and in wet exercise clothes and went right to the shower. Not ready to get dressed to go "out," but eager to put my dirty exercise clothes in the washer, I put on the closest thing I could lay my hands on – a clean pair of spandex bike shorts and a matching top which exposed a bare midriff, and then set out for the laundry room. "After all," I said to myself, "nobody is in the hall this time of day, so who's to see me?"

And I was almost correct. There were no other residents in sight, but I had forgotten that the hall nearly always has a cleaning cart parked somewhere along its length. Housekeeping cleans every apartment once a week, and the Ranch has a large staff of housekeepers, all of whom seem to be young, female, and Hispanic – many with a limited command of English.

I had made a couple of trips up and down the hall, one to start the wash and another to put the clothes in the dryer, without encountering anyone. On my third trip, as I exited the laundry room carrying my basket of clean clothes, the housekeeper emerged from the apartment she had been cleaning. She took a long look at my garb, clearly not typical Ranch resident wear, and said politely, " 'Scuse me Miss, OK I ask you somethin'?"

So dumb, unsuspecting me, I said, "OK," and then she threw the curve ball: "How old you are?" I'm not sure why, maybe because I was so stunned, or maybe because I knew she did not understand that she had just been totally inappropriate and unthinkably rude, I told her. She took another long look, nodded, and said, "Pretty good."

So there you have it. It's just "Life at the Wrinkle Ranch: The Pretty Good Housekeeping Seal of Approval!"

Life at the Wrinkle Ranch: Trivial Pursuit

One of the employees in the Activities Department at the Ranch is a prima donna named Patricia. She is truly a prima donna; back in the day, she was an opera singer. She still has a strong, lovely soprano voice. She has been here working with resident "activities" since the Ranch opened years ago so she has a fair amount of power derived from time in grade. Furthermore, every year she organizes a major production, which includes many of the residents in all the various aspects required to put on a stage performance. There are set builders, and artists, and actors, and chorus members all assigned to the appropriate tasks, and after months of preparation, the results of Patricia's creative talents and management culminate in an original production written and directed by her, performed by residents, and attended by everyone else including many of the folks from town. The proceeds are used to augment the scholarship fund maintained here to benefit the employees, especially the young people who work in our food services area. The entire process amounts to a lot of fun and positive activity for Seniors, and all for a good cause.

Patricia does a terrific job with this type of event; however, the Activities Department is responsible for far more and different types of activities than the annual theatrical production. For example on this particular week Activities had scheduled a Trivia Night in the Auditorium. Notices went up in the elevator and were published in the Weekly. Teams of four to eight residents were invited to complete for prizes.

Well, count me in! Even though we were fairly new at the Ranch, I was able to troll about and collected a splendid team, which included two people from Sarasota, that storied capital of cultural and literary excellence; a retired librarian; a very intelligent attorney; a former Jeopardy contestant; and My Hero, a scientist and engineer. I felt confident that no other group at the Ranch could compete with our team's broad base of knowledge and our ability to work together to ferret out tough answers.

Then one of our Sarasota team members, Anna, who must have been alerted by previous experiences with Activities, went to Patricia to inquire about the format for Trivia Night.

To her distress, she was told each team would have a Trivial Pursuit Game at its table and would play together as a team. In the end, the team that completed the game first would get muffins in the Bistro! This was not what our team had in mind! We wanted full blown competition! Our Sarasotan went to work to "assist" Patricia in finding alternate ways to organize this activity. She researched 120 questions on the Internet, including categories that would be appropriate for people of our age and experience, and she voluntarily withdrew from our team in favor of her goal of holding a more enjoyable event for everyone. Although she thought her efforts were proceeding splendidly, at 4 P.M. on the afternoon of the Big Trivia Night, she had a phone call from Patricia.

Patricia had decided to run the event another way. She thanked our teammate for all her help and informed Anna that her questions were not going to be used. Patricia was worried that if all the teams received the same question at the same time, teams would overhear the deliberations of the other teams, since many residents here are hearing impaired and speak loudly, and since some are vision impaired, the conferencing could not be carried out in writing. So instead of Anna's logical and efficient format allowing for real competition, each team would get a different question in rotation from the Trivial Pursuit game provided by the Activities office and would answer it aloud....

There would be one person on the stage with a Trivial Pursuit board. She would roll the die to pick a category, Patricia would read a question from that category, and the designated team would have two minutes to confer among themselves and come up with an answer, which would be delivered by the team captain via microphone held by Patricia – all these details are important as you will see later, so hang in there with me. A correct answer resulted in the team's receiving a colored card matching the color of the category. The team that collected three cards of each color in each of seven categories would be the winner and get the free muffin. If you think this sounds complex, convoluted, and time consuming you are correct. "Unworkable" is another word we could have used.

Three teams were signed up for this event, and I did not need my degree in mathematics to compute that a requirement for answers gaining three cards in each of seven categories, each taking up to two minutes to deliver for three teams, was going to create an environment that would last for hours! Remember, the card is only awarded for a correct answer. What about all the time spent giving incorrect answers? What about the fact that the categories were going to be chosen at random by the roll of the die? What if your team never got a single question in one or more categories?

Our team ate dinner together in the Emerald Room. The Emerald Room is green and so were we, green with concern about how to rescue what was sure to be a disaster of an event and could even preclude holding any more such games. Then we learned the worst news of all. No bar had been set up in the auditorium! We did not mind paying for drinks, but we were being denied the opportunity to purchase any. How were we to remain sharp with no lubrication? No beer? No wine? Nothing?

Fortunately, we still had time to fortify ourselves before the appointed hour, and we all made a bee line to get to the Tavern before closing time only to discover that the bartender had taken down the bar five minutes early, and we could not even buy a drink to go.

Undeterred, Anna went to her apartment for plastic glasses, and I went to ours for wine! Not wanting to appear in the auditorium holding multiple wine bottles, I took out our medium-sized cooler and filled it with all the open wine bottles from the refrigerator and threw in a couple that were not yet opened, just in case the evening dragged on longer than we projected. Then I added a few bottles of club soda and a bag of ice and headed for the auditorium. The cooler was heavy, but my heart was light.

"What are we going to do about the other teams? Do we have enough to share?" asked My Hero, always concerned for decorum and good manners. "BYOB!" I responded emphatically, and the rest of the team solemnly nodded their agreement. We broke out the glasses and the various wine bottles and settled ourselves to wait for the start of the Big Event.

It had not occurred to me that there would be an audience, but lo and behold! There they were. And they continued to filter in until at 7:30, the appointed time, there were about fifty people seated in the audience rows. We were Team Three and were seated at the table with our number neatly written on the folded paper tent. Teams One and Two did not come in as a group, and there was a strong effort to rip off our former Jeopardy competitor – a last-minute, strategic add-on for us – by a loud bully on Team One who complained that teams were only supposed to have six members, and we had seven. Fortunately, one of our teammates was President of the Residents' Council and had some standing in this community, even with the Prima Donna. So when he assured Patricia that the printed notices said teams were made up of four to eight people, the bully was denied access to our sleeper!

On each table there were sheets of paper containing incomprehensible rules for the competition. I do not know who wrote them, but I am sure she would have failed any fifth-grade class in expository writing. To make matters worse, Patricia proceeded to "explain" the rules in a manner that would have gone under the heads of slow third graders. Did she realize this group was not the general public? This was a group of people who thought they could answer questions – in front of an audience – Seniors who still had their wits about them. The requirement for three cards in each category was changed to two on the spot in response to the unanimous demands of the teams, most of whom wanted to be back in their apartments before midnight!

At 7:30 as Patricia still continued to repeat her instructions for the fourth time, I began a rhythmical clapping, which was picked up by other members of our team. "I don't respond to that sort of thing," our moderator announced testily. "We are not going to start until 7:30! What time is it?" Well since it was 7:30, it turns out she actually did respond to "that sort of thing," and we got underway.

For some reason my team had asked me to be the team leader and spokesperson. I guess they wanted to buoy my confidence, so I was the one who had to deliver our final answer into the microphone held by Moderator Patricia. The first few rounds went swimmingly for all three teams with puff ball questions and correct answers, but then the other teams began to miss as the difficulty of the questions was random, and some were actually tough. When our question in Arts and Entertainment was "What was the name of the girl with whom Running Bear plunged to his death in the river," I pulled the microphone out of Patricia's hand and without any consultation with my team, began to sing, "Running Bear loved Little White Dove...." Patricia, who cannot abide being outdone, especially musically, grabbed the mike back and began to sing with me, "with a love…" My team was stunned, since the only other person on our team who knew that song was My Hero. Those types of ditties are not popular in cultural havens such as Sarasota, you know. Since I alone knew the answer, I gained considerable status with my teammates.

We continued to pull in the colored cards, marching inevitably toward victory, and we continued to pour wine at our table, much to the envy of the other two teams and of some in the audience as well. As our empty bottle count mounted, so did our good humor. At one point when Patricia announced that the winning team would each get a free muffin in the Bistro, I called out in mock horror, "I thought we got a free *Stud* Muffin!" My team, and anyone in the audience whose hearing aids were working, cracked up. Patricia was not amused.

I must admit our team missed a couple of toughies. Do you know what fruit is used to make the USDA stamp on meat? We did not. And we did not know much about Marie Antoinette's vital statistics. It seems she would have given Jane Russell a run for her bra! Then My Hero, our aviation expert, forgot that Wiley Post was the first man to circumnavigate the globe by air, but at that point he too had consumed several glasses of wine, and besides Post was not in a fighter plane, so I forgave him. Besides we still had a big lead.

By this time, it was apparent that the game would never be over unless the questions were chosen from the missing categories since we had the required number of cards in all but two categories and had not had a single question in either of those two. So again, by unanimous agreement of the teams, Patricia changed formats in mid-stream and began to ask only questions in categories where cards were still needed.

We continued to drink at our table and eventually emptied everything I had brought in the cooler. Fortunately, it was a short run back to our apartment, and My Hero dashed off to retrieve reinforcements as soon as we answered our question, giving him time during the other teams' turns, to run up the two flights of stairs, grab a bottle, and get back; however, the other teams were quicker than we had expected, and I had to stall until he rushed back holding a bottle of red, again annoying Patricia. By now we were clearly the audience favorites because we were the only team having any fun. I was a little annoyed at how long it took my bar man to return, but he redeemed himself by answering the next question. So I gave him a little hug and said in clear voice, "You're going to get lucky tonight!" That really went over well with the audience, many of whom still remembered what that means! Patricia glared at me darkly. I wondered if she were going to reach into her operatic past, call an assassin like Verdi's Sparafucile, and put my name on his list of targets.

After a few more turns, our team collected all fourteen of the required cards, and we were named the Winners! Patricia announced that we could each receive the previously offered muffin or, Ta dah! A free drink in the bar! "Which do you prefer?" she asked. Everyone in the room, looking at the empties on our table, laughed; and even she had to admit she knew the answer. The next day, I picked up our free drink tickets.

I intend to enjoy my cocktail courtesy of the Activities Department; however, I intend to keep looking over my shoulder for a *basso profondo* with an assassin's dagger. I am pretty sure I am still on Patricia's list! So there you have it. It's just "Life at the Wrinkle Ranch: Trivial Pursuit."

Life at the Wrinkle Ranch: Evasive Maneuvers

Don't misunderstand. I love the theater. I have eagerly attended amateur theater, professional theater, and Broadway productions. I have been to the Kennedy Center, the Los Angeles Music Center, and Lincoln Center. For years we had series theater tickets to the Play Makers at UNC. I saw *Hair* at the Pantages Theater in Hollywood in the 1960s when I went in style wearing my white lace mini dress with the flesh colored body stocking underneath, all the while fervently believing in the Age of Aquarius.

I had a period when I loved theater of the absurd, but Shakespeare always was a favorite although My Hero vowed the actors were speaking a foreign language. I am a life-long fan of Gilbert and Sullivan. In my theater experience there was *Virginia Wolfe, The Cherry Orchard, The Glass Menagerie....* I could go on and on about my love affair with the theater.

And then I moved to the Wrinkle Ranch. In other essays I have written about the amazement with which I greeted theatrical productions by the residents here at the Ranch.

Eventually I learned to love and appreciate the efforts of my fellow residents, so even if the production was poor, the lighting and sound systems intermittent, and the actors could not remember their lines or stage directions, I could enjoy the experience because it was all in the family.

So I do not know what came over me one night. We had been looking forward to attending the latest production of our Ranch House Players. Our resident playwright is brilliant and had come up with several very enjoyable plays in the last few years. I knew almost everyone in the cast and am quite fond of them.

As usual we showed up just before the scheduled show time and took a seat in the very back of the theater portion of our auditorium, and we found ourselves sitting with our backs to the panne velvet curtain that surrounds the seating area and next to our good friends, George and Gerri, who were mounted on their comfortable, go-anywhere electric scooters.

We greeted our friends and sat back in our seats, ready to enjoy the show, but from the time the curtain went up – late – the tempo dragged, and dialog was strained because of poor timing and missed cues. The framework of a plot, just an excuse, really, to feature a variety show, was not developed although it was well-conceived and ripe for doing so.

The show was framed as amateur night at the Moulin Rouge where various performers – residents – sang, "imported" children tap-danced, and some of our older ladies did a burlesque of the cancan.

There was a "rehearsal" for a cooking show featuring "Julia Child." The connection between that "act," as amusing as it was, rubber chicken and all, and the amateur night at the Moulin Rouge was at best "a puzzlement."

Toulouse Lautrec painted a portrait of Van Gogh in the corner of the Moulin Rouge, and Vincent himself stopped by to toss off a few corny jokes about missing ears. It just went on, and on, and on.

Despite the fact that this was "amateur night" at the Moulin Rouge, "Edith Piaf" sang – lip synched really – and stripped – well, stripped off her long black gloves. At her age, she is ninety-five, that was more than enough skin to bare. "Marcel Marceau" made a surprise appearance and mimed his way across the stage in gestures that were too obtuse to decipher.

Finally when the imported, little girl tap-dancers reappeared with a friend who made a valiant effort to belt out a song too big

123

for both her voice and the limited acoustics of the microphone, I whispered to My Hero who was also squirming in his seat, "I can't take this a minute longer!"

And then I thought about it. If I get up and walk out, everyone in the room and on the stage will know it. My friends and fellow residents will be annoyed, disappointed, hurt...whatever their reaction, it will not be good, and I have a position of responsibility and leadership here. How can I resolve the warring factions in my head and heart? My esthetic senses were screaming, "Out of here, now!" and my better judgement was warning, "Do not hurt your friends' feelings. They have worked long and hard on this effort!"

Then survival instincts took over, without thinking really, I slipped out of my chair and onto the floor. Stretched out prone, I wriggled behind my chair and George's scooter and rolled, gold leather jacket and all, under the beautiful panne velvet curtain onto the dark, empty dance floor behind. Now safely out of the view of the audience and the performers, I stood up and tip toed out!

But once in the elevator lobby I realized, I did not have a door key! My Hero, still seated, had it in his pocket. It seems I did not have long to worry. Once a successful tactical maneuver is demonstrated, any good naval aviator is game. It was just a matter of minutes before I was joined outside the auditorium by my also-agile companion with the key in his hand, and we made our escape as the sound of slightly out-of-synch taps wafted through the auditorium door.

After Action Report and Preemptive Damage Control: Since now I am a politician of sorts, I thought it might be wise to do some damage control. The next morning, I called George, realizing that he must have noticed our maneuvers right next to his wheels, and secure in the knowledge that my loyal friend would not squeal on me if I asked him to keep that little caper just between us. I forgot Rule One of preemptive damage control: first assess if there is damage to be controlled. Turns out George and Gerri were so involved in the show they never noticed the two of us rolling out of formation, executing a classic "tail spin," and heading for the base. Oh well...It's just "Life at the Wrinkle Ranch: Evasive Maneuvers."

Life at the Wrinkle Ranch: The FU Grad School

Our excellent CCRC, aka the Wrinkle Ranch, offers a variety of classes presented in a six-week Senior enlightenment semester every year under the name, Freedom University Graduate School, or FU Grad School for short. Now a person with a twisted mind like mine would not have chosen that name. But like so many potentially serious mistakes I discover here, nobody asked me before they ventured into the abyss. More's the pity.

Given my past professional experience, My Hero signed "us" up to teach a computer course. I considered the potential student body carefully and decided to offer a very basic course on using the simplest options in e-mail. I entitled it "Loving Your E-mail."

I told the Trustees of Freedom University we would take the first twelve students. They needed to have lap tops and some familiarity with e-mail. I made the serious error of not writing those provisions into the course description, which was published to all the Ranchers. The Registrar signed up thirty-six people! A few actually had lap tops, and some had even sent and received e-mail in the past. Others had not! They had Apples and PCs with various operating systems and represented a large number of e-mail providers: AOL, Roadrunner, MSN, Yahoo, Google, Hotmail, Verizon...the list goes on and on. And so do the problems with giving these people hands-on instruction!

In desperation I offered to break the class into two sessions, and so "we" agreed to teach two mornings a week. And still we had 'way too many unqualified students. Then once the classes were all set, the problems associated with the registration process began to appear.

What follows is a message I sent to a fellow instructor who does not live here and is a personal friend. I trusted he would not turn me in to the faculty disciplinary committee.

Dear Fellow FU Professor,

Since you and I are both FU professors and you seem to have tenure in the FU organization, I thought I would consult with you. I don't know what the registration process is for classes at FU. But I can attest that it certainly seems totally FU'd.

Grace swears she signed up for our e-mail class but was (inadvertently?) enrolled in Conversational Spanish instead. She had no interest in that class and only discovered she was enrolled when she accidentally wound up in the elevator with Maria who is teaching it and congratulated her for enrolling.

Grace went to the FU Registrar and demanded that she be allowed to take our class, and over my objections to adding another person she was assigned to my Friday roster. My hands are tied since My Hero refuses to let me bar additional students, tell anybody off, or quit, and slitting one's wrists, if unsuccessful, can leave ugly scars.

A neighbor from our hall, Carole, was due in class on Tuesday and did not show. I saw her in the hall today and asked if there was a problem. Carole assured me she is in the Friday class.

However, I am in possession of official documents with both the Tuesday roster and the Friday roster on two separate pages. These were given to me by the Official FU Registrar.

Carole assures me that nobody called and told her there were two sections and that she was assigned to Tuesday, not Friday. Then she told me she went to a Tuesday computer class at 9:30 yesterday!

Since there is not another FU computer class besides the e-mail class we are teaching, I told her that was impossible. After some discussion during which she vowed she went to a FU computer class yesterday, she finally realized she had gone to your FU Bridge class!

This raises a lot of questions:

1. Did you not tell the students the name of the class before you began your lesson?

2. Are you perhaps teaching by using a computer and therefore confusing students and hiding your true subject matter?

3. Do you think they will find your "computer" class easier to comprehend than your bridge class?

4. What Internet service provider are you using? Baron Barclay Bridge?

5. Is there any need for Carole to take my class given that she thinks she has already attended a computer class and probably thinks she has "learned it all" already?

To make matters even more confusing, one of my Tuesday students mentioned that they missed me in the Tuesday Writing Class. His wife is the FU instructor for that class, and it is held at 9:30 A.M. on Tuesday. Does this day and time sound familiar? It is the time both you and I are to teach computer classes (or some FU subject.) I did not sign up for a single FU class! I am FU'ed enough. I am teaching two FU classes and don't need any more FU time I can assure you. How did I get enrolled in the FU Writing Class? Nobody seems to know.

They tried insisting that I enrolled myself, but since I enrolled in nothing and signed nothing, it will be difficult for the FU Registrar to prove otherwise, and it is totally illogical to expect me to be in two places at once, unless of course Carole told them that you were teaching the computer class Tuesday and they figured I was at a loss for what to do with my time, and at a loss for a subject about which to write — I understand that the FU writing instructor in that class always provides one. *I know you have been involved with all this FU business before and am eagerly awaiting your enlightenment.*

I signed my message, "The FU E-mail Instructor"

As you can see it's just "Life at the Wrinkle Ranch: The FU Grad School."

Life at the Wrinkle Ranch: Loving Your E-mail

When I taught computer classes in the 70s for a computer manufacturer, the companies that purchased our machines sent their best and brightest male – remember, I said the 70s! – computer professionals to the classes we offered.

I frequently found myself struggling to stay ahead of the class with the material at hand since many of the students were very experienced and knew a lot more than I did about the system I was teaching!

For this reason, whenever I got into real trouble in a class, I wore miniskirts, turned my back, and wrote up high on the blackboard. That usually won the men over and restored my class control since although some came to class to pick up new technical material, others came to pick up the instructor. But these days, miniskirts are out of style and so are my thighs; blackboards are no more, and this time, much to my relief, I do know more than my students! The following is a message I sent to my friends in the midst of teaching our first class at the FU Grad School.

Teaching "Loving Your E-mail" at the Wrinkle Ranch has been a real adventure in instruction. Course prerequisites included such stringent guidelines as "must have sent and received e-mail in the past." Sadly, the students were not properly vetted, the prerequisites were not stressed, and one student didn't even have an e-mail address.

It seems that many Seniors have very nice laptops usually given to them by their children, in the usually vain hope that they will be able to communicate with their aging parents via these modern marvels by sending pix, Skyping, etc. It also seems that most Seniors are terrified of those sleek little boxes with their large color displays.

Here is a list of problems and questions I have encountered but had not anticipated (foolish me).

One lovely and intelligent woman said she couldn't bring her laptop to class because there was no place to plug it in. She had no idea it contained a battery and was portable!

Mouse skills are almost non-existent in this group, and for some, almost impossible to develop. When I suggested being "more gentle" to one student who was pounding his left mouse button with such force that the entire mouse jumped uncontrollably, he informed me that he has a severe tremor and neuropathy in his hands! Others are quite arthritic. And most just never practiced using a mouse so even those with "feel" in their hands, have no "feel" for the mouse. To make things worse, very few have a plug-in mouse and are using the laptop touch pad, which I find more difficult.

One woman insisted she didn't have to plug in her mouse because she had WiFi all over her apartment. She had no idea that her wireless mouse had a battery and a Blue Tooth connection, which had nothing to do with her WiFi.

Only one of our original thirty-six students, a professional engineer, had any idea about how WiFi or networks operate, and most had had their computers hooked up by the cable provider and had no notion of how any of the equipment worked. There is no building-wide WiFi, but we hold our class in a conference room that does have WiFi access. There was chaos in the classroom when we explained to our first class how to connect to the Internet in the conference room. Performing that operation was much too complicated for the students, and My Hero had to make the rounds, setting up the WiFi on each laptop. Now we insist they have to come early so we can make sure they are on the net before class starts.

To further complicate things we have users of Road Runner, Yahoo, Gmail, Verizon, MSN, and AOL. We are demonstrating on our laptop using AOL and projecting our display image onto a large pull down screen. For many of our students, the screen on the computer in front of them looks nothing like what we are projecting on the big screen. Of course most have poor vision and can't see the big screen anyway, and if I didn't have a microphone, few could hear me, so maybe the difference in the systems doesn't matter so much....

After covering the fact that you cannot edit or modify e-mails sitting in your in-box – both in class discussions and in several of the numerous e-mails I send out each week, as well as in many one-on-one sessions – students continue to tell me the Copy, Cut, and Paste options are "faint" in their Edit menu and don't work. I continue to remind them to hit Reply first! To say that my instruction falls on "deaf ears" may be more often literal than figurative.

One student, who answered all of her homework questions correctly, apologized for her e-mail response containing her answers. It seems that when she numbered the questions in her response, the numbers didn't automatically start on a new line. Her message had no spaces except the ones between words, and one line of text just ran into the next. Apparently she had no concept of the Enter key on the keyboard. It hadn't occurred to me to tell them about that. Sigh.

Another observant student noticed that when My Hero and I e-mail each other, AOL.com does not show in our e-mail addresses. I explained it this way: When we make a phone call in our neighborhood, we don't dial the area code first, and if we are all AOL users we don't have to add that suffix. I think she understood that, but I have really had to stretch to find analogies that will get through to this crowd!

Another lady wanted me to make a house call to assist her in finding her e-mail Address Book. She said her system didn't have one. I explained that there is no such thing as a commercial e-mail system without access to e-mail addresses. Once she learned that "contacts" is another word for "address book," the missing option was revealed! Just for the record, I had pointed that out in class several times previously.

This same woman then told me she could not do the homework because I had asked that she highlight her e-mail responses in color, and she didn't have a color computer. I pointed to the program icons in full color arrayed on her screen and asked what was that, if not color? But she was adamant. She got up, grabbed her cane, hobbled across the room, and picked up a lovely picture of herself – in black and white. "You see,'" she said triumphantly, "when I printed this out there was no color!" She had no concept of her computer as separate from her printer. It is difficult for an instructor to anticipate these problems.

But the most baffling teaching problem was presented by the student who asked me to make a "house call" because he had written an e-mail to me to satisfy a requirement for his homework, but it just sat on the screen and didn't go anywhere. He complained that he had typed my e-mail address in the 'Send To' block, a Subject – I insist on a completed subject line – and then had typed his message, and still it sat on his computer screen. I asked him if he wrote a letter, put it in an envelope, addressed it, added a stamp, and left it on his desk, would it be delivered to the addressee? He confirmed that he would have to drop it in the mail box first. Then I showed him the little "button" marked "Send Now.'" Another day, another real world analogy.

So you can see that teaching this class is harder than we ever imagined it would be, and My Hero is under constant fire – from me – for volunteering "us" to do this; however, we are both actually glad we took on this challenge. These people need us. Some, about half of our students, are learning, if not "to love" their e-mail, at least not to fear it, and the few who already knew their way around their e-mail and just signed up for fun are having fun.

I am getting feedback from people who are not in the class that "they heard..." – there is a very active grape vine at the Ranch – and then they *tell us the students say they enjoy the class and that I am a "wonderful" teacher.*

Well you all know I never met a microphone I didn't like, and I have spent a lot of time designing this course. I think they mostly like the lessons where I warn them of ways to embarrass yourself by not paying attention to what you send. And then I give real life examples from my long and faux-pas-fraught Internet past. They also seem to like the new vocabulary words I have taught them:

e-barrassment: to send an e-mail you are sorry you sent.

e-versations: back and forth, Send and Reply messages.

And My Hero's "favorite:" e-nagging, which is e-mail intended to provide wifely inspiration and e-couragement, but often received in a different frame of mind by a husband.

I'm sure the next time the Ranch holds classes, we will be asked to do this again. Next time I will insist that the class size be limited, and I will interview each prospective student personally. But if we live through the next three weeks, I'm pretty sure there will be a next time – after all, my public needs me!

I signed it, "The Frazzled E-mail Instructor." It's just "Life at the Wrinkle Ranch: Loving Your E-mail."

Life at the Wrinkle Ranch: Another Red Car!

So what is it with red cars anyway? Surely you remember my account, "The Run Down," in which I told of the red Mercedes that aimed at us as we walked down the golf cart lane along the boulevard during our morning exercise walk.

Well, it happened again. This time I was without the protection of My Hero, who had escaped the rigors of exercise with me in favor of Geezer Golf at the country club.

Of course I was walking in the prescribed manner, fully in the golf cart lane and facing the traffic, when the big red Cadillac convertible sped at me with both of his passenger side tires firmly entrenched on my side of the cart lane markings.

Of course I gave him the universal sign to move over. No, not that sign; I know what sign you're thinking of. I mean the sign where both arms move repeatedly in a synchronized motion, indicating the direction in which the vehicle should travel.

And of course I had to jump onto the grass to protect myself when the driver did not choose to veer out of my cart lane; however, this time I was prepared – I remembered to turn around immediately and note his license plate number.

Not having anything with which to record the six-digit number, I made up a little rhyme which I chanted to myself until I completed my exercise and could report the miscreant's license plate to the Front Desk. It went like this:

> ES3 and 9ND,
> You are blind and you can't see.
> You drove in and aimed at me!
> Once I know who you may be,
> I'll give your name to DMV.

By going through this process, I accomplished two things. First I was able to give the correct license plate number to the Front Desk fully half an hour later, so now they could determine if this person is a resident here. Second by using this clever mnemonic device, I proved to myself that I am not yet a candidate for our memory unit. Both of these outcomes were reassuring.

But just in case this rhyme thing does not always work, I think when I go out for my morning walks I should either start carrying pencil and paper, or maybe an AK-47! I guess I should not be surprised. After all, it's just "Life at the Wrinkle Ranch: Another Red Car!"

Life at the Wrinkle Ranch: Dining Debacle

One night I went into the Tavern to chat with my successor as Wrinkle Ranch President. She was having a well-deserved Scotch at the bar. It is a tough job, as well I know, and we both agree that a nice cocktail at the end of the day seems to help.

As long as I was standing there, I ordered an appletini, which the bartender expertly mixed in a shaker and poured into a handsome martini glass. After all, having a fancy glass is at least half the fun of drinking martinis! The President suggested My Hero and I should join her group for dinner because they had reserved an eight-top in the Aloha and still had two open seats. I demurred since we had a date with another couple, and we were eating down the hall in the Green Room. The bartender, hearing this, took one look at my very fashionable three-inch peep toe patent leather platform pumps and astutely made me "an offer I couldn't refuse."

"Would you like me to deliver that drink to your table?" she asked knowingly. I gratefully accepted that offer because although it is really cool at my age to be able to walk in such fashionable three-inch peep toe patent leather platform pumps, it would not be cool to slosh my green appletini with every gracefully undulating step down the hall – and a very long hall at that.

When we arrived at my table in the Green Room, our table was empty since my dining partners were still finding their way through the chatting groups of friends in the Lobby.

As the bartender set my drink at my assigned place, a woman at the next table erupted and verbally assaulted the bartender, "She," she barked, pointing at me, "hasn't even sat down yet, and she has a drink. We ordered our wine twenty minutes ago, and it's still not here...." That was the opening salvo, which she hurled angrily at the undeserving young woman. It got worse.

Both the bartender and I hastened to explain the special circumstances of the situation, and the defenseless bartender retreated as quickly as possible while I offered to get the rude woman "a supervisor," which is how we are supposed to deal with issues in the dining rooms.

Off I glided on my quest, in my very fashionable three-inch peep toe patent leather platform pumps and immediately encountered a dining services supervisor in the hall.

"Could you come in and speak to a woman in the Green Room?" I began politely. The supervisor said, "Not right now. I have a Dining Debacle in the Aloha!"

A "Dining *Debacle*?" I did not know the young woman knew that word, much less that she would resort to using it under stress, and of course I was dying to know the nature of the "Dining Debacle!"

Since I have friends all over the Ranch, there was bound to be some resident who would "spill" – no, not my appletini, but the "beans." All I had to do was wait a few minutes, return, and ask the right questions of the right residents.

And return I did, ten minutes later. Remembering that the President was sitting in the Aloha, I figured she would be the best source of G2, so I turned toward the end of the room where that imposing eight-top table is located and was surprised to see she was not holding court with her group at her usual position overlooking the room. Instead I found her and the "First Man" sitting with only one other couple at a standard four-top in the center of the Aloha.

Approaching, I said quietly, "The supervisor told me there was a 'Dining Debacle' in here! What gives?"

"It was us!" she replied. "We take turns signing up for the eight-top, and Doris had signed up for every Tuesday night this month, and when we came in tonight someone else was sitting there! My husband walked up, and strangers were sitting at our table! I think someone erased Doris' name! At any rate we were not happy about it, and I let the supervisor know it."

When the Ranch President gives a dining supervisor an earful, it could certainly qualify as a Dining Debacle – a great disaster, Wrinkle Ranch style. So now I understood the expressive term the supervisor had used to describe the issue in the Aloha. If someone else had appropriated the President's table...well, just suffice it to say that the supervisor would have been distressed, even if the President had not "let her know it." Without further comment I retreated to the Green Room, my very green and perfectly mixed appletini, and my three charming dinner companions.

But the next day I discovered which resident had actually been seated at the highly desirable, one and only, eight-top in the Aloha. It was a lovely couple in their 90s who had six family guests. The wife in this couple is a delightful lady, a native of England, and very proper and well bred. I found it extremely unlikely that she "erased" anyone's name in any reservation book at any time in her entire life. So I asked her what happened.

She told me her family announced their arrival quite late, and she rushed to the Dining Table Reservation Book to see how, or if, she could accommodate them all at one table. She said in her elegant British accent, still quite strong after all these years in the States, "To my great surprise and delight I saw that no one had reserved the eight-top that evening so I wrote in my name forthwith."

So we are faced with a conundrum. What is the real truth of this matter? Did some disgruntled resident, perhaps annoyed that the Presidential party has made a habit of reserving the highly desirable eight-top table repeatedly and to the exclusion of other residents, whip out an eraser and make the Aloha eight-top available again? Did our lovely British nonagenarian's eyesight fail her such that she did not notice the other name in the book? Did one of the President's group fail in her assignment to reserve the coveted table?

Any one of those explanations could be accurate, and I have learned an important lesson from this Dining Debacle: When reserving a table in the "Book," always write in ink!

Oh, and what of the rude woman who was so angry about waiting for her wine? The Dining Room Manager soothed her, explained the ordering procedure for drinks, and provided her table with two complimentary glasses of wine. All fixed. It's just "Life at the Wrinkle Ranch: Dining Debacle!"

Life at the Wrinkle Ranch: Le Beau of the Ball

For those of you who are interested in what passes for night life in a Senior Community, I will give you a report on the splendid dance we had one evening here at the Ranch. The live music was outstanding, and the attendance was excellent. There were two other couples from the dance studio where we study, both much more advanced than we, and lots of regular dancers, many of whom are quite accomplished. Three marketing guests were there. All the prospects had a wonderful time. Did I say, "Successful"? It was certainly that.

The white haired, handsome Senior who is our Ranch's "Le Beau of the Ball" came in about 8 P.M. He was dressed in an elegant white suit and wore a tie. He was pushing a cart of the type used here to haul groceries to our apartments after shopping trips. The last time he came to the dance with such a cart, I thought he must have just come from the store and stopped by on his way to his apartment. How naive of me! It seems, according to a good source, that he forgets that we do not bring our own snacks and booze to our dances, since that is *de rigueur* over in town, and he goes to town for many dances; he shows up prepared to be generous.

Here is a man who always needs a little support for ambulation. He uses a walker to traverse our halls, and now he shows up leaning on a Senior style shopping cart that has more than a dozen long stemmed roses, a bottle of wine, a potted Easter Lily, and all manner of snack foods, unopened. Is it any wonder that I thought he had just come by on his way from the store?

He stood by, but once the music stirred him, he stepped onto the dance floor, repeatedly and sans cart, to dance with a young woman from town known for her exotic and erotic moves, and he danced and danced. Between dances he handed out long stemmed roses to all the ladies. His potted lily languished in the cart along with the wine. This is not a BYOB event – we have a bartender and snacks.

The dance floor was the center of everyone's attention as our skilled resident dancer, Le Beau, danced the rhumba with the lithe and sensuous miss from town, who was wearing a tight, short, white fringed dress. As a matter of fact I am pretty sure his right thigh will never be the same again. My guess is he was first in line the next morning for Physical Therapy to work on that area which was bound to have a huge lump after all the hot massage his partner provided – and she never even used her hands! It was a sight to behold. And we all did!

At what point should we apply the "public decency" measures that surely would be supported by the U.S. Supreme Court and certainly by some of our leading lawyer residents? On the other hand, as long as this activity does not cause a heart attack, what mean spirited person would want to spoil an old man's fun? It's just "Life at the Wrinkle Ranch: Le Beau of the Ball."

Life at the Wrinkle Ranch: The Red Arrow

At the Ranch residents and associates alike have name badges. Associates all wear their badges and so do most residents. In the case of resident badges, they are helpful to staff and to other residents since recall can be a challenge as we age, and peoples' names seem to be one of the first things we have trouble digging out of our memories.

Sometimes special symbols are added to the badges. A green dot indicates that the resident is new. A top hat was added for residents who have recommended ten other residents. As we learned in "The VIPs," the orange dot lets us all know that the wearer is vision impaired and may need additional assistance.

One day My Hero and I were sitting in the Bistro enjoying our breakfast when my friend Barbara scooted up. "Join us," I said to my friend on the motorized scooter. After all the best thing about eating in the Bistro – besides the food – is sitting at one of the tables right off the main hallway where everyone passes by and can easily be hailed and chatted up.

Barbara manipulated her scooter into a convenient place at the table, and we began to talk. The conversation was running along the lines of so many Senior conversations these days – who was taking which medication, how much the health insurance had gone up, and what the prescriptions cost in the "donut hole."

I was listening attentively and looking directly at Barbara. I am a very observant person and noticed right away that she had a red arrow on her badge. At an appropriate pause in the conversation I asked, "What's with the red arrow? I never saw one of those before."

"Oh," said Barbara, "I told you I was diagnosed with age-related macular degeneration last week so I e-mailed the VIP chair, and he enrolled me in the group and sent me this to go on my badge."

"I wonder why we switched from orange buttons to red arrows?" I asked pensively, thinking of the handbook for new residents we would need to change, among other things. Just to make sure I was seeing what I thought I was seeing, I asked Barbara to remove her badge and pass it over so I could examine it more closely.

In the process of passing the badge, she handed it to My Hero who was seated between us. Since he is an engineer, he felt required to inspect it carefully before handing it to a mere – but observant – non-engineer. Then he started laughing. "Who installed this 'arrow' on your badge?" he inquired.

"My husband. It came on a card in the in-house mail, and he removed it and stuck it on my badge," Barbara replied.

So now it was my turn to have a close-up view of this red arrow, which was growing in interest by the moment. The heart or center of this arrow was a dot, a perfect, round, raised dot, and it turns out it was not really red after all, but more like red-orange. The part which looked arrow-like at a distance was just extraneous material surrounding the raised dot. It became obvious that the installer had failed to remove that superfluous material.

Now this *really* was a job for an engineer, one who did not worry about damaging a fingernail. My Hero applied his unbreakable thumb nail to the problem, and the extra soft, extraneous plastic material fell away. Unlike the dot the extra material had no mastic on the back and only remained on the badge because it had not been separated from the dot.

Barbara regarded her modified badge. "Look at that. It's an orange dot!" she declared.

A quick phone call to the VIP chair confirmed that a new source for orange dots had produced a redder, less raised dot that is not identical to the previously ones. He informed me that the dot is distributed affixed to a card with large print directions for installing it. The card was prepared with vision impaired people in mind, but nobody seems to have a solution for people who do not read the directions. It's just "Life at the Wrinkle Ranch: The Red Arrow."

Life at the Wrinkle Ranch: Talking Turkey

Thanksgiving is always turkey day at the Ranch, just as it is all over the USA. The tradition of eating turkey on that holiday has persisted through the generations, and turkey is certainly a resident favorite here along with dressing, gravy, cranberry sauce, green bean casserole, squash, sweet potatoes, pumpkin pie, pecan pie, and all the other fixings that usually accompany it. This particular year along with that sumptuous feast, the dining room had offered the option of ham or an excellent Orange Roughy.

Even though we have full size ovens and fully functional kitchens in our apartment homes, very few of us cook a turkey or even a turkey breast for that special day. None of us has more than two people in our resident household – two old people. And how much turkey can two old people eat anyway? Granted a few folks have large families who come to visit, and some residents still cook a holiday meal to entertain them, but that sort of do-it-yourself activity is rare here.

Most choose to reserve a private dining room on the main floor, or to depend on the willingness of our Dining Services Staff to put tables together to seat large family groups on holidays,

So how, we were all asking, did the large, whole, uncooked turkey in the disposable foil roasting pan wind up in our construction dumpster a few days after Thanksgiving?

Did someone having a senior moment look at the calendar and, in an arthritic knee jerk reaction, buy a turkey and after a few days of having the bird sit around in the kitchen, undressed and unaddressed, realize the enormity of that error and seek to dispose of it?

Perhaps that same undressed and uncooked turkey started to be a bit smelly, so the trash room down the hall did not seem like a good place to dispose of it.

Did a Senior swain thinking he would woo one of our lovely single ladies to his apartment with the delicious odor of roasting turkey, buy this bird and the shiny aluminum pan and take them home, only to realize he did not have a clue what to do with it, or even sadder, only to discover the object of his affection had made a date for Thanksgiving dinner with another gentleman, one who invited her to the full repast in the dining room with no strings attached and no dishes to wash? And then what to do? What to do? Certainly he would not want the evidence of his thwarted fantasies to waft back toward his residence from the trash room.

Did some lucky Rancher win the turkey at the bingo game or a raffle in town, and then, although fully intending to donate it to a deserving family, forget until it was too late – in so many ways – to give it to one of our hard working associates who would actually have cooked it and served it to the family on Thanksgiving?

Holidays are open season on Seniors when it comes to health crises. It is always possible that someone intended to travel to a friend's house for the holiday and was going to bring the turkey, only to have an illness strike and wind up in the hospital. Maybe days later the resident called from her hospital bed and asked someone to rescue the turkey and dispose of it.

All of these scenarios are possibilities, and given my knowledge of Ranch life, no particular one is more likely than the others. But the real mystery is why and how did the turkey and its final resting pan wind up in the dumpster? This dumpster is a temporary one, set prominently in front of our Villas. It is there to receive the carpet and other debris resulting from the renovation of all the common spaces in those buildings. It would not be there for much longer, but since it is neither a garbage receptacle nor a regular fixture, most of our residents would never think about it for the disposal of a long dead turkey.

And pray tell, how did the culprit transport the turkey out of the building and into the dumpster? Did she wait until the dead of night and do the turkey trot down the hall and across the street? Was she tall enough to place the turkey ever so carefully in that green but open grave? Or was it just an incredibly serendipitous heave that found our fetid friend still breast side up?

By all accounts the turkey was not wrapped in the ubiquitous plastic shield that normally protects super market turkeys from the hands of butchers and shoppers. Old fashioned meat markets, like the ones of our childhood that sold chickens and turkeys we carried home swathed in butcher paper, are few and far between these days, and there is not a turkey farm within miles of here. So did someone actually unwrap the plastic enclosed turkey, certainly a start on the cooking process, if a very preliminary one? For some reason, perhaps one of those reasons identified previously, did the preliminary process come to a screeching halt in a case of *turkus interruptus*? Or did freeing the turkey from the packaging begin without a firm plan for ending the process to the satisfaction of all involved, and so was what we might call a *premature evacuation*? Who can say?

More mysteries: given that someone, the purchaser or a "foreign" agent, so to speak, decided that the fowl was foul and had to go, and given that the fowl was too foul for the building trash room, did the dumpster became a turkey target of opportunity? Can anyone explain to me how the ordinary Rancher could lift a fifteen- or twenty-pound turkey in a pan over her head and deposit it, pan-side-down, breast-side-up, in the dumpster?

Because that is exactly how it was discovered on the Tuesday after Thanksgiving – breast-side-up in the dumpster. And this is how that discovery came about: The dumpster was nearly full of debris, so although it was almost five feet deep, the turkey was near enough to the surface that when one of our dog walkers happened to come close to the dumpster, his dog began to sniff about in the manner of a mighty canine hunter on the scent of his favorite prey. Never mind that this particular canine is well into her 80s – in human terms – is blind, and suffers from diabetes, getting his daily injections of insulin, just as many of our other Ranchers do. In response to the sniffing, our dog walker looked around, expecting to see a squirrel but instead saw the unexpected source of his dog's excitement. There in the dumpster was last week's raw turkey – just lying there – its white, plucked skin exposed to the Florida sunshine, and without a hint of a tan or even a sun burn.

The startled dog walker grabbed his unseeing, all-smelling pooch and headed home for the phone. He called Maintenance and reported an abandoned raw turkey, now roasting in the dumpster in the rays of the hot December sun.

Wednesday morning arrived, and once again the Rancher and his "hunting" dog ventured forth for a relieving walk. This time our dog walker made sure he took a turn by the dumpster,

139

believing the turkey was long gone thanks to his call to Maintenance, but deciding to check – just in case. Imagine his consternation when he saw the turkey, still breast up, still gleaming in the confines of its shiny pan. He returned to his apartment, once again he called Maintenance only to find that the Maintenance Department had wisely determined the turkey was beyond both preventive maintenance and repair; therefore, the turkey was outside their purview. In the manner of corporations everywhere, they had kicked the turkey down the organizational road, so to speak. They had referred the unpleasant issue to Housekeeping.

Housekeeping management dutifully sent the message down their chain, but apparently the chain had broken. The vigilant Rancher was fully aware that our 140+, well-wooded acres contain a regiment of raccoons, squadrons of squirrels, an army of armadillos, and several battalions of buzzards; so he called Housekeeping and stirred up some action before those troops moved in to attack the kill which was lying there more like a "sitting duck" than a turkey.

As he watched from his window later that day, two five-foot-tall females from the Housekeeping staff approached the dumpster wearing surgical gloves. They stood on tip toe and peered into the dumpster with trepidation. Then they recoiled, their disgust apparent, even from his window across the street; despite their distaste for last week's turkey and the task at hand, they clearly recognized that retrieving the turkey was their job, and they continued to take on the turkey task. Then the reality of their vertical challenge set in. In the manner of women from time immemorial when challenged with height issues and dead things, they found a *man* for the job. He had to climb into the dumpster to retrieve the raccoon bait, but basking in the praise and gratitude of his fellow female associates, he persevered until the turkey extraction was accomplished.

Now we are left with just the lingering scent of over-ripe turkey and the mystery of who, and why, and how. Of course the questions and rumors, unlike our erstwhile turkey, are still flying around the Ranch. It's just "Life at the Wrinkle Ranch: Talking Turkey."

Life at the Wrinkle Ranch: Wardrobe Malfunction!

As everyone at the Ranch knows, old age is not for sissies! Even those of us who have been healthy and meds-free up to now can develop medical problems as we happily age in place at the Ranch.

And that "aging in place" is the reason I found myself wearing a heart monitor for a two-week diagnostic test.

The real problem with a heart monitor is not the annoyance of making sure you have the transmitter with you at all times, nor connecting and disconnecting the electrodes when you shower, nor even the seemingly constant alerts about required battery changes. The really, really annoying thing is trying to find something to wear that does not advertise to your solicitous friends and your gleeful enemies that you are undergoing a medical test, so you will not have to explain the intimate details of your health concerns to everyone who notices that you have a device the size of a cell phone hanging around your neck, electrodes stuck to your chest, and a veritable tangle of wires criss-crossing your upper body.

Fortunately, loose fitting tops are "in" and if nobody notices the small black strap around your neck, you can fly "wired," as it were, and under the radar most of the time; unless of course there is a special event where you have planned to wear a particular outfit that does not conform to the "loose fitting top" description.

Naturally such a revealing event came up right in the middle of my heart monitor period. It was the Veteran's Organization Annual Dinner Dance, and the theme was "South of the Border." My Hero was wearing a gaucho style black and red shirt purchased some years ago for a "hoe down" themed event. This town is nothing if not theme-oriented for every possible event. I had ordered a splendid "senorita" outfit with an off-the-shoulder peasant top, an elasticized cinched waist, and the traditional tiered long skirt. My plan was to augment this dress with a huge, faux-bejeweled crucifix – borrowed from a fellow Ranchette who has an endless supply of accessories – a Spanish style comb for my hair, and an authentic black lace mantilla from Spain, a little holey after spending the last fifty years wrapped in tissue paper and stashed in the scarf box, but the real deal nonetheless.

None of this was going to work with a heart monitor competing with my jeweled crucifix for accessory of the evening, but I am nothing if not creative when it comes to wardrobe. After rooting around in my lingerie drawer, I produced a twenty-five-year-old strapless bra, a remnant of more glamorous times and more attractive décolletage. Removing the neck strap from the monitor, I secured the monitor under the middle of the strapless – where the cleavage used to go   and moved the electrodes down just a bit lower, thus managing to disguise as a bust line the tacky tangles of electronics and wires running across my chest.

In no time at all we were off to the BYOB dinner dance in full South of the Border regalia.

My goal was to drink no more than one small glass of wine since wine seemed to be one of the culprits which sent my heart and the reporting monitor into overload, and I was desperately trying to convince the cardiologist, *"no hay problemas aqui."*

This particular event started at 5 P.M. with a social hour, a typical Senior cocktail time! It consisted of one full hour with only tortilla chips to eat and a lot of drinking. I consumed two ten-ounce glasses of water and no wine. Then came the program. It began with toasts at 6 P.M. We toasted the flag, the Commander in Chief, the Army, the Navy, the Marines, the Air Force, the Coast Guard, and moved on to other service-oriented subjects. The more we toasted, the more wine my tablemates consumed, and the more besotted they became; sadly, I just became more waterlogged.

At 6:15 we sang the service songs. In keeping with tradition we started with the Army, the oldest of the services. Of course the words of the Army song have changed. Now it seems it is the "Army" which "goes rolling along." There are no more "caissons." You might ask in a paraphrase of Peter, Paul, and Mary, "Where did all the caissons go?" I do not know, must be that technology insertion thing. Oh, and there is no more unstoppable "Army Air Corps." That was another generation; now it is another service, and so we sing, "Nothing can stop the U.S. Air Force." There are many changes to the old service songs, but at least the Marines Corps Hymn remains inviolate. For that we can thank the Mexicans and the Pirates of Tripoli, both of which continue to be on our radar in one way or another, insuring the words of the Hymn remain constant and current.

At 6:30 there was a hint that dinner might be in our future. By then I was the only sober person at my table. My Hero, aware that wine hastened the assault of my elevated heart rate, made a masterful, if totally unnecessary effort, to save me from myself by drinking all but one glass of the bottle of wine we brought – and all before dinner too! Guess he did not notice that I was doing the waterlogged thing and that the level of liquid in my wine glass was not decreasing with time. Instead he and the British Brigadier on his left were sharing lies and matching gulps. Bless her heart, the wife of the Brit swapped seats with My Hero and tried to chat me up. By that time I was totally divorced from the mood that had seized the table, and the room for that matter. After all I was sober, cold – but not delightedly – sober; but sober all the same. And I was totally in the minority!

Suddenly as I sat at the table, I heard a popping sound. Not a loud sound, but surely an audible one to me. Then nothing happened. So I kept smiling and dodging the personal questions lobbed at me by the tipsy Brigadier's wife, and then it happened again – that popping sound. Without further fanfare the right cup of my strapless bra went rushing toward my right elbow while the left cup flew toward my left armpit! The heart monitor, suddenly unsupported, plummeted toward my nether regions. Fortunately, it stopped at my cinched in waist. Remember I was cold sober and still fully coordinated. I pulled my arms together, elbows bent into the compression phase of a chest stretch maneuver, drawing the two cups back toward the center, and hissed to My Hero, "Wardrobe Malfunction – Ladies Room."

I beat a hasty retreat to that nearest source of privacy where I surveyed the damage. The strapless was designed to accommodate a deeply plunging neckline and was held together in the front by clear plastic strips that had served quite well for twenty-five years, but given the pressure exerted by the heart monitor that had been tucked under the strips, the aged plastic had stressed out and burst, separately freeing both cups, the monitor, and "the girls."

Without duct tape, a replacement strapless, or safety pins there was no hope of saving the current approach to heart monitor support. So I moved to plan B. I threw the old, and now totally useless, strapless bra into the trash, arranged the mantilla to hang over the front of my costume, rather like long hair arranged over each side of my bosom, said a few very bad words, tucked the monitor into my stretch panties, and returned to the festivities.

Needless to say after dinner and a few – very few – dances with my now rather uncoordinated and significantly inebriated dancing partner, I dragged him away from the sea stories and the party, and we went home where I shed my costume and accessories and restored the monitor to its usual neck harness.

Let us hope this is the end of the heart monitors so that we can avoid another similarly exciting episode. It's just "Life at the Wrinkle Ranch: Wardrobe Malfunction!"

CHAPTER

8

All the World's a Stage

One of the principle resident activities at the Wrinkle Ranch involves the theater. It seems half the world lives a normal, every-day, non-theatrical existence, all the while quietly longing to be in the theater; once these people move to the Ranch, they jump at the chance to participate. That never occurred to me before I became a Rancher. Oh sure, I had attended a few little theater performances, but never did I feel drawn to act, direct, write a play, do set design, or get into the production business. Maybe I was just too busy being the star of my own life for the past 70+ years, but it quickly became obvious to me that at the Ranch there is great participation in The Theater. This Ranch was fortunate to have on staff a woman who was a wonderful writer, had once been an opera singer, and loved to stage theatrical performances. Her approach to Senior theater was a little old fashioned as you will see, but she was a genius at using the talents of the residents and in working with what others might have found stumbling blocks, like walkers and other assistive devices. A few years after we arrived, a couple with lots of amateur theater experience moved in and introduced a more modern approach to Senior theater. Thereafter we had both forms of theater on our stage.

What follow are stories about some productions as seen from the eyes of a person who was usually not involved in any aspect except audience participation. Some very interesting things happened on and off our stage, and some very funny things too. The show must go on in "Never a Dull Moment," a story that explains the need to watch one's step on stage.

"The Odyssey Revisited" incorporates many of the old-fashioned approaches to Senior theater practiced for years at the Ranch before the talented and experienced community theater-savvy residents moved in and brought along a new paradigm.

"When Push Comes to Shove" describes the difficulties that can arise when getting so many residents involved and how a strong leader with a wide range of impressive talents can manage to make it all work. In "Comedy Night" we learn that some of the funniest parts of the show sometimes happen "behind the scenes."

Life at the Wrinkle Ranch: Never a Dull Moment!

Because My Hero and I took ballroom dancing lessons we were asked to perform a small dance segment in a Wrinkle Ranch theatrical production. The event was a musical play built around memorable show tunes from three favorite shows: *Annie Get Your Gun, Fiddler on the Roof,* and *The Sound of Music.*

Our dance number was to be a re-creation of the Austrian folk dance, the Ländler, danced by the young, naive Maria and the very military Captain von Trapp in *The Sound of Music.* We took the challenge seriously and asked our dance instructor to watch the original movie video clip on line and choreograph something we could manage. She did a wonderful job, and after three hours of instruction and a lot of practice, we had a routine. My Hero wore a tux, and I wore a costume appropriate to the scene, borrowed from a member of the German Club.

There were a few minor glitches as one might expect when performing a complex show employing ancient actors for whom ambulation is a challenge and Senior chorus members whose voices have definitely aged but not necessarily mellowed.

Naturally there were a few technical difficulties. At one point the tablet computer containing the downloaded overtures and connected to the sound system failed! A long and very pregnant silence ensued. A few people missed their cues here and there, and the narrator's microphone did not always work. But the most exciting glitch, certainly in keeping with my "Never a Dull Moment" title, came in the very first scene. Frank Butler from *Annie Get Your Gun* threw up on stage! Fortunately, being an experience thespian, he barfed discretely behind the edge of the curtain and nobody in the audience even noticed.

Of course the odor lingered, and during our dance we had to be very careful not to step in anything which might have compromised our footing and given new significance to that show business admonition, "Break a leg!" If you recall one of the most memorable tunes from *Annie Get Your Gun,* "There's No Business Like Show Business," it has the refrain, "Let's go on with the show." And go on we did!

The performance was complete with the usual curtain call, thanks, and awarding of flowers to the writer/director and the choral leader. "Frank" however had missed the rest of the show. He was home with a stomach ache and did not get to take a bow. All in all, it's just "Life at the Wrinkle Ranch: Never a Dull Moment!"

Life at the Wrinkle Ranch: The Odyssey Revisited

A good Senior Community provides all kinds of activities for the residents. There are games, both indoor and outdoor, athletic and intellectual. There are trips to "big league" cultural and athletic performances. Artistic efforts of all kinds are part and parcel of life at a proper Wrinkle Ranch like ours.

Residents are encouraged to paint, write, and sing in the Ranch chorus. A special effort is made to recruit residents to participate in theatrical productions, which are designed, scripted, and produced by the talented and creative Lifestyles staff on a regular basis.

In this culture, the product is not nearly so important as the act of producing it, and if Seniors, new to these crafts, create less than professional results, who cares? Keeping the residents busy, happy, and learning something new also assists in keeping them healthy – mentally and physically. It is all part of the job of running a successful Wrinkle Ranch.

With that firmly in mind, come with me to the Monday afternoon production of "It's Greek to Me," a half hour, one-act play with a set built by members of the residents' wood shop and music provided by a resident, on a harpsichord he assembled himself from a kit – Homer to the accompaniment of a harpsicord, now there is an anachronism! – a Greek chorus, aka the residents' choral group, costumes created by someone who was clearly never an understudy to Edith Head, and masks, courtesy of the art group and designed in the best tradition of the ancient Greek theater.

And there are actors! Do not think for a minute that all the artistic talent at the Ranch is of the behind-the-scenes and support variety. There they are, right out on the stage with their masks, and there is all the dialogue one could ever need, thanks to the writers' group and the poets' association right here at our Wrinkle Ranch.

So what sets this afternoon apart from your standard matinee at any theater on Broadway?

Well...first of all there are a lot of canes, walkers, and electric scooters parked in every nook and cranny of the theater. So, OK, the audience is of the older variety, and many cannot hear well and sport large hearing aids. And even though the play was very short, I noticed a number of the audience nodded off; three o'clock is nap time at the Ranch, you know. But that bespeaks the audience, not the production.

What makes this production different?

Not a one of the stars or supporting cast utters a word! A mime production, you say. "No!" Actors at the Wrinkle Ranch never speak a line in these plays. They either lip synch, or in the case of handheld, two-sided church fan style masks, they (hopefully) flip the appropriate face to the fore as the behind-the-scenes voices, reading into the mike from their well-hidden position, recite their lines for them.

Look at the problems one avoids using this approach. No prompter is required. Amplified voices assist hearing impaired audiences to appreciate the performance, and no old people have to remember a word!

This does not, however, avoid the necessity for rehearsals. The actors need to be schooled in when to flip their masks from comedic to tragic, where to stand, when to sit, and of course in the overuse of gesticulation. Granted this is more difficult to do when one hand is permanently attached to the tongue depressor handle of the church fan mask. One of the stars confided to me in the after-the-play party that our super diva Lifestyle leader in these activities, "...told us there is no such thing as *over* acting!"

So over act they did, with long, sweeping, one-armed gestures and extreme body language accompanying each line read from the hidden microphone.

But what of the play itself? What about the plot, the story line, and the action?

It seems that Homer had it all wrong. First of all Ulysses was not gone for twenty years, but only for ten.

During this time although his loyal wife, Penelope, remained faithful despite the plethora of greedy, freeloading suitors who swarmed over her estate, she did not weave and unweave a tapestry as a stalling tactic. Once again Homer was off base. Penelope just hung out with her devoted servant Columbine and dished the dirt on the suitors.

The Ranch audience was treated to a window into the private audiences Penelope held with a few of these suitors. There was Atlas, the muscle man; Hippocrates, the hippy who dispensed recreational drugs along with his medical advice; Midas, who promised endless riches but was actually looking for a slush fund; and finally, Adonis, the sexy lothario for whom Penelope lusted but had no desire to marry.

At the end, Penelope decides to leave everything behind in dear Columbine's hands – everything except her money that is, and go off to Rome – or was that "roam"?

As she exits stage right, Ulysses enters stage left. It seems Homer did not have a clue. Ulysses had been sailing aimlessly around in the bay for ten years in order to have the opportunity to duck ashore periodically to tryst with Columbine, who was his true love.

So you can see that the Trojan War had nothing to do with any of this and all of those fanciful stories about the Cyclops, Circe, et al. were just that – fanciful stories. The real scoop is much more believable. Ulysses was just a guy looking for a way to cheat on his wife without getting caught.

The play was full of clever and humorous lines that clearly showed that the writers were familiar with the original, if erroneous, account by Homer.

Even Chef got in on the act by providing an after-the-play feast of Greek olives, pita triangles, and feta cheese served up with gallons of rosé, but no retsina. Since most of our Ranchers are originally from the Mid-West, they probably never developed a taste for retsina, so it was just as well.

There you have it, a Monday afternoon where it's just "Life at the Wrinkle Ranch: The Odyssey Revisited."

Life at the Wrinkle Ranch: When Push Comes to Shove

The leader of our Wrinkle Ranch theater group, the Ranch House Players, is Pierre, a very talented man. He has a wonderful, deep booming voice and can sing and act. He not only has years of experience in community theater, he also has an extensive background in public education. At one point in his career he was the superintendent of education in a large school system. His experiences in life, education, and business stand him in good stead in the leadership job he has accepted with our Seniors' thespian organization.

One of the reasons that theater, especially original theater, is so important in a Senior Community is that it provides a wide range of opportunities for residents to contribute and stay active. Besides the obvious requirement for a playwright, actors, a producer, and a director we use the Art League and Woodworkers to create sets.

The chorus and various musicians are worked into the script. The more able-bodied residents can be stage hands and open and close the curtain. Others create the program, usher, take tickets, and provide valet service for the walkers and other assistive devices belonging to the audience; there is lighting, sound, costumes, make up, and the all-important prompter. The list of people who can be utilized goes on and on.

You will not be surprised to learn that the more Seniors who are involved, the more difficult it is to manage all the interacting egos and personality quirks. Take for example this small vignette: Bob volunteered to do the lighting. He had experience; years ago he had worked with lighting in community theater. Bob was not familiar with the computer-based lighting system we use, but he was sure he could learn; however, he became more and more frustrated and agitated as the project developed and his ability to operate the lighting system did not. After a few rehearsals, the lighting scheme was simplified so he could manage the job, and Bob had to admit to himself he could not perform as he had in his younger days. He had fallen victim to denial.

Through my observations I have come to believe that denial and falls are the two worst enemies of Seniors, and many times it is denial that is at the root of falls. Denial certainly leads to accidents and frustrations as it did in Bob's case. As we grow older, sometimes we just cannot do the same things we did before – things we used to do easily. We are not so agile, cannot see or hear so well as we once did, do not remember things, cannot memorize scripts, or even keep our place if we are reading. Wonderful singing voices no longer have the same quality and range; arthritic fingers do not move over the keyboard with the same ease they once did.

One of the worst manifestations of denial among our Seniors is the insistence that they can still operate an automobile safely. "I've been driving for 70 years. I'm fine behind the wheel, and I will not give up my car" is the sort of declaration we frequently hear the day before a Senior confuses the accelerator with the brake or turns the wrong way into traffic. Experts in the science of aging advise that we note and accept these changes and modify our activities and expectations accordingly. If we do so we run less risk of falling off that ladder, or having an accident in our car, or being frustrated by the technical details of that new-fangled lighting system.

But I digress; let us get back to the theater and Bob. Bob was already on a short fuse, one that was more frequently obvious these days to his wife and friends, when suddenly he noted Mike angrily removing the "reserved" signs from a group of chairs at the front of the auditorium.

Mike has been diagnosed with Alzheimer's, and although he still functions in an Independent Living environment, his wife keeps a worried eye on him much of the time, manages his appointments and meds, and apologizes for his sometimes brusque and illogical comments at dinner.

The reserved seats had been paid for by the Marketing Department, eager to bring in prospects and to show them how much fun we have here at the Ranch. Who knows why Mike was angry about the "reserved" signs? He probably does not know either. That sort of anger is a common symptom among Alzheimer's sufferers. Bob observed Mike removing the signs and intervened. Bob yelled at Mike; pushing and shoving ensued! Seeing the distressed reaction of the on-looking theater workers, Bob said, "Let's take this outside!" and into the hall they went. The stalwarts had just squared off and resumed grappling with each other, pushing and shoving, when Pierre appeared!

The brouhaha was immediately interrupted by the leader of our merry band of performers. Pierre stepped between the sparring pair, and exhibiting the splendid experience in adolescent behavior he had gained working in the field of public education, he separated them. Speaking in his deep, authoritarian voice, he commanded, "Knock it off. I have a show to put on here." They complied, so fortunately order was restored. I guess you might say, it's just "Life at the Wrinkle Ranch: When Push Comes to Shove."

Life at the Wrinkle Ranch: Comedy Night

Although most of the theatrical productions at our Wrinkle Ranch strive to involve as many Ranchers as possible, there was one show that did not involve the voices of our chorus and a cast of little old ladies trundling behind their walkers like the ones recruited to be flower children in *Hair*, or members of the Greek Chorus in "The Odyssey Revisited."

This show, organized and produced by the Ranch House Players, not by the Activities Department, was named, *Comedy Night*, had a relatively small cast, and featured three different comedic skits. The first was an adaptation of Neil Simon's *Sunshine Boys* in which two old vaudevillians try to patch up their tumultuous, long-dissolved partnership in order to participate in a major network comedy retrospective only to have their efforts fail when they fall into their old patterns of squabbling and insults. Two of our better actors took on this task and did quite well with it. Those of us who knew them were not surprised. They were type cast.

The second was entitled by our resident playwright, "Guess Who's Coming to Dinner," and was not at all related to the famous movie and play of the same name. The Ranch Activities Manager, ever on the alert for anything that might be politically incorrect, was nervous when she saw the playbill until they showed her the script. This is the same racially sensitive Activities Manager who brought us the hoop skirt event in "honor" of Black History Month the year before I arrived and who later staged a Management approved spoof on *Gone with the Wind*, complete with actors in blackface and called "Gone with the Breeze." Oh well....

This "Guess Who's Coming to Dinner" is a skit about a widow whose "busy" and "important" son keeps promising to come to Sunday dinner but always makes last minute excuses. Somehow, week after week, he does not show. Every time he stands her up, the frustrated mom presses the pendant she wears in case of medical emergency and pours out her pain and frustration to the sympathetic woman at the medical alert company on the other end of the phone. This touching and audience-appropriate story was nicely handled by two of our female residents, much to the delight of the audience, many of whom could relate first hand to the situation.

But it was the third part of the trilogy which was truly original. It was the brain child of our resident stand-up comedian, Abe. If truth were told, Abe has always mourned the fact that he never got to work the Borscht Belt. Born in Brooklyn just a few years too late for all the action in the Catskills, he has imagined himself, I am sure, performing at Grossinger's many times.

He wrote an extremely imaginative rendition of that old favorite, "Little Red Riding Hood," which he named, "A Sheep in Wolf's Clothing." In this version "Red," who was played by the author's red haired wife, wearing a very short and sexy hooded red cape, is in cahoots with "Granny" in order to rob unsuspecting strangers. After Red lures the mark to Granny's house, the scheming pair draws him in with the "sick Granny" routine, and then the two women mug the poor fellow. Of course the Wolf falls for the scam and is soon relieved of his valuables. The two hucksters then cry out to be rescued from the Big Bad Wolf, and the nearby Woodsman – played by My Hero, who has no acting talent whatsoever and who muffed his lines every time he delivered them – rushes in with his rubber axe and does what heroes do – another example of type casting. Thanks to my excellent Amazon.com shopping skills, his Woodsman costume was authentic, so he looked the part anyway.

After the Woodsman wrestles Wolf into submission, the sheriff is summoned, and poor Wolf is summarily arrested and ordered to appear in court.

Now the fun really begins, there is a jury made up of just three jurors – the Three Little Pigs! They are an unsympathetic jury to say the least. They have a genetic distrust of wolves and are definitely prejudiced in favor of the "victims," Red and Granny. One of our retired attorneys did an excellent job of playing the judge; experience shows. The corny jokes were myriad including "here come de judge" and lots of other predictable lines. However, the third time the attorney for the accused came through carrying his brief case – this time with a ladder – and proceeded to announce that he was taking his case to a higher court, even the most jaded members of the audience were reduced to gales of laughter.

The jury had lots of one-liners too. And they looked the part. Those cast in the pig parts were very short and a little porky – we have a large pool of residents to draw from there – and they wore the most adorable pig noses. Thanks again to Amazon.com, not even those famous Redskin fans, The Hogettes, had more authentic snouts!

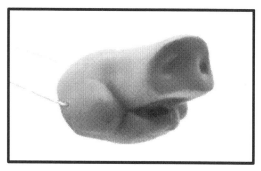

At the dress rehearsal it all went famously, although the pig played by Dean, an eccentric male resident, did seem rather nervous and throughout the rehearsals repeatedly told anyone who would listen that he had never acted before and that the bright lights on the stage hurt his eyes. Of course everyone just wrote it off to stage fright and assumed he would get over it.

Then two hours before Show Time, the Front Desk called Pierre, leader of the Ranch House Players, with a strange message. It seems they were in possession of a brown paper bag addressed to Pierre and containing a pink shirt, a pig nose, and a note. When Pierre collected the bag, he read the terse note, "Lights are too bright. I don't want to go blind. I cannot perform. Dean."

Well, you can't just cast a pig in a poke! It takes time to train a pig! These pigs had lots of lines. The obvious solution was to Shanghai someone already in the cast, someone who was familiar with the play, and who could at least wing the pig part. Nobody knew the lines better than Abe, but he was too tall and too thin. There was nothing in the least porcine about him, even the snout did not suit him.

It fell to Pierre to fill in for the missing porker, and that turned out to be serenpigidous since as an experienced actor, he made a much better pig than Dean could ever have been. You might even say he took advantage of the situation to hog the limelight!

Of course the audience did not know that one of the three little pigs had scooted out of the barn at the last minute, and since hardly anybody ever reads the playbill and no one pays attention to the pre-show announcements, most of them never found out about the pig caper, which in some ways was one of the funniest parts of the show! It's just "Life at the Wrinkle Ranch: Comedy Night."

CHAPTER
9

Managing the Ranch

When we moved to our Wrinkle Ranch, unbeknownst to us, the Executive Director was a Theory X manager with few of the true prerequisites for heading up such a complex, extensive, and people-oriented business enterprise. His experience in the major corporation that owned our Ranch was mostly in finance. As I quickly came to find out, he seemed to know little or nothing about managing people of any age. His understanding of gerontology was nil, and his people skills were pathetically lacking. His major criteria for decisions were usually financial, regardless of how inappropriate the criterion was to the situation, and to make matters worse, he was a bully, raising his voice at residents and associates alike. The result of such a management style at the top was just what you would imagine. Subordinates were not empowered; they lived in fear, and although the corporate mission statement vowed that they were here to "enhance" our lives, it seemed more likely that they spent their time and efforts just trying to stay out of trouble with the boss.

Given this environment, it was no wonder that we encountered such maintenance situations as those that led me to pen "The Harvest Moon Syndrome," "Excuse My Dust," and "Leaky Lanai."

Unfortunately, our early issues did not end with the Maintenance Department. "Transportation Distress" describes the difficulty I experienced with my first encounter with the Transportation Department. Providing transportation is a necessary part of Senior living, but unfortunately finding the right people to handle the jobs in that department is an on-going challenge since those positions are not counted among the more complex and higher paid jobs at the Ranch. After reading this account, you may think Management should "re-count." Unfortunately, my second experience with Transportation did nothing to offset my lack of confidence. Join in my frustration as described in "Transportation Mysteries."

My first encounter with a major meeting run by the Executive Director is the subject of "Not Ready for Corporate Prime Time."

Let me hasten to say that within a couple of years of our arrival, Corporate Management, which had clearly been actively pursuing the exit of this inappropriate executive, succeeded. One day he was escorted out of the building by his direct supervisor, a Vice President, and he was never seen or mentioned by Management again. Although the Ranch House Rumor Mill had grist for months, appropriately none of our residents ever knew what events actually precipitated his leaving; however, I can say without fear of contradiction that absolutely nobody here missed him!

After a lengthy search the former Executive Director was replaced by a wonderful man, one who had all the experience his predecessor lacked, was dedicated to the well-being of the residents and the associates, and managed his staff by being a coach, a mentor, and an example. If this Executive Director had been in place when we moved to the Ranch, I am convinced that we would not have had to deal with the unfortunate management issues we initially encountered.

All of this just emphasizes how important leadership and proper community management are in your "Forever Home." We were wise to have chosen to live in a community owned by a fiscally sound, reputable corporation, one dedicated to the lives and well-being of Seniors, one that would not allow the situation we encountered to continue.

The resident upset caused by the events reported in "The Silk Forest" was overcome by events when, a year or so later, a massive renovation project completely eliminated the referenced arboreal collection.

Management makes plans, but their plans are not always timely. The excitement caused by "An Unscheduled Fire Drill" underscored the need for a new alarm system. As you might imagine, after our late-night sleep interruption, we all supported that particular expenditure.

Nonetheless being owned by a giant corporation, even one whose only business is Seniors, has its pitfalls. It is easy for the folks who work in corporate offices far away from the communities to forget who the customer is, and so situations like the one described in "Hop on the Bus, Gus..." do happen.

"Powerless" points out how important it is, even with proper management, to have residents who are observant and participate in their community. "Helping Management See" is a valuable tool, and the successful management team encourages input from those extra Senior eyes.

The best of intentions do not always find solutions to resident problems, as we learn in "The Shell Game."

"Driving Miss Daisy" is a story that explores how the staff in a good Senior Community treats their Seniors. The associate in this story received a commendation from the highest level of the Corporation. I made sure of that. At the request of the lady he had rescued, I acted as the ghost writer for her account of his service, which she submitted to Management.

Other times, when faced with a difficult situation like the one described in "The Changing of the Guard," Management finds a way to implement changes in the best interests of the community in a smooth manner, negotiating the minefield of residents who are protecting their turf with vigor and sometimes with a dash of dementia thrown in.

Life at the Wrinkle Ranch: The Harvest Moon Syndrome

After living at the Ranch for a few months, I detected a management attitude about dealing with resident issues – an attitude I have decided to call The Harvest Moon Syndrome after one of my favorite songs. If you recall it starts, "Shine on, shine on...."

The Harvest Moon Syndrome is the first line of any organizational defense against complying with requests and usually begins with Plan A, a common response, found in bureaucracies everywhere and in many different situations. I like to think of it as the Sacred "Status Quo" Statement, but you may also recognize it as the "**Take it or Leave it**" **Lemma**.

Many times when raising an issue or a problem, residents at the Ranch are told, "That's just how they do it here." "They are all that way." "It's always been that way," or "There is no way we can address that now."

When that approach is not applicable, the Ranch staff member frequently invokes Plan B: The **Gas Light Gambit**, which involves the non-validation of the resident's perceptions.

It unfolds like this: Resident goes to the appropriate staff department manager and reports a problem and/or asks for a service. The well-trained management person then has a wide variety of tried and true responses from which to choose. All of these responses are designed to minimize, trivialize, or even deny the existence of an issue or problem. So when asked to address an issue that might call for the expenditure of resources or budget, management responds, "That's not really a problem," or "It's not what you think," or "That's the way it's supposed to work."

If I were a serious subscriber to conspiracy theories, I could draw the conclusion that this approach, when taken to the extreme, is eerily akin to a psychological plan to drive someone to the brink of serious emotional distress. After all, having an organized effort to convince Seniors that their valid perceptions are erroneous is surely a form of elder abuse, don't you agree? But on a more realistic note, I think the intentions of the staff are much more mundane. They just do not want to spend the resources to address the residents' requests, and any little ploy they can use to avoid or delay the expenditure is doubtless encouraged by their Executive Director and rewarded at bonus time.

The third strategy falling under the Harvest Moon Syndrome is Plan C, which we will call the **Defer Defense**. In this maneuver the manager defers dealing with the issue "until...." It could be "until the weather changes," "until the new equipment is delivered," or "until Joe comes back from vacation." There is no end to the "until" scenarios that will defer dealing with a problem.

A favorite example is to defer the solution until higher management approval is obtained. Everyone knows that senior management is always on travel, in meetings, or otherwise unavailable to deal with the "little" things. This is one of the best and most effective Defer Defenses because it assures the resident of the willingness of the person with whom he is dealing to affect the desired solution. Should "approval" not be eventually forthcoming, rest assured, it certainly was not the fault of anyone at a lower level!

Remember these are old people who are coming forward with these issues. Old people forget things, or they may have a major change of status – for instance moving to Assisted Living, or even departing for the Hereafter. Such changes in circumstance may permanently defer the request. So Defer, Defer, and Defer, and with any luck at all, the whole thing will just go away.

For example: The first day I looked out of the window in my new bedroom – which is actually four windows grouped together – there were three perfectly clear windows and one cloudy one. The Maintenance supervisor was there, and I explained to him that we needed to replace the damaged window. "Oh that's just dirt on the outside of the window," he replied smoothly. "No, I don't think so," I countered. He responded with his final offer of the day, "I'll have Joe look at it. He's an expert with these windows."

A week later Joe arrived and continued the party line, reiterating, "The window is just dirty on the outside and doesn't need to be replaced." After another chat with the supervisor I was told the window cleaners would be here "soon," and then I would see that it would all be fine, just fine. I was unconvinced, but since I was still in my self-declared "don't make waves" period, I decided to wait for the window washers who were coming "soon."

Months went by, but I was caught up in other issues such as the ones described in "Excuse My Dust," "Leaky Lanai," not to mention the lack of consistency in laundry room signage, and the runaway rabbit, so I just kept the blind at half-mast on that window and non-confronted the foggy view.

Then the window washer came. Much to my surprise, it is not necessary to use a scaffold to wash these windows. The windows themselves are athletic – contortionists actually. They all fold down, turn around, and lift out easily. In other words, we could have cleaned this window ourselves and resolved the question, but who knew? Not us, anyway. The window washer washed the foggy window carefully and announced, "This window has moisture trapped between the panes and needs to be replaced!"

I felt validated, elated, triumphant! I was right all along. I had been temporarily victimized by the Harvest Moon Syndrome Plan B, the Gas Light Gambit.

But now girded with a new and substantiating "professional" opinion, I called the supervisor to say that the window had been washed and definitely needed to be replaced. The next move on his part was to tell me that the window would have to go to the glass company and be refitted with new panes. He quickly invoked Plan C again and deferred any action until...; however, by then I had analyzed the patterns here. I knew that I am supposed to wait until the right employee can come and remove the window, and that is just what I was told, but hold on! Surely then I will be informed that we cannot leave an uncovered window in the midst of rainy season, so I expect to be instructed that we will have to wait until.... Do I get this stuff, or what?

However, I am prepared. My next counter will be: they can just take a window from an empty apartment and replace mine – after all, they are all identical. Except, of course, some of them are clear, whereas my window – like some people's judgment – is clouded.

I am prepared to take this up the management chain. I am a master of the effective e-mail, the revoltingly repetitive request, and the elegant art of escalation. Maybe they will even learn that it is better to address my reasonable requests in a timely manner than to sing me another chorus of "Shine on, shine on...." It's just "Life at the Wrinkle Ranch: The Harvest Moon Syndrome."

Life at the Wrinkle Ranch: Excuse My Dust!

The building we live in here at the Ranch is referred to as "the Tower," and it is over twenty years old. To our knowledge, the HVAC ducts in this building have never been cleaned. We know for a certainty that the ducts in our 1400 square feet of the Tower had not been cleaned since the renovations made to the bathrooms, and the kitchen, and the completion of the very dusty construction project we funded to install a wall of built-in cabinets in our bedroom, all before we moved in.

After a month or so of dusting every other day and still being able to scrape a quarter inch of thick, stand-up-on-its-own, fuzz from the top of the night stand beside my pillow, I e-mailed the head of the Resident Health Committee and asked if she struggled with dust in her apartment. Her answer stunned me. "Yes," she replied, "it's always been that way ever since we moved in seven years ago, but my husband doesn't care if I dust or not, and so I just ignore it. You know, Florida is a very dusty place, and that's just the way it is." Being a friendly, helpful woman, she signed her e-mail "Dusty in 465."

"Dusty" did, however, ask around, and she discovered that everyone in the Tower to whom she spoke battled heavy dust problems. Then she took it up with her committee. They deliberated and agreed there was a dust issue and resolved to look into it.

In the meantime, unwilling to put off my issue while the committee deliberated and resolved, I waited the requisite two days and once again gathered the dust from the top of the 2' x 3' nightstand. This time I placed the collected dust in the center an orange piece of paper which I folded neatly around it and set off to call on the building Maintenance coordinator.

"Show and tell time," I announced cheerfully. He peered at the orange paper I had deposited on his desk and which I proceeded to open for his viewing pleasure. "What's that?" he asked hesitantly. "Two days of accumulated dust from the nightstand beside my pillow," I replied. "I might have brought you what has accumulated in my lungs since I have been here, but I thought I would start with this."

Two-day dust accumulation before duct cleaning

Needless to say, he was nonplussed. It seems that residents of the Ranch are not usually so assertive, and he was not sure how to deal with me. But the people who work here always start a response to a problem in accordance with the Harvest Moon principle. "Did you know that most household dust is really just skin cells shed by the people who live there?" he inquired. When I told him that was ridiculous, and I did not believe it, he tried another tact. "You have all those rugs; the dust probably is coming from them." I explained that those rugs are antique Oriental rugs and did their shedding long ago. Furthermore, they had all been professionally washed and cleaned before our move. Finally, unable to come up with another explanation, he moved from the Deny Approach to the Defer Defense. "I'll show it to my boss," he promised. "Perhaps he will have a suggestion."

And so the issue was escalated up the management chain. I received a call promptly from the head of Maintenance, who reverted to the Deny Approach and wanted to reassure me there was not really a problem. After I explained calmly that My Hero and I arrived here in perfect health and that it was his job to see that we did not succumb to respiratory failure because of conditions in his building, his response was that he would look into the situation.

And then the "fixes" began. Fix #1: change the filter – it was only 2 weeks old – no improvement. Fix #2: clean the coils of the heat exchanger and change the filter again – no improvement. After I offered to bring more dust samples, Management decided to bring in outside assistance. Then, voilà, a professional duct cleaning service appeared and spent several hours cleaning our ducts.

So far the dust is down about 75%. I was hoping for something equivalent to the environment created for the Bubble Boy, but I guess I should be satisfied with the improvement we have.

It is sad to think that intelligent people accept such conditions without a murmur. Is it just age that somehow prompts them to think, "That's just how it is"? Would they feel the same way if they were still living in their own houses? Is this attitude "Ranch Mentality"? Well, I was not having any of it.

I believe with a little humor, logic, and persistence we can change things that need changing, and I intend to keep working to that premise. I wonder what the Resident Health Committee will think when they hear that I have battled the dust monster and have a clean win. I wonder if other residents will ask to have their ducts cleaned also. And I wonder what Management will think about that. So far, it's just "Life at the Wrinkle Ranch: Excuse My Dust!"

Life at the Wrinkle Ranch: Leaky Lanai

One of the most beautiful features of the apartments at the Ranch is the lanai. Every apartment has one. The lanais have floor to ceiling windows that open and are screened. Our windows along the bottom half lift out, and although they are very heavy, it is possible to remove them entirely from their channels and raise the middle set of windows creating a wonderful screened porch.

We chose an east-facing apartment on a higher floor with a lovely view of the golf course in the daytime. At night we can see the lights of the local town.

The fact that the windows open is actually not of particular interest to us. We have hardly ever opened a window in thirty years. If it is not too hot or too cold, we fear the pollen and other floating particulates, which incite our allergies to riot.

So we did not hesitate to furnish our lanai with the latest in sun protective floor-to-ceiling fabric blinds, a beautiful oriental rug, and elegant rattan furniture. We knew the windows would remain closed, and everything on the lanai, protected by the Low-E blinds, would be safe from the elements.

For the first three months we were here, drought conditions reigned. We had precipitation only a couple of times, and it was neither heavy nor long-lasting. Then one night in late June a storm came in from the east, and heavy rain poured, blowing sideways and aimed directly at our windows. We did not pay much attention until the next morning when we went to our lanai to have breakfast and discovered a totally soaked oriental rug and two inches of water standing on the lower side of the slightly sloping floor!

After mopping up the water and spreading the rug to dry in a safer place, I called building maintenance. They explained that it is really not possible to keep the windows from leaking when it rains heavily because of the way they are designed, and furthermore, Marketing should have informed me of that fact *before* we moved here.

Then I explained that it was totally unacceptable to have a major part of one's dwelling that leaked when it rained. Once we understood each other they sent a team to inspect our problem. My Hero was there armed with all his engineering expertise to lead the discussion.

After a meeting of the minds, directed by My Hero, the Maintenance supervisor told us that they would order a "high boy," and in a couple of weeks when it arrived, they could raise it to the level of our lanai and drill holes in the outside metal channels, which hold the bottom windows in place. That procedure should allow the rain water to run out and not collect and spill over into the lanai. We approved their plan.

The high boy arrived, the holes were drilled. My resident engineer oversaw the entire process; and then we waited, with my lovely oriental rug still rolled up under the bed. We waited for the next onslaught of driving rain from the east to make sure the "fix" actually fixed the problem.

In the meantime, I experimented with making paper boats to float in a "show and tell" for Maintenance, in case their contention that "the fix is in" was not correct, and it was *still* just "Life at the Wrinkle Ranch: Leaky Lanai."

Life at the Wrinkle Ranch: Transportation Distress

One of the nicer aspects of life at the Wrinkle Ranch is that transportation is provided at no additional cost for all medical, dental, and financial advisor appointments within the two neighboring counties. This is clearly spelled out in all the literature given to prospects and new residents.

This fact encouraged us to move to the Ranch with only one car, leaving our 15-year-old sedan behind.

When I decided to make a "get acquainted" appointment with the doctor of internal medicine at the local University up the road, the doctor who was recommended to me by a physician from my previous health provider, I called Transportation several days in advance and asked to schedule a ride to my appointment.

The doctor's appointment clerk had requested that I arrive half an hour earlier than my scheduled appointment so that I could complete new patient paperwork, and I gave the earlier time to Transportation as my actual appointment time. I also asked if they were familiar with the route to the building on the University campus where my new doctor was located. The Transportation manager assured me that they take people there all the time and the drivers knew exactly where it was.

Confident that I had followed all the correct procedures, I showed up at the front door precisely on time, forty minutes before my desired arrival time. When the driver said, "We have another passenger, is that all right with you?" I said, "Sure as long as I get to my appointment on time." After years of working in the aerospace industry, supporting the military, and being married to a career military man, the only acceptable alternative to "on time" is "early," as far as I am concerned. The driver shrugged and said, "I was told to drop her off first."

So it was with trepidation that I climbed in the back seat of the big white sedan which had the Ranch name and logo on the door, and the three of us started north on the Interstate. After we dropped my fellow rider, I had only five minutes left to get to my destination. "You do know where this place is, don't you?" I asked testily. "Not exactly," he admitted.

"You do have GPS don't you?" I inquired even more testily. "Yes, but it's not finding it," he admitted. So I had to whip out my smart phone and do the navigating myself. It turns out we were quite a distance away from my destination, and I was thirty-five minutes late!

When I finally filled out all the paper work and saw the nurse who took my blood pressure, my usually low BP was sky high! I wonder why?

On a subsequent morning I dispatched My Hero – who had his own "get acquainted" appointment – to the Transportation Office. He made it clear to them that whatever departure time is required to get all those being transported to their destinations on time is fine with him. He also made it clear that *late* is always unacceptable. In instances like this he can be quite persuasive. He has even been known to use "command voice."

Somehow I think the message was received, but just in case, I am glad we have our very own dependable car with our very own GPS in the carport outside. If necessary in the future, we will be prepared to provide our own transportation in case it's just "Life at the Wrinkle Ranch: Transportation Distress!"

Life at the Wrinkle Ranch: Transportation Mysteries

After my first experience with Ranch Transportation I wanted to make sure there were no glitches with the ride to my new periodontist, who was about forty-five minutes away. I sent the Transportation Office an e-mail with the name, location, and phone number of the dentist along with the appointment time, and I made sure I had programmed my smart phone to find the destination before I showed up in the Lobby at the appointed hour. This time I would not agree to another passenger to be dropped off first, and I had the route guidance in my own smart phone GPS app, ready to go. I was confident I had all the bases covered.

Ted from the Transportation Office was there and explained to me that it was necessary to give them the address of my destination in advance! He then went on to tell me that "we" were fortunate that he had a directory that allowed him to find the location from the phone number which I had provided. He seemed very proud of his performance!

I was so beside myself, I did not even bother to respond. What part of the e-mail I had sent to him two weeks before was he not able to read? How could Transportation not know all the details of the appointment? I had certainly sent them. This was a Transportation Mystery.

The trip was uneventful, but I could not wait to get home to resend my original e-mail message to him. One of my many neuroses has to do with being complete in my communications and being very upset when people perceive that I have not been complete, and Ted was certainly convinced that I had not been complete. I found the e-mail in question and – resentfully – resent it with a tactful message about how sorry I was that there had been a misunderstanding that caused him extra work. If he could read between the lines – which by then I doubted since he did not seem able to read the lines themselves – he would certainly see that my "sorry" was actually a statement of how disappointed I was by his "sorry" performance.

Nothing further was heard from Ted until almost a month later. One Friday afternoon after working hours, I checked my voice mail and learned that Ted thought I had an appointment Monday morning and was reminding me to be in the Lobby on time. That would have been a splendid example of follow-up except to my knowledge, I had no appointment. Not that Monday, nor any Monday in the future – as far as I knew.

I was distressed. Another of my many neuroses has to do with being on time and being where I am supposed to be when I am supposed to be there. Failure to execute in either department makes my stomach hurt. Even contemplating failure in such situations makes my stomach hurt. What appointment? Had I forgotten something? How could Ted just make these things up? This was another Transportation Mystery!

I called his empty office and left a message disavowing any appointments and any transportation requests.

Monday morning came and as I was exiting the building for my morning walk, Ted hailed me and said cheerily, "I figured it out! It was all my fault!" I could have told him that; as a matter of fact, I thought I had.

"I wrote all the information about your dentist appointment last month on the calendar page for this month. I didn't have it last month so that was why I thought you didn't tell me where you were going. But I did have it for this month, except you didn't have an appointment this month. I figured it out. It was all my fault."

And that cheerful admission should make me feel better? I now know that no amount of transmitted information is sufficient to inform the Transportation Department of my destinations and my appointments. I also know that Ted is not overcome with shame nor does he make abject apologies when he screws up royally. He, who clearly is not burdened with the same neuroses I have – the performance ones, the ones that make my stomach hurt – is happy that he figured it all out. He can smile and say it was all his fault. I admire his emotional good health. I, on the other hand, will always approach transportation opportunities at the Ranch with trepidation, reminder e-mails, and the potential for a stomach ache. It's just "Life at the Wrinkle Ranch: Transportation Mysteries."

Life at the Wrinkle Ranch: Not Ready for Corporate Prime Time

I worked for thirty-five years in the military electronics industry. A number of my employers were among the Fortune 500 – you might say I worked in Corporate Prime Time.

After I had served an appropriate length of time in the trenches, I reached a level that allowed me to attend some important meetings in the Board Room, meetings where CEOs and Division Presidents butted heads, where I saw multi-million-dollar project managers destroyed with a single glance and grown men cry; I learned first-hand the meaning of Theory X management and was fed to the wolves along with the "guys" – equal opportunity at its least attractive!

So it was with some interest that I attended my first Quarterly Residents Meeting at my new Senior Community, which is owned by one of the largest purveyors of Senior care in the nation, and heard the Executive Director speak to the assembled residents.

There was a rumor that he was going to announce a monthly fee hike for the next year, and I was interested from several angles: finding out how much he would be taking from my pocketbook and learning how a professional Senior Community Manager tells his fixed income residents that he is raising their monthly service fees.

First he told a couple of "Senior" jokes. Well, making fun of one's self can be endearing, but he is not so old, so maybe he is just making fun of us. He did express his appreciation and surprise that he got a few laughs. I found that strange, but stranger things came later.

Next he gave a corporate service award to some of his employees, doubtless a "feel good" activity, intended to put us all in a mood to appreciate Management and the parent corporation. He told us that they had acted in accordance with the corporate mission statement, which has to do with "enriching the lives..." of the resident; however, as you will soon see, I am not so sure that is what happened in this case.

Surely all of you who have worked in an organization with a corporate mission statement can fill in the blanks of the corporate directive. So you too will be qualified to evaluate the explanation that came later.

Our Leader explained that what he was about to describe happened as a result of a situation in which he was unable to cope with a scheduled event – in part because of his self-confessed total lack of patience – an event for which he clearly had not done adequate planning. Then he went on to tell the assemblage that he had to call four managers to leave their daily posts for the entire day in an emergency move to bail *him* out.

Now I know his peers and superiors were not present to hear this confession of inadequacy; however, schooled as I am in the killer culture of corporate America, I was so stunned, I almost fell off my chair. And please explain to me again, whose life did these loyal employees enhance? I think it was that of the Leader, but then I may not be seeing things from the proper perspective, i.e., from *his* perspective.

The feel good(?) awards out of the way, we moved on to a lengthy discussion of dog poop – how despite the installation of refuse stations around the property, he had personally seen and confronted two residents who, at different times, had accompanied a dog that pooped, and he had noted that the resident in question did not scoop! He recounted that when confronted, the one resident twice denied not scooping and then slunk back to scoop later. How did he know?

He also said the second resident asserted that since the dog had pooped in the grass, it was natural, and therefore unnecessary to scoop. But after a lecture from our Fearless Leader on the Rights of Others, etc., etc. – Could he be a disciple of Rousseau? – he told us this resident also came back later with a shovel and deposited the unwanted natural gift into one of our lakes! Of course this constituted an additional environmental sin, but again, how did the Fearless One know this happened?

I am coming to the conclusion that not only has this man confessed to the inability to plan for standard events, he spends all his time patrolling the property for "poop, no scoop" crime. No wonder he cannot plan properly for corporate missions, he is too busy with his surveillance activities. Perhaps in an effort to make his points, he speaks in fables..., but as you doubtless have seen already, this guy is no Aesop!

There was one more dog story... it seems that someone lets his dog out into the hall – forget this walking outdoors with a leash and the problem with outside clean up. This dog just uses the hallway rug!!! If we know this is happening, why have we not called PETA, the ASPCA, local animal control, The American Alzheimer's Association, or a dog poop flash mob to deal with this situation? Another fable? Or just fanciful fiction?

But then, gratefully, the poop issues seemingly out of the way, we moved on. We moved on to the topic of redoing the trash rooms on each wing of the Tower building.

Our intrepid Leader informed us that all the trash rooms had to be redone because of uncorrectable odor issues involving their carpeting.

Give me credit for restraining myself; I did not leap up and call out, "We have *no* carpet and no pervasive odor in our trash room!" Those of you who have been with me for the long haul can refer to my initial vow not to make waves in my new home. I stuck to that strategy – with some difficulty.

There are more than a dozen trash rooms in this building. How could he say they all have to be redone because of the carpet??? Has he ever toured all of them? But, moving on, the real point of his discussion, as he was quick to explain, was to identify the source of this problem: The invasive and irreversible result of so many used Depends being deposited in unsealed containers in the trash rooms.

Depends Disposal: A distasteful idea which had never occurred to me! You can bet your bottom dollar, now that Paul had brought it up, I wanted to wipe it from my mind. Who discusses an odiferous idea like this in a formal meeting? Perhaps he thought the budget and the ultimate issue, "How Much Will This Cost Me?" would be less odious in comparison.

Eventually after we had dealt with all the possible distracting, distasteful, and disgusting issues he could dispense, our Executive Director blurted out the bottom line, the *piece de resistance*: There will be a major increase of monthly fees in the next year. This was not unexpected. As in any closed community rumors swirl and precede any major release of information. Nonetheless, it is good he got a few laughs *before* his presentation because none of the residents was laughing afterward.

I can assure you this manager and his presentation style would not have lasted five minutes in the DoD or at any major corporation where I have worked. I think it is safe to say that it is no wonder he was employed here in this little backwater, surrounded by apparently helpless old people. It's just "Life at the Wrinkle Ranch: Not Ready for Corporate Prime Time."

Life at the Wrinkle Ranch: The Silk Forest

In some places people cannot see the forest for the trees, and at times our Wrinkle Ranch seems to be among them.

Before we held the marvelous 20th Anniversary Paris Park event on that special Tuesday, we had silk trees, many decorated with tiny white lights, positioned outside the elevators and at the ends of the halls on various floors in the Tower.

In order to provide the proper ambiance for the special anniversary event, the creative Lifestyles Department gathered up all our trees, stripped off the lights and grouped them artistically in the auditorium. Can you say Bois (de soie) de Boulogne, Boys and Girls? But the more creative among us are not necessarily the most organized – or thorough – and after gathering up all these trees and holding a wonderful event, there seemed to be no determined effort to return the trees to their original locations. In fact many months later, a number of the trees were still grouped behind the stage, homeless!

One resident was incensed that the beautiful tree outside the elevators on our floor, the one with the tiny bird's nest, was replaced by a hulking, ugly tree with a chopped off limb. Somehow she found our original tree, and then we had two trees where once we had only one. Are the former owners of the chopped tree "pine-ing" for its return, even though it is a ficus?

One of our residents was very upset because, as the decorating chairman of an upcoming Holiday Dinner, she had already picked out the lighted trees she wanted to borrow to create the requisite Winter Wonderland environment in the designated dining room and had already obtained permission from the floors involved. Now nobody knew where the original trees were, and no trees appeared to have lights anymore.

Apparently the Lifestyles Department had no idea how we had bonded with our trees or how proprietary we felt about them. The Sierra Club has no more devotion to their redwoods than does a Senior at our Ranch to his floor's silk ficus.

I believed this tree issue is a Housekeeping Committee appropriate topic and suggested that Committee launch a Search and Rescue mission to find the trees that were, pre-Paris Park, on the various floors, inventory them and mark them with an unobtrusive tag so that this tree misplacement resulting in a new

169

growth behind the stage – this tragedy, this Birnam Wood event, if you will – will never be reenacted. It's just "Life at the Wrinkle Ranch: The Silk Forest."

Life at the Wrinkle Ranch: Powerless!

Many residents of the Wrinkle Ranch have their own golf carts – some because they can no longer pass the Florida driver's test and do not have a license to drive an automobile – but they are in denial about their driving abilities and so persevere by driving their golf carts. Others use the cart as a second vehicle for running around town, and some, including us, are actually golfers and find owning a cart more cost effective and convenient than renting a cart each time they play.

The Ranch also owns carts. Multi-passenger carts are used to drive residents from one building to another and to the parking lot; maintenance people drive golf carts and electric utility vehicles; and even Marketing has a cart used to drive prospects from the Tower to the outlying parts of the Ranch – the South 40, if you will.

All these carts must be charged regularly and housed in a space protected from midnight requisitions by the enterprising and unscrupulous people who lurk outside our gates, just waiting to prey on the innocent Senior citizens inside – or so we have been told.

For the purposes of charging and protecting our carts, the Ranch has provided little tents, just big enough to cover a golf cart, and tiny, lockable storage cabinets that house chargers for the carts. The chargers belong to the individual cart owners, but plug into power provided at no additional cost by the Ranch. The entire cart tent complex is surrounded by a chain link fence, and the gate is locked every night.

We had owned our new Yamaha golf cart for less than a week, plugging it into our new charger each time we parked it under our cute little tent, when My Hero, always watchful in such matters, announced to me that the cart had not charged the previous night! After one more try the subsequent evening, he drove right back to the Golf Cart Store and suggested that either our new battery or our new charger must be at fault; however, after extensive testing at the store, he was satisfied that both were working properly.

For his next move, he went to Robert, the Maintenance Director at the Ranch, and explained the situation: the power to the golf cart area was not sufficient to charge the carts! This was new news to Robert, and clearly, if true, would have serious implications.

Visions of multitudes of old, white-haired people at Winn Dixie, Home Depot, and Wal Mart, stranded by the dead batteries in their golf carts flashed before his eyes. And they could be the lucky ones. What about the carts that would die just as their drivers were crossing the State Road that ran through town? Would it be only the cart that died there in the intersection?

The best possible scenario involved dozens of phone calls coming in to the main switchboard with angry Seniors on the other end of the phone demanding a pick up and a tow for their carts. Even this scenario qualifies as one of a Wrinkle Ranch Maintenance Manager's worst nightmares.

Robert immediately went out to check the validity of this unwelcome information and determined that indeed, the power was not working. The golf cart area was powerless!

After calling the local power company, he and their representative began to diagnose the problem, cutting the power line to the cart area in two places in an effort to pinpoint the exact location of the break. My Hero dropped by to monitor their progress.

Now that several days had gone by without power to the carts, we took our charger to the Ranch golf course and plugged into their power, which came off the main power line before the line to the residents' cart area. Our cart was charged; however, it was the only resident-owned cart that was.

"Do you think we should put out a memo and alert everyone that their carts may not have a charge?" Robert asked My Hero. He was asking the right person. Having managed large organizations and been "in charge" for much of his life, My Hero was certainly the right person to give advice concerning this "charge" problem. He astutely recommended that since no one else had reported it, it was far better not to announce a problem without a solution in hand. Such an announcement was sure to make Robert and indeed, the entire management team, the object of widespread complaints and criticism.

On the other hand, once the problem was fixed, a memo explaining how the attentiveness and quick response of Maintenance had avoided disruption to golf cart usage at the Ranch could garner kudos. Such are the lessons learned in command positions.

Sure enough, by the afternoon of the second day of diagnostics, and after some serious trenching along the power line route, the disruptive root that had grown through a portion of the cable was discovered, and the line was quickly repaired.

No Seniors were stranded, no complaints were filed, and no memo was sent.

If it had not been for the vigilance and attentiveness of My Hero to all things electrical, mechanical, and associated with safety, who knows what the end of this root-through-the-power-line story would have been. One thing is clear: they need us here, or else the residents may discover it's just "Life at the Wrinkle Ranch: Powerless!"

Life at the Wrinkle Ranch: An Unscheduled Fire Drill

The Main Ranch House Fire alarm system was installed more than twenty years ago when the building was constructed. It was state of the art then, but that state has changed! Periodically there have been glitches with the alarm system, which was "aging in place" right along with all the residents. Although there had never been a fire in the building, and despite the fact that the building is a certified hurricane shelter and built of concrete and rebar – with thick walls and a fire safety door on each apartment home – the alarm system would sometimes just "go off." This particular night it sounded at 2 A.M. for thirty-five long minutes. Front Desk had no idea what to do. The local Volunteer Fire Department finally came and turned off the alarm. Later we were told we may, or may not, have had smoke in the kitchen, or perhaps a short in the alarm panel.

Despite last spring's "Defend in Place" directive by Management – appropriate, and recommended by fire safety authorities for concrete and steel construction – Front Desk personnel told people who called them during the aberrant alarm period to "come to the Lobby!"

Many other residents went into the hall and waited for instructions per the old, rescinded protocol. Among Seniors, old memories stick; new information – not so much.

It was your basic Wrinkle Ranch fiasco. I pulled a pillow over my head and went back to sleep. At that point I was not only the President of the Residents' Association, I was co-author of the *Resident Orientation Handbook,* and we were fully informed on the latest protocols in our apartment home! My Hero put in ear plugs and slept peacefully beside me.

It was upsetting to learn that many hearing impaired residents heard nothing. You would have to be really, really deaf not to hear that alarm! When the subject came up the next day, they had no idea that the alarm had gone off. The P.A. system – a vintage technology companion of the alarm system – did not work. Whatever could go wrong did. It was a wonderful, unplanned training exercise!

Thank goodness, no one was hurt in the confusion, although one uninformed care-giver bumped her charge's wheel chair down the stairs for three floors, from 6th to 3rd, before encountering someone who stopped that particular brand of foolishness.

Everyone in Management is back to the drawing board to study "lessons learned." It's just "Life at the Wrinkle Ranch: An Unscheduled Fire Drill"

Life at the Wrinkle Ranch: Hop on the Bus, Gus...

Paul Simon, the gifted musician and song writer, has many catchy lines in his songs. One that always resonated with me was "Hop on the bus, Gus...." It comes to mind whenever I think of getting away from it all, taking a fun trip, or having an adventure.

At the Wrinkle Ranch we frequently "hop on the bus." OK, OK, so we do not "hop" so well these days, but we do enjoy getting away from home for a while. Sometimes we want to go to a ball game, or a cultural event, or to a nice restaurant. Other times we may be off to a community outing, or to pig out at the regional Chili Cook Off, or to view the festive decorations in the local neighborhoods at Christmas time.

At our community individual transportation to medical, dental, and financial appointments within a given area is included in our contracts and transportation to group events is provided; so with over 500 residents, many of whom no longer drive, we maintain a regular fleet of vehicles – vans, small busses, middle sized busses, wheel chair busses, and even a big bus for the more popular trips.

The transportation aficionados among you will understand what this means in terms of expense and wear and tear on our vehicles – vehicles making numerous short trips and having multiple drivers.

Multiply this by the large number of communities in our corporate family, and certainly the requirement for a corporate transportation directorate is obvious. It takes a group of knowledgeable business people to negotiate contracts, select and procure vehicles, and manage this sort of activity in a cost-effective manner so that "Gus" and the other Ranchers can "hop on the bus" and get away for the afternoon to enjoy the ball game.

The vehicle experts in the far off corporate office are required to focus on such parameters as good mileage, reliability, maintainability, and cost. Local management cares about all those items too, and they are the ones who must deal with the day to day issues of resident safety, ergonomics, comfort, and feedback; unfortunately, it sometimes seems as if the corporate transportation people have forgotten who the customer is.

After all, our vehicle procurers are, on average, young and agile. In contrast, our vehicle users are, on average, old and halt. There are issues for which the procurers and the users may be focused on different goals. For example, to the procurers, a vehicle built on a truck chassis means durability. To the user it means a stiff, uncomfortable ride, one from which old bones will suffer for days afterward.

The number and height of the steps for mounting the bus are not an obvious barrier to the procurers, but they are a "show stopper" for many of the residents. A trivial first step for a younger, fully ambulatory person is literally insurmountable for a Senior who has had a hip replacement or who needs one. So let us explore what happens if the corporate transportation experts act without sufficient focus on user considerations:

There was a lot of excitement among our residents when the long awaited, super-duper new bus arrived! It was indeed big and shiny; it looked cool and had the new corporate "wrap" with the familiar corporate logo and this year's catchy branding phrase emblazoned on its broad sides. All our Seniors wanted to be the first to ride on the cool new bus. Then reality set in.

Right away, that first step was a stumbling block for some – too high. Then it became apparent that we must mount four steps to board the new bus, not just three as on the previous model. The aisle was farther above us, and the angle was steeper. Next we determined that the depth of each step was not sufficient to contain a complete adult foot, making balance on the steps more of a problem, and if we thought the first step was too high, all we had to do was wait until we reached the last one. It was higher still!

Once safely up the steps we learned that one side of the aisle had plenty of knee room whereas the seats on the other side were too close together for comfort, setting off a Senior scramble for the wide side.

Sitting down, we quickly discerned this bus was inhospitable for Senior motion sickness sufferers because there was no horizon to be seen looking forward. The designers of this bus had put the driver in a "well." Well, it's like a well. The driver sits well below the level of the passenger seats and aisle, and since the front view is deemed more important to the driver than to the passengers, the windshield is far below the passengers' view – hence, no horizon is to be seen. For those who need a reference to fend off that queasy feeling – or worse, the serious nausea of motion sickness – this bus is not the answer.

Then there is the ride itself: No more soft-sprung, coach-like ride for our Ranchers. Our vehicle procurers did indeed chose durability of equipment over comfort, and the new bus is mounted on a truck chassis, with all that implies for the suspension system: springs, struts, and shock absorbers. When we ride on this bus our Ranchers get a true Western style ride, bouncing along in the "saddle" as it were, like real cow pokes. Never mind that for the next few days a sore body will be the souvenir that reminds us of our trip.

But first, before we can return to the Ranch and chase down a handful of Senior M&Ms – aka Advil – with a stiff adult beverage to ease the stiffness we feel rapidly approaching in our joints; before we can soak our old bones in hot water to ward off the aches caused by our jarring jaunt; before we can do any of that, we must deboard.

Deboarding – that presents yet one more problem. Yes, the steps are the same steps we struggled to mount and somehow we did manage, but for many of us a big step down is much more difficult than one in the opposite direction. Bracing our bodies against a premature arrival on the pavement below is no small problem, especially when the stabilizing pole at the bottom of the steps on which we depended in the old bus is no longer to be found. Our only hope is to hold on to the handrails for dear life and pray that the driver is there at the foot of this daunting stairway to brace us – or to catch us if all else fails.

Oh yes, I almost forgot to explain the other problem with the driver. Not any particular driver, just any driver of this vehicle. You see not only is the driver sunken in the well, he or she must enter and exit this super new bus from the opposite side. Facing the bus, the passengers' door is on the left side of the bus and the driver's door is on the right!

This peculiar arrangement must have made sense to the vehicle engineers who designed the after-market coach addition to this truck chassis, and my guess is they had no idea that the driver would have a bus full of Seniors, Seniors who might need attention at any time, Seniors who would have to wait for the driver to deboard on his side, walk around the bus, and only then get into position to assist them.

How well would that work in an emergency? Is there a back door? Not on this vehicle. It seems our helpful friends at the US DOT have mandated against that feature for this size bus. What would happen if "Gus" and his friends needed to "hop" off the bus in a hurry? Someone mentioned an emergency window exit, but I think neither I nor corporate legal want to contemplate that situation.

I do not know what the impact of this, this latest corporate offering in Senior transportation, means to resident enthusiasm about Wrinkle Ranch trips; however, as far as I can tell, as long as our trip is scheduled on the cool, shiny new bus, none of us is eager to follow Paul Simon's suggestion. It's just "Life at the Wrinkle Ranch: Hop on the Bus, Gus...!"

Life at the Wrinkle Ranch: The Shell Game

As we have discussed in our other stories, our Ranch is populated by indigenous critters. Why not? They were here first. Certainly the armadillos, the "little armored ones," were present in the New World as early as the Cenozoic Era, and so they certainly date well before even the oldest resident here. Armadillos are the only land mammal that has a shell, and the nine-banded armadillo, of the genus Dasypus, is the only type of armadillo found throughout Florida.

Armadillos are prolific sleepers, dozing away in their burrows sometimes as long as sixteen hours a day, but when they do emerge in their search for beetles, ants, termites, and other insects, they dig holes, and of course, given the high cost of housing these days, they dig their own sleeping burrows too. So armadillos and holes in the ground are usually found in the same area.

Although we have a number of armadillos, our Ranchers rarely see them since they forage for bugs early in the morning and avoid the heat of the day; however, sometimes in the early evening, as we eat in our beautiful dining rooms with the floor to ceiling windows, we see a little armada of armadillos, deploying among the tropical plants and digging for insects with their huge fore claws, in an effort to find their own dinner. They really look quite appealing from that distance, and some of our residents think they are "cute."

As it turns out, armadillos do not have to be seen to make their presence known. Many of the residents on the first floor of our building have dogs, and dogs can smell armadillos. Even the best behaved pooch can erupt in a frenzy of barking upon the realization that one of these strange armored beasts is prowling around outside the door.

Pity the sleeping dog owner who is awakened repeatedly at night by the alert his dog is sounding, and more's the problem when the nearby neighbor has no dog and actively resents the barking. Besides that annoyance, the dog walker must beware because an armadillo who has been about during armadillo prime time probably has dug holes in the ground while looking for grubs and other little delicacies, holes that are just lurking for the unsuspecting dog walker to step into and fall. We at the Ranch know all about the danger of falls to Seniors!

Another significant fact about armadillos is that they have the ability to produce liters of four, eight, or even a dozen genetically identical offspring from one fertilized egg! "So what?" you ask. If you see one, siblings are bound to be nearby somewhere, and since we do not feature roast armadillo on our menu and there are no natural predators in the area, armadillos unchecked can multiply rapidly.

Unlike our buzzards, armadillos are not protected by law and if they are a nuisance, may be trapped or even killed "humanely;" therefore, when one of our Seniors complained to Management that the armadillos were harassing her dogs, the dogs were barking, the dogless neighbors were harassing her, and furthermore, she had fallen when she stepped in a hole just outside her back door – a hole that was doubtless the work of an artful armadillo – while walking the dogs, one of our brave Directors went to work on a solution. Skipping any armadillo foreplans, he jumped directly to "Plan T." He announced that he had resolved to *trap* the disruptive Dasypus!

For days our wary Senior dog walker not only had to look for armadillo holes when she exited her back door, she also had to be careful that neither she nor the dogs would trip the armadillo trap and thus interfere with the successful completion of Plan T! And for days, although she looked ever so carefully, she saw no indication that Plan T was in place.

Then one day a few weeks later our beaming Director informed her, "I caught the little fellow in the trap and released him into the woods."

"Where was the trap, I never saw it," she asked puzzled. "On the other side of the building!" was the proud reply. Thanks to Plan T, one suit of armor was retired from the armadillo army to a more bucolic life in the woods, and it is highly unlikely that the fellow wearing that armor was the same one causing the problem on the opposite side of the building. Since many of our resident armadillos are identical quadruplets, it is difficult to tell one from the other, but never mind that it is a big building and we have a number of armadillos; after all, Management strives to be nothing if not reassuring.

Apparently with a deft sleight of hand move, just like the con artists with their walnut hulls in the age-old shell game, Management has tried to confuse our Senior and convince her that the armadillo trapped on one side of the building is actually the same armadillo who spent his waking hours upsetting her dogs on the other side. That's a tough sell to a savvy Senior. It seemed to her it's just "Life at the Wrinkle Ranch: The Shell Game."

Life at the Wrinkle Ranch: Driving Miss Daisy

Imagine for a moment that your beloved spouse was not only quite elderly, he was very ill. Imagine that he was not only suffering from dementia, he had also recently experienced several heart attacks and some serious falls. What if, while still able to decide how he wanted his final days to be managed, the two of you placed Do Not Resuscitate (DNR) documentation with Management here at the Ranch, our skilled nursing facility, and at the local hospital.

Imagine after a long day by your husband's side at the nursing facility, you went home to dinner only to get this frantic message from a neighbor whose spouse was also being treated there, "Your husband has just fallen, and they have rushed him off to the local hospital in an ambulance."

Think how your heart would have been racing if you, unable to drive because of advanced macular degeneration, had been required to search for a driver to take you in pursuit of the ambulance. Think about that, because what happened later was unthinkable.

This was the situation in which one of our Ranchers, Daisy, found herself. Her husband, Jim, had been in the nursing facility for treatment. She had spent the day with him and had just gone home to dinner when her neighbor rushed in to tell her that Jim had fallen, was unresponsive, and had been taken by ambulance to the local hospital around the corner.

After Daisy had located one of our uniformed Ranch drivers, who immediately took her to the hospital, she was told Jim was being loaded onto a helicopter to be transported to a regional hospital for tests. She objected strongly telling the hospital staff about the DNR and insisting that she did not want him transported; hospital personnel told her it was too late, and they could not stop the process. Much to her upset and frustration, the helicopter took off with Jim inside and Daisy wringing her hands down below.

Although he was supposed to be off duty, the Ranch driver volunteered to take Daisy to the regional hospital, and they set out, chasing the helicopter across town.

At the larger – but apparently not more responsive – hospital, Daisy was thwarted again by hospital personnel who seemed more focused on their goals than those of the patient and his next of kin. They insisted on doing an MRI and other tests. Daisy was shuttled from person to person, waiting room to waiting room, all the while the supportive driver never left her side.

After an unpleasant encounter with an arrogant physician who insisted that they should operate on the comatose Jim, despite the paper work that had accompanied him in the helicopter, Daisy finally gained assurances that no surgeries would be performed and Jim would be returned home "soon." But this happened only after the doctor called Daisy's son in another state, also a physician, who reinforced her demands for Jim's release.

One of the most upsetting events that night for Daisy was the fact that one of Jim's hearing aids had been removed during transit and was given to her in a package marked with the name, "Jim Energy." Jim's paperwork clearly provided his complete name, but the EMT who retrieved the hearing aid, apparently did not note his full name and made one up. Talk about insensitive!

It was 11:30 P.M. before Daisy and her faithful driver left the hospital that night.

Several days later Jim was returned, still comatose, to the nursing facility and it was several more days before Daisy was able to secure a space for Jim in hospice accommodations. He died after three days in the caring environment of hospice. He never regained consciousness, but on the third night as she sat by his bed and whispered to him, "It's all right; just let go," he squeezed her hand, and he let go.

Our Ranch administration is not responsible for the errors in procedure or judgment on the part of the two hospitals. We are all victims of "the system" in experiences like this. The proper paper work was on file and accompanied Jim at every turn. One hospital administrator told Daisy that she would receive a bill for about $5,000 to pay for the helicopter – the helicopter she tried to reject – but so far no one has had the chutzpah to send her one.

We are very proud of our driver who spent hour after hour of his own time supporting a visually impaired, distraught, and overwhelmed woman who was caught in a nightmare. He emerges the only hero in all these actions and certainly deserves a commendation.

Postscript: I asked the driver why although officially off-duty, he took on the task of driving Daisy into the night with no idea of how long it would be before he could go home. He told me, "I treat the people here like I would want my own parents treated. I would certainly want someone to comfort and stay with my mother if she were in that situation. How could I do otherwise for Miss Daisy?"

So far My Hero and I can drive ourselves where ever we want to go, even at night, and we do not need the nursing facility, nor are we expecting to be airlifted to a hospital in a comatose state any time soon, and we are certainly are not ready for hospice care. But we, like all our fellow Ranchers, will continue to age in place, and eventually these things may happen. That is why we are so glad we live here. It's just "Life at the Wrinkle Ranch: Driving Miss Daisy."

Life at the Wrinkle Ranch: The Changing of the Guard

The Changing of the Guard at Buckingham Palace is such a major event that tourists from all over the world put it on their "must see" list when they visit London. The "Changing of the Guard" that is the subject of this story did not attract much interest at all, but it may have required almost as much planning as the London version!

It was in the Wrinkle Ranch *Weekly* – just a few lines thanking Joan for all her years of devoted service and hard work on the Movie Committee "on behalf of her fellow residents."

To the casual reader this small notice did not seem especially noteworthy. But to those of us who knew....

Here is the backstory: When this community opened over twenty years ago, many couples in their 60s and 70s flocked to move in. They had listened to the sales pitch and understood that dinner was provided, the maid came once a week, the golf course was beautiful, and a chauffeur took you to your doctors' appointments. There were fun activities galore, and when you got too old to play golf, go to the horse races, or live on your own, there was Assisted Living right next door.

The place filled quickly with vital, interested, and active Seniors, and in those early days some lines of volunteer responsibilities were drawn; for better or for worse, as the years went by, some of those lines turned into concrete barriers.

Fast forward twenty years and consider the case of Joan, the Queen of the Movie Committee. Actually they called her the "chairman" of the Movie Committee, but she really was the Queen because she had absolute authority, and she exercised it when it came to the selection of movies to be shown at the Ranch on Saturday nights.

In case you have not thought about it, movies in America have changed over the last generation. They are faster paced, full of special effects, sex, violence, racy social situations, and language that would have made Clark Gable blush.

Many of the older crowd have continued to view movies as these cultural and technical changes have occurred and so are not surprised or offended by much that is available on the Big Screen these days.

But not so the Queen! Over the years she had become not just the Queen of the movie committee, she had become the Queen of Censorship! Not a movie got by her with today's foul language, hideous violence, and vile sex, but how many times can you show *A Dolphin's Tale* and still pack them in?

She had not only come to think of the Movie Committee as her private fiefdom, she believed that she was the sole proprietor of the sign board on which she posted the movie information every Saturday outside the Dining Room – although the Executive Director foolishly thought it belonged to him – and furthermore, she had locked in her apartment the box of little white letters with which she painstakingly spelled out the movie name and its stars and refused to allow anyone else to have access to it. I know because I tried. Permanent "tenure" is an awesome thing!

I do not know how they brought it off, but somehow Management found a way. Queen Joan retired from her throne. They published a lovely thank you in the *Weekly*, and for all I know they may have scheduled a limo to treat this now almost 90-year-old Former Queen to dinner and a movie somewhere out in town.

I wonder if they could find an appropriate one, you know one that the Queen would have approved for her fellow Ranchers. I checked to see what was playing: *Dark Shadows*, a horror thriller about vampires; *Think Like a Man*, an "adult comedy" with lots of steamy premarital sex; *The Avengers*, a Marvel cartoon character-based flick – all violent action, all the time; and *The Hunger Games*, which is described as, "intensely violent thematic material and disturbing images all involving teens."

On second thought, maybe they could just rent her a copy of *Mary Poppins* from Netflix and microwave some Orville Redenbacher's.

Regardless of Joan's reward, I see this notice in the *Weekly* as a hallmark of progress. Hurray for Management! It's just "Life at the Wrinkle Ranch: The Changing of the Guard."

CHAPTER
10

Stepping Up to Lead

Where I come from, if you do not like how things are going, you step up and work to fix them, or you keep your mouth shut. Since I am no good at the latter, I frequently have been inspired to do the former.

Shortly after moving to the Ranch, I made a small and limited foray into Ranch House change when I ran into a logical inconsistency in some laundry room signage down the hall. In retrospect, it is clear from my reaction that at that point I did not begin to have enough to do with my time. That reaction is the subject of "Uniformity."

My first major effort to address a community-wide problem is described in "A Paradigm Shift," in which I am asked by an African American resident to get involved to encourage Management to give proper recognition to Black History month. I jumped in with both feet. After that successful effort into making a difference came the holiday season. This time nobody asked me, but I firmly believed somebody needed to step up, and so I did. Read "Tree Lighting Party." Then I decided to try the Ranch House yoga class. To see how that went read, "Yoga Transformation."

Later, after only one year here, I found myself serving on the Residents' Council, even though I was not sure what was going on in the community, or why, and had no clue about the "how." The year after that, I was "elected" – if you can call it that – in an unopposed "election" to be The President of the Residents' Association, a job nobody else on the Council wanted.

It was a difficult job. As far as I could tell, given the lack of cooperation from the previous Executive Director and the failure of former resident "leaders" to maintain records and enforce the by-laws, Council affairs were in a difficult state. When I assumed the position, I received no turn-over file and had very little useful guidance about what to do or how to do it. It turns out that although the Council and I were involved in many serious efforts, there were some very funny things that happened to me in my role as Floor Leader and as President. Some of them are chronicled here.

It is interesting to note that "An Illusion of Autonomy," which discusses the impotence of the Resident government, and "A Paradigm Shift," which talks about the staff approach to Black History Month, were written before Corporate Management installed a truly competent Executive Director, one who respected the residents and understood Seniors. If he had been in place, I doubt I would have encountered those situations.

Next you will meet the Butler, who is a key character in the short vignette, "The Butler Did It!"

In my new position as Council Member, representing my floor, I had to figure out what to do and how to do it in every situation. In those days, unlike now, there was no handbook for Council Members, only the old tried and true on-the-job training (OJT). "Talking Trash" describes how I learned to work within the bureaucracy and not be disruptive, and "A P.I.T.H. Event" discusses how scatology became part of my Floor Duties.

In "Butler Battles" we see what happens when rules are waived for some people because it is easier to do so than to enforce them. If a stronger Management team had been at the helm, "The Butler Battles" would not have required clever adjudication by Sylvia, who eventually convinced Carolyn to "donate" the Butler to the Activities Department and so effected his departure from our hall. After the new ED arrived on the scene, Sylvia, as Executive Assistant, no longer had to "run everything" but was allowed to do her job because her boss did his.

In North Carolina there is a company that, for a price, can produce from its humongous warehouse almost any piece of china, crystal, or silverware ever on the market. This phenomenal place, which I have used to add to china patterns or replace out-of-production items that were broken, is called "Replacements Limited," although it might more aptly be named "Replacements Unlimited." In this chapter my story entitled, "Replacements Limited," is a lament about the difficulty of filling volunteer positions at the Wrinkle Ranch. Sadly, unlike the namesake of this story, at the Ranch we have no warehouse of qualified volunteers just sitting on the shelf waiting to be called into action!

Being President of the Council did not relieve me of the responsibility of being the Floor Leader on my hall, and "A Toothy

Luncheon" discusses how a noon-time floor gathering unfolded on one memorable occasion.

"Tracking Intruders" describes my efforts to defend our "Forever Home" from the invasion of contractors who acted – well – like contractors.

The new fire alarm system was the impetus for a couple of hours spent at my computer, monitoring and seeking to deal with a distressing, real-time situation. Note our Executive Director also hung in there, communicating with me all the way, all the way that is until at the end of the "event" I sent him the Wikipedia article on torture. Read all about our Saturday morning in "An Alarming Event!"

The last essay in this chapter, "Persistence Revisited," deals with one of my pet projects, or pet peeves, depending on your point of view, and how even as a past President, I still strove to encourage Management to answer my "Whale Mail." It turns out that shortly after I sent my e-mail, my goal was realized, although I doubt my message had anything at all to do with the resolution, which had been underway for some time.

It is important to understand that in a Wrinkle Ranch an individual resident can always make a difference, and if you are the type of person who wants her home to be the best possible place to live, when you move to your Wrinkle Ranch, you will follow in my footsteps. You too will find yourself "Stepping Up to Lead."

Life at the Wrinkle Ranch: Uniformity

Early on in our Ranch residency I became perturbed by the erroneous signage in our laundry room and not knowing how to deal with the situation, I wrote to the knowledgeable Executive Assistant.

Dear Sylvia,

I am a person who values uniformity – where it is appropriate. And I strive for accuracy at all times.

Regarding the sign in the floor laundry room on our wing: As we discussed, the sign was in error. It stated that one should "take all laundry supplies and turn off the light upon leaving." Since there is a hard plug in place of the light switch, one cannot turn off the light, no matter how diligently one tries. I know, because on my first trip there, I worked for some time in an effort to comply with the posted directions, but to no avail.

Based on your approval of the plan we discussed, My Hero and I made a splendid new sign with wording identical to that of the old one, except for the deletion of the reference to the impossible task of turning off the light; however, in keeping with my compulsive nature, before I replaced our laundry room sign, I did a brief survey of some other laundry rooms on various floors in our wing.

Here are my findings:

7th floor - wooden frame 8 x 10, no glass, hangs from a single screw, at eye level just right of the door to the hall

6th floor – same as 7th.

5th floor – no sign, but the screw is still in place

4th floor – no sign and no screw, but the place where the screw used to be is still visible although, it has been patched and painted over.

3rd floor – no sign, no sign of a sign, and no sign of a screw to hang a sign.

2nd floor – same as 3rd.

Several of the laundry rooms have a number of tacky, 8.5 x 11 computer-generated signs discussing the amount of detergent to use, the softness of the water, and admonishing residents to clean up spilled detergent. There seems to be no specific place allocated to post such messages, and different floors have put them in different places on the walls. Most of these (tacky) signs are in (tacky) plastic sleeves, but some are not covered at all and look water-spotted, which adds nothing at all to their general attractiveness.

One observation that may not have significance is that the lower the floor number the more numerous the tacky signs. Would it be appropriate to draw a correlation between the number of the floor and the orderliness of the residents? Or should one conclude that this lower level profusion of (tacky) signs is just a coincidence?

Surely someone is responsible for signage in our community spaces. Surely there should be an approval process before anyone is authorized to post a sign in those community spaces, and surely if the residents of one floor need to be reminded to "take all laundry supplies upon leaving," so do they all.

Have we thought of having a bulletin board in every laundry room and putting identical messages that are checked and updated regularly? Unless of course each laundry room is designated as an area to highlight the individuality and "personality" of each wing and its residents. In which case uniformity is not only unnecessary, it would be totally inappropriate.

Since I am so new and do not really understand how processes here are organized, I hope you can direct me so that we can either work for uniformity of signage, elimination of tacky signs, and eradication of erroneous direction, or encourage each wing to expend more energy *expressing their individuality and creativity in this important and frequently used community space.*

In the meantime I have designed an attractive, legible, and accurate sign that we can laminate – I assume we do not use glass in the frames because of the danger of breakage. I will put this new sign in our laundry room in place of the old one.

We would be happy to do the same for all of the laundry rooms in the building, but since many are obviously missing frames as well as screws, perhaps the signs have outgrown their usefulness, and because we are not people to waste time doing useless tasks, if the requirement for the few remaining signs has indeed been overcome by events, perhaps an authorized person should remove all the remaining signs containing this message.

Please advise.

I signed my message, "A concerned new resident!" Thus, spurred by my neuroses, I began my career as an activist in my new home.

It's just "Life at the Wrinkle Ranch: Uniformity."

Life at the Wrinkle Ranch: A Paradigm Shift

Before our arrival in this Senior Community of over 500 people, only one, lone Black person, Clarisse, lived at the Ranch. After years of being "the only one," Clarisse had become tired of fighting to get respect and recognition for things African American especially when it came to Black History Month (BHM), which, right before we arrived, was "celebrated" by an afternoon cocktail party for the residents at which the ladies of the staff dressed in antebellum style hoop skirts and the mostly minority wait staff served mint juleps to the assembled White Ranchers!

In the fall Clarisse came to me in frustration, seemingly near despair. She had been informed that for the next BHM "celebration" Management had booked a one woman show – one *White* woman show – in which a monologue presented the story of a White pioneer's trip over the mountains in the 1800s and her meeting with a Black woman along the way. It was a show that Corporate had booked, and since it was being performed at other Wrinkle Ranches in our Corporate family, it must have seemed the perfect, cost-effective way to handle the entire bothersome Black History Month situation, avoiding the blow-back from last year's hoop skirts.

Is our Management racially prejudiced? Are these intended to be token, dismissive, and degrading activities in place of what is supposed to be a celebration of accomplishments and success by Americans of African descent? No. I don't think so. So why hoop skirts and mint juleps? Think about it. February is a short month with lots of special occasions. There is Super Bowl, Valentine's Day, Mardi Gras, President's Day, Groundhog Day, and International Condom Day to list just a few of the special observances. So few days in the month, so many opportunities to celebrate; then on top of it all, by act of Congress, the entire month of February is Black History Month.

Now if you are the manager of the Activities Department at a Senior Living Community, how are you going to deploy your limited budget and your small staff to address as many of these important celebratory opportunities as possible? Add to your consideration that events where booze is served get the most participation and the highest ratings of all social activities at the Ranch. Naturally a party with adult beverages would be the first thought of a busy activities manager, especially one who has not been schooled in diversity or sent for minority sensitivity training as might be the case at a Fortune 500 company.

I mean, how could Black History Month possibly be of as much interest to a bunch of old White people as Mardi Gras, Super Bowl, or Valentine's Day? Come to think of it, including a celebration of International Condom Day might get quite a rise out of some of our Ranchers. Wonder why we do not celebrate that one? I could certainly come up with some interesting activities for the residents in line with that theme. I would bet we could persuade a manufacturer to donate samples. Hmmmm....

Clearly you cannot fault a performer for catering to her audience. Besides there are lots of pretty ladies who work here, and they probably all loved getting dressed up in hoop skirts. It must have been a lot of fun for them. The mint juleps probably went over really well with the residents also.

There was no insult intended, but we can certainly do better. Now in the case of the scheduled one woman show, that was an easy solution for the Activities Department. Since Corporate had arranged it, no additional planning was required. And the price was right. Obviously it was appropriate. After all, surely the folks at headquarters always set the right tone.

Of course they wanted Clarisse, as the "duty" African American, to approve. And of course she did not approve, but by the time she came to me, she was tired of fighting and losing. I decided it was time for "A Paradigm Shift."

"The Marines have landed!" I assured my new friend. Being ex-Air Force, she knew the significance of that statement. Then I moved out in my best Marine Corps Quick Reaction Capability (QRC) style, organized an *ad hoc* Black History Month Committee, and designated Clarisse the chairman. I recruited a former social worker and two retired school teachers – there is no shortage of bleeding heart liberals here – we just needed a community organizer! And so our committee moved forward. In short order we presented the Activities Director with a list of twenty things appropriate to do during the *month long* celebration of Black History.

It included buying books for our library by African American authors. We did not have a single one. Not even "Roots!" We recommended a Black dance band for the monthly dance, a soul food buffet one night, and a theme appropriate Saturday night movie, "Something the Lord Made."

We kicked off the month with a discussion in the "Timely Topics" group entitled, "Do we really need Black History month?" I figured, just get it out there and talk about it right up front. It was well attended. Clarisse, My Hero, and I stayed away, dispatching surrogates instead, so as to be sure not to impede discussion.

The Opera Club listened to an opera featuring Leontyne Price; the Writers' Group wrote on the topic, "My most memorable Black person," and some of their essays were very touching. The Poet's Corner bulletin board posted poems by Paul Laurence Dunbar. Our committee infiltrated almost every organization and activity at the Ranch.

I created the "Name that Person" contest in which we posted a picture of a different famous African American in the Lobby each week in February accompanied by a few obscure clues about the person. People could guess the identity of the "mystery person," and after some encouragement from me our Executive Director "volunteered" to give a prize each week for the winner. At the end of the week we posted the identity of the famous person with a detailed bio.

By the second week people were crowding around the easel in the Lobby guessing and arguing, and everyone wanted to see the answers. OK, so a lot of them thought the young Ella was Aretha, and that G.W. Carver was Frederick Douglass, and hardly anybody recognized Paul Robeson even though the posted photo showed him dressed for his role in Othello, but by the end of the month I felt we had given some folks a little education, and I knew we had an overall victory for our committee when at the next Management meeting, the Activities Director demanded to know how to prevent the formation of future *ad hoc* resident committees!

Our coup de grace was having the Poet Laureate of a nearby major city in the area come and do a reading of his works for us. We had suggested this event to the Activities Manager early on, and she tried several times to reach him, but he did not return her phone calls or her e-mails.

It was time for me to deploy my reserves. So far My Hero had stayed out of what he called "my project;" however, I knew if I dispatched him to reach out to the poet, Big Man to Big Man, we could get his attention, and it worked! One Saturday night in February, the celebrated poet and his wife came for dinner with the BHM Committee, and he spent over an hour doing a reading for our residents. His visit was well received, even though there was some grumbling from the old timers about canceling the Saturday night movie, but most of the residents were delighted to have a local, famous poet come here and perform for us. Even some folks from town attended, including members of the small, neighborhood African American Club.

If our Activities Department does not want any more ad hoc committees, I guess next year they should pick up the ball for both Super Bowl and Black History Month, two events important to me.

Besides there are two more Black residents who just joined our ranks and pretty soon we will have them surrounded. It's just "Life at the Wrinkle Ranch: A Paradigm Shift."

Life at the Wrinkle Ranch: Yoga Transformation

The first time I went to yoga class here at the Ranch, as I was laying my personal purple yoga mat on the floor, the substitute instructor informed me that this was "chair" yoga.

"Am I required to sit in a chair?" I asked. Well that question brought him up short! And finally he 'llowed as how I could sit on the floor if I wanted to – like he could stop me.

The next week the regular yoga instructor returned, and he was more astute. He realized that the staff does not dictate to the residents in such matters. He was happy to have me sit on my mat and participate from the floor. He even gave me cues as to what "real" poses he was trying to achieve when he gave direction to the other ten or so folks all sitting in a circle in their arm chairs.

Fast forward a month or so. Bill now sat on the floor beside me and had for the last month. He was not an experienced yoga practitioner, but he could get up and down all by himself, and he was game for this new approach.

One day, Marilyn came for the first time since I joined the yogis. She has her own yoga "quilt" and sits on the floor. She does her own practice in her apartment with a tape every morning, but once she heard I sat on the floor, she packed up her quilt and came to class.

It seems she had come once some time ago, and when she saw that everyone else sat in a chair, she did not want to be different....

She told me that the next week Wilma was coming too. Wilma will sit on the floor. I have 'splained to My Hero that he will be coming to yoga with me. He had done yoga for years, and he too has his very own personalized mat.

That made five of us on the floor! We now constituted at least one third of the class. At that point the instructor did a number of standing poses including two warrior poses. He began giving specific instruction to "those of you who lie down on the job," as he put it. Everyone was doing what they could do, and some people made an effort to do a little more than they had done in the past. It was a good thing.

It is interesting that the people who came to yoga, even though at least three of them were well over ninety, were welcoming and warm to me. They did not seem in the least unhappy that I could get down on my mat – and up again. This set them apart from many of the Ranch residents who seemed to resent those of us who walk quickly and confidently without assistance. I believe that yoga loosens more than just the muscles, the tendons, and the joints. I believe it broadens the mind and softens the heart. I also believe that I single-handedly transformed this yoga class. Today yoga, tomorrow the South 40! It's just "Life at the Wrinkle Ranch, Yoga Transformation."

Life at the Wrinkle Ranch: Tree Lighting Party

December is a busy time at the Wrinkle Ranch. There are parties, special programs, and holiday dinners all month long.

Early in the month there was a party entitled, Marketing Bakes for You. This extravaganza of sweet treats – cookies, cakes, rum balls, brownies, and a variety of other scrumptious looking goodies...all created in the kitchens of the Ranch Marketing Department – was bundled with the annual Christmas Tree lighting and caroling in an afternoon celebration that also offered spiked and virgin egg nog and coffee to wash down the thousands of sugar-laden calories served to the residents.

Frankly the whole event gave me heart burn! What could be wrong, you may ask, with such a sweet celebration? First of all the general organization of the event did not seem much like my idea of a party.

Picture this: The Lobby, which normally has half a dozen conversational groupings of sofas and comfortable chairs, is surrounded by rows of tightly packed folding chairs with absolutely no space between them. The party is scheduled for a 2 P.M. start and a 3 P.M. tree lighting and will continue for two hours. Residents start to arrive early to grab the relatively few soft seats before they are gone.

Since many of the Ranch residents are not cocktail party mobile, that is they cannot stand and mill about for an hour or two, and certainly most cannot balance a plate and a cup and simultaneously stand and mingle, they all sit down – many in the uncomfortable folding chairs – and except for the necessary trip(s) to the tables of food and drink, there they remain for the two hours of the "party."

What kind of party has you essentially trapped between two other people in hard folding chairs for over two hours? And frankly eating while balancing a plate of food and a cup of egg nog is not much easier in such a seated position than it is standing. Remember, this is not a performance or a presentation – it's supposed to be a "party."

The people who garner a seat in one of the regular seating areas are the lucky ones because there are a few occasional tables in those areas, and so there is a place to deposit a drink while using one hand to eat from the plate of goodies balanced by the other.

Those of us who are fully ambulatory and want to visit with other attendees have constraints. Anyone stopping to chat with first one group and then another, leaning over the folding chair rows to greet friends and generally working the room, needs to be slender and agile because there is very little space to maneuver and no proper place to sit and visit once the groups are assembled in semi-permanent configurations.

Fortunately sofas and easy chairs have arms, and I am able to perch first on one arm and then another and chat with many of my fellow Ranchers, but then I am not burdened with balance problems. Sofa arm perching is not for everyone.

Aside from the logistics of holding a party for a crowd with limited mobility – a crowd sporting a stunning collection of walkers, some wheel chairs, and lots of canes – I have a far bigger concern. Many of the residents here are diabetic. Not only are we tempting people to eat thousands of sugary calories and drink fat-laced alcoholic beverages, which probably should not be on their diets, we are tempting fate with their metabolic responses to these indulgences!

And eat they did. Since getting up and working one's way to the food tables was not an easy task, most people went only once, and they stocked up for the duration, piling their plates high with an assortment of treats. Be assured, once a morsel was on the plate, it was consumed. This is totally unlike the grazing approach of a more mobile cocktail party crowd where talking and moving from group to group competes with eating as an activity.

In my typical low-key, subtle style I asked our resident nurse who was dispensing coffee, "Whom shall we call when all these old people go into sugar shock?"

"I'm afraid I am the one," she replied ruefully. I looked around the room. Part of the mission statement of our leaders here is to promote our well-being. So how does this celebration of fat food, this sugary sit-down social, fit in with that pledge? Where were the checks and balances that should have been provided by a meeting of the minds by the Directors of Wellness, Activities, Marketing, and Administration?

If I sound very much like the Grinch, I hasten to assure you, I did not expect to gain general popularity by casting aspersions on a social gathering offering homemade cookies to old people. Especially not a social gathering featuring professional carolers and a Christmas Tree lighting; nonetheless, I plan to lobby for cheese, nuts, and fruit to be added to the party menu for subsequent years. Since I intend to be here for many, many more tree lightings, and because I am extremely persistent, my expectations of success for my vision of balanced party food are high. Reworking the stadium seating will be next....

For now it's just "Life at the Wrinkle Ranch: Tree Lighting Party"

Life at the Wrinkle Ranch: An Illusion of Autonomy

Many Senior establishments have a residents' governing body that purports to have some authority over resident affairs and to wield influence over management action that impacts residents' lives. Indeed in Florida a state statute mandates such an organization for CCRCs.

At our Wrinkle Ranch we have a residents' association that is governed by a residents' Leadership Council. The Council is made up of "elected" representatives, most of whom are, in fact, unopposed volunteers. This organization lends support to the myth of resident self-government and provides at least "An Illusion of Autonomy."

The Leadership Council also has committees which have names that mirror the organization and roles of the management departments. There is a Health Committee, a Dining Committee, a Safety Committee, and an Activities Committee – to name just a few.

Committees meet with department heads to make suggestions, support activities, and generally provide feedback and interaction with the staff.

For example the Activities Committee works with management's Activities Department, which has a manager with a limited paid staff. The Committee provides input regarding activity planning and assists in the support of these activities. It is a good way to expand the resources available to management, and it also gives residents a productive way to spend their time.

It is only natural that there will be conflicts between residents and Management in a Senior Living Community. Residents want only the best. Management has budgets, financial requirements, and must meet corporate profit and loss targets in order to provide a continuing, economically viable environment for the residents – many of whom have sunk their life savings into the community with the plan that they will live there with appropriate care for the rest of their lives.

When the goals of these two groups come into conflict, Management usually wins. This can lead to a feeling of impotence on the part of residents.

Long term residents who have seen countless battles lost, whether over the redecoration of the Lobby, the lack of a full time medical person on staff, the hiring of a social worker to deal with problems of the aging population, new audio/visual equipment, or even personnel issues can become cynical about a Resident Council they see as a mere illusion of residents' autonomy.

This is a dangerous situation. It discourages the best qualified residents from participating in the residents' organization, robs Management of valuable resident resources, and fosters resentment, and this occurs at a time when residents may already feel helpless and discouraged by more and more personal limitations such as failing eyesight, hearing, mobility, and even financial woes.

Promoting the idea that residents' associations are powerless should be assiduously avoided by the savvy management team to the extent that can be done while still running a safe, secure, and fiscally viable community, and at the same time meeting corporate requirements.

In other words Management in Senior Care environments should shun any unnecessary attempt to control issues that rightly should be under the jurisdiction of the residents' association alone.

For example at one point in our community history, a corporate directive changed the name of the Activities Department. The new name was announced as the "Enrichment Department." This news was conveyed to all residents in the weekly newsletter delivered to everyone's door. Along with this announcement was also the news that henceforth the corresponding official residents' committee would no longer be the "Activities Committee" but would have a name change to "Enrichment Committee."

Ooops! It seems that this arbitrary pronouncement was made independent of any consultation with the Council or its officers. Now clearly Management is entitled to name its departments as it sees fit but not Council committees! What message does Management send regarding the importance and autonomy of the residents' self-governing organization if the Council has no say even over its own committee names?

The Council president was livid and refused to accept the Management edict. He vowed to do battle with the Executive Director over the issue. I, on the other hand, firmly believing that this false step by Management was a thoughtless faux pas and not part of an insidious plan to disenfranchise and humiliate the residents' organization, wrote the following e-mail to our Executive Director, a man with a financial background, and perhaps one lacking in certain sensitivities to the social and psychological issues of Seniors.

Dear Paul,

When I read in the newsletter that Management had made the decision to change the name of the Activities Department and, along with it, the name of the associated Council committee, it never occurred to me that the Council committee name had been summarily changed by Management without any dialogue whatsoever with the Council.

An e-mail I received from our Council president disabused me of that viewpoint.

If we assume that the more active and involved residents are the ones who volunteer to work on the Council and its committees, this kind of action on the part of Management could be perceived as a deliberate effort to make those residents, of whom I am one, feel impotent and ineffective.

This type of unilateral action only serves to discourage residents from Council participation – why bother? Our organization has no influence – and furthermore it builds resentment about the lack of consideration shown to the residents and their representatives.

I can't imagine that those are your goals. You seem far too intelligent to operate in such a destructive manner. Perhaps you could let our Council President know that name change was inadvertently announced and was in error.

I gave some thought to the difference in our two approaches, the Council president's and mine. Then I realized, women in male-dominated businesses such as the one in which I spent my career, rarely are successful with a head on, aggressive, confrontational approach. My tactics were the result of learned behavior. Over the years I had adopted the "give the other guy the benefit of the doubt" approach. I try to solve problems by presenting a different point of view without making an accusation or a frontal attack. I developed that style when I discovered again and again that if a woman goes toe to toe with a person who is physically bigger, more imposing, has a deeper, louder voice, and more organizational status, she does not have a winning strategy. Alpha males on the other hand naturally revert to the angry confrontation, frequently with raised voice and aggressive table pounding, because it works!

Somehow between the direct, angry, and confrontational face-to-face meeting demanded by the Council president and my more tactful missive, Management got the message. The edict was reversed. The residents' right to name their own committees was reaffirmed, but the damage may have been done. Those residents who pay attention noted once again that the importance of the Council was denied. It's just "Life at the Wrinkle Ranch: An Illusion of Autonomy."

Life at the Wrinkle Ranch: The Butler Did It!

After I was selected, but before I began my tenure as Floor Leader, I sent the following message to the head of security here at the Wrinkle Ranch:

My floor Emergency Action Group Representative has informed me that she believes the Butler shown in the picture below may present a problem in case of emergency.

At least one resident who lives near the Butler's station at the end of our hall by the stairway door has voiced the same concern.

197

It seems that during the fire drill today, he froze and did nothing to assist any of our residents. Indeed, I was told he just stood there in the hall as useless and unresponsive as his cousin, the local cigar store wooden Indian.

As the upcoming Floor Leader I certainly do not want to infringe on the civil rights of any of our residents or impose my sense of decor unilaterally; however, I believe it is appropriate to be concerned for the safety of everyone on our floor in case of emergency.

If this Butler's position is indeed a violation of our safety regulations, perhaps someone in charge of security for the building should step up and banish the Butler. We would certainly not want to have an issue with a safe evacuation from our floor and be forced to admit that "the Butler did it."

So there you have it, my latest concern. It's just "Life at the Wrinkle Ranch: The Butler Did It!"

Life at the Wrinkle Ranch: Talking Trash

Once I was elected to represent my Floor and became a Representative to the Leadership Council here at the Wrinkle Ranch, I began to get "helpful" suggestions from all my constituents. The very first suggestion in my official tenure was that we get a magnetic door stop on the metal trash room door.

That was actually a good idea since if you use a walker and are trying to dispose of your trash, opening and holding the metal door is something of a problem. The downside of the magnetic catch is that Ranchers are bound to forget to close the door, and the next thing you know, we are all looking into an ugly trash room and being invaded by trash room odor; however, we will deal with that problem when it occurs. "One day at a time" is a good mantra when one lives at a Wrinkle Ranch.

I went to Mary in Maintenance and asked for this modification, and she willingly put in a work order. I felt very official and very efficient. My constituents ask, and I provide. So far, so good in this Floor Leader business.

But a number of days went by and not only did the trash room magnet not appear, the one on the laundry room door went missing! Alas, my first official act, and it was not working out well at all.

Then I saw the maintenance man in our trash room. "Aha," I thought, here we go with magnet installation, and then I made a mistake. I told him that we were also missing the magnet on the laundry room door. Of course at the time I did not know it was a mistake to tell him that, and I went away secure in the knowledge that we would have a magnet on each door when I returned. Again I felt confident that I would be a success in my new Council role.

Shortly thereafter I discovered that the laundry room door was again able to stick to the wall, but the trash room door had no magnetic catch and still required too many hands for our Seniors to handle disposal of their trash successfully. Then I had a second "aha."

And I sent the following message to Mary:

To: Mary

Subject: Talking Trash

Let's talk trash; well, trash rooms; uh, well, trash room door stops to be exact.

Just wanted to make sure we didn't get confused between the door stop for our laundry room and the one for the trash room.

The work order you put in when I spoke to you the other day was for our trash room, which has never had a magnetic door stop.

However, I saw your man in our hall the other day and pointed out that our magnetic laundry room door stop had ceased to function. (The magnet was missing.) He said he would replace it, and it is now replaced. This is a good thing, but it is not the whole thing. The trash room door still needs a magnet installation.

Just making sure that somehow we don't confuse that magnet replacement with the request for a new magnetic door stop on the trash room door.

Thank you for talking trash with me.

To which she responded:

Yes! he did confuse fixing the magnet in the laundry room with the trash room w/o. He crossed off trash room on the w/o and wrote in laundry room, so I will let him know you still want the trash room magnet done. I was wondering why he did the laundry room instead of the trash room like I had put the w/o through, now I know.

I am getting the hang of this job, and I learned an important lesson. The Ranch is a bureaucracy. It works by utilizing systems – in this case, Maintenance Work Orders. Interfere with the system at your own peril. I should have put in a second Work Order for the Laundry Room Door, instead I inserted myself into the system and that did not work. It's just "Life at the Wrinkle Ranch: Talking Trash."

Life at the Wrinkle Ranch: A P.I.T.H. Event

One day as I was leaving our elevator lobby and heading toward my hallway, I noticed something on the carpeted hallway floor. Although I did not execute the spider man maneuver of golfer Camilo Villegas and sniff this lump on the carpet, I immediately sent an e-mail to the head of Housekeeping. Entitled, "Oh Dear!" it read:

There is a two-inch smear of something brown and sticky on our hallway carpet between the elevator lobby and the place where the corridor joins the hallway. It is on the north side of the hall near the wall.

To my knowledge none of our people up here has a dog. I would hate to speculate as to the nature of this smear, and I'm sure when you see it you will be as eager as I am to have it removed and the spot sterilized.

To her credit, our splendid Head Housekeeper deployed her best carpet man with the appropriate equipment, and in mere moments only the yellow caution sign placed on top of the wet carpet indicated that there had been a problem.

While he was diligently cleaning I asked the carpet man, "Is that what I was afraid it was?"

"Yes, M'am!" was his immediate response. And so I had my first ever, Poop in the Hall, or P.I.T.H. event.

I knew immediately I should identify this as a P.I.T.H. because some years ago when I was on the Fitness Committee at our country club, we had repeated instances of a similar experience when the little ones did not wear their swim diapers in the pool and then "made deposits" in the water. At that point we were required to empty the pool of swimmers, close it for some period of time, and "shock" it with expensive chemicals. I personally take credit for naming such an event a P.I.P. which looked so much more genteel in our minutes and club messages than the phrase, "Poop in the Pool"

Since I have moved here I have heard reports of P.I.T.H. events on the first floor where residents have dogs. Despite the rumors, we never quite figured out which one of our residents or which one of our dogs was so out of control.

But I live on a higher floor. No dogs live above the 1st floor, and so up until that very day and time I was unsuspecting, and yet...there it was, the brown smear. We have no seriously impaired residents on this floor, so when added to the fact that we have no dogs, the presence of this deposit remains a mystery. Besides, I am pretty sure the local armadillos and racoons cannot operate the elevators, and so I continue to be completely baffled as to how a P.I.T.H. event occurred on our hall carpet.

But it did; now I have added that concern to my Floor Leader duties as I check the laundry room, the hallway bathroom, and the trash room every day, keeping a sharp eye out and stepping carefully along the way. It may never happen again, but at least this time it's just "Life at the Wrinkle Ranch: A P.I.T.H. Event"

Life at the Wrinkle Ranch: The Butler Battles

The longer I live at the Wrinkle Ranch, the more evident it becomes to me: Age and maturity are not synonymous. In fact, I have some excellent anecdotal data that show that they are actually inversely related, and divergence may be continuous. As an example I offer the following account.

The Butler, as seen above, appeared one day outside the door of one of the residents on my hall. After a few days he migrated to a station at the end of the hall, in front of the windows. From this position he could be seen silhouetted in front of the windows for the entire length of the hall.

I had shared my concern with Management fearing that he might get in the way of our people during an evacuation, should we ever have one; however, after checking with the building security manager, I was assured that the Butler was acceptable where he stood, and even though I was certain he was undocumented, that assurance was every bit as good as a green card as far as I was concerned – The Butler was hired!

Don't ask me what would happen if every single resident on the hall decided to invite a four-foot tall friend to stand guard in the passage way. Some residents have "friends" but they stand very close to home, and I thought that was the Rule.

But as I have discovered, the local Rules at the Ranch have as many bends as a French curve, and as Floor Leader, I do not make the Rules, I just research and relay them and try to keep the peace.

As I quickly discovered, the Butler's mistress, Carolyn, was not universally popular on our hall. Indeed her immediate neighbors seemed to believe she was the cause of every hallway problem. One resident told me that Carolyn was the person who repeatedly overflowed the trash basket in the laundry room, although the accuser offered no evidence of this crime. Another told me that years ago, when Carolyn moved in, her moving company had used a contaminated dolly which irrevocably stained the hallway carpet! What more do you need to hear? Clearly Carolyn bore watching.

A couple at the end of the hall had regularly complained to me about The Butler. As I said, Carolyn was not in the running for Miss Congeniality. Of course when I first arrived at the Ranch, I found all such hallway creatures, decorations, and ornaments just amusing, if tacky, manifestations of Wrinkle Ranch life; however, once I was the Floor Leader...well, you understand, I had to take all of these issues seriously. Because Lord knows, at least one of the other residents would have a hissy fit before all was said and done.

After my first concerns about The Butler, the reassurance of the Security Director, and the receipt of some doubtless unavoidable smart alec comments from my friends and neighbors – One wag asked, "Is he a silent butler or just a dumb waiter?" – I paid no further attention to the Butler until Carolyn announced to me that we were having a "Battle over the Butler."

It took a while to get the complete story since some people, Carolyn among them, seem to get great pleasure from speaking in allusions and enigmas. However, the bottom line of her announcement was that Helena, her neighbor across the hall, a small, frail, white-haired widow who eschews a walker and prefers instead to drag her hand on the hallway wall the entire seventy-five yards to and from the elevator each day, had repeatedly moved the Butler from his station in front of the window back to Carolyn's door.

In addition, Carolyn alleged that Helena had authored not one, but two notes that she left on The Butler's tray, demanding that he retreat to Carolyn's doorway.

Furthermore Helena claimed that in a face to face confrontation Carolyn had told her that she had *permission* to place The Butler in front of the windows and that Helena had better not move him again! It was at that point Helena, allegedly threatened to "call Sylvia!"

Now it is very important, if one lives here at the Ranch, to know and respect Sylvia. She is the assistant to the Executive Director. She had been the assistant to the Executive Director for many years and had held her position through the tenure of many executive directors.

The bottom line was that Sylvia runs this place. I figured that out early on in my residency here, and after that I never made a move without consulting with Sylvia first.

So a threat to "call Sylvia" was a "biggie!" But Carolyn said she was not fazed since she had "permission."

Hearing all of this, I called and gave my ally Sylvia a "heads up." Interestingly enough she did not know a thing about any of it and vowed to be ready when the assault came. And when it did, it turned out to be anticlimactic. Because on my way to the parking lot I came across Helena who stopped me to talk about, you guessed it, The Butler.

I let her vent about him for quite a while before I delivered my speech indicating that my main concern was for the safety of everyone who lives on our hall. Then I ran through the chronology of checking with Security and finally reminded her that we all want to live together nicely and respect each other's needs and property.

Perhaps if I had been a kindergarten teacher, I might have developed better skills for dealing with this sort of thing. However, surprisingly, before I was released to continue to my car, Helena assure me that she did not care a bit about The Butler, and he certainly does not bother her in the least!

Later that same day Sylvia engaged Helena in a more confrontational manner at the Quatro de Mayo Sip n' Social. OK,

OK, so most people celebrate *Cinco* de Mayo, but since Cinco de Mayo fell on Saturday that particular year and most staff is off on Saturday, the Ranch decided to serve up margaritas and mariachis on the 4th instead. Despite a heavy barrage of interrogatories from Sylvia and at least one margarita, Helena denied ever writing any notes or moving The Butler. After all, The Butler "does not bother her in the least." She told me so herself.

That afternoon The Butler was in front of Carolyn's door. That night about 10 P.M. it was in front of the windows. The next morning it was again in front of Carolyn's door.

I have a feeling this feud is not over yet, and although all is quiet on the other end of the hall, I prayed once this feud ended, we would not then start the Bird and Indian Wars. What can I say? It's just "Life at the Wrinkle Ranch: The Butler Battles."

Life at the Wrinkle Ranch: Replacements Limited

I knew it would be hard. I knew all-volunteer organizations can be difficult. After all, I headed the 180-strong Women's Golf Association at our country club for two whole years. And I figured older volunteers had less get up and go, and more dig in and drag than the younger set, but I totally forgot about the Big Gotcha – if they are not on the Departure Table because they are in hospital or the nursing facility – then they are there shown in a picture frame between the other two lists, along with the vase holding the requisite rose and baby's breath. In other words, they die on me!

So far in my first year as Council President, a position I assumed in March, by April I had one Council member resign because he could not manage to get out of the nursing facility. He had been there for four months – broken hip and all – and it was downhill from there. Another one died of cancer. One who was in hospital with pneumonia – a favorite malady here at the Ranch – when he was elected, came back for one meeting, was not really ready for duty, and was now...you guessed it, back in hospital. Out of the seventeen of us, I had to replace three in the first two months of my job. To make matters worse my VP went north for the summer.

There were thirteen Committees reporting to the Council. At least they reported to the Council on paper. But since apparently no Council President in memory ever pointed that out, no committee thinks they are beholden to the Council. They meet or they do not meet. They rarely have an agenda, and minutes, which are required in the Bylaws, are, like a "Woman" in Gershwin's famous lyrics – "a sometime thing."

Our Golf Committee was suffering from the Idi Amin, or Chairman "For Life," Syndrome. That is the condition in which someone is elected to Committee Chair and since no one else wants the job enough to face him down in an election, the Chairman just ages in place, growing crabbier, more imperious, and less effective with each passing term. There are no committee term limits, and no one actually knows when these bit players came to power. The Council can review their service and deny an additional term; however, someone would have to keep records and take the initiative. "Initiative," now there is a novel idea!

Remember! I had to be careful! I live here; furthermore, I have to live here for the rest of my life. If I just up and Donald Trump-like, fired too many people, my life could get really ugly. These people have friends here at the Ranch, and it is just not a good strategy to gore too many pet oxen right at the get-go. Besides I would have to find replacements.

But back to the Golf Committee and our Chair for Life, Rich. So when management hired a new Director of Golf named Fred, Rich, the "old timer" morphed into Rich, the "hard liner." He did not like Fred and essentially told him so to his face. Part of my job was to see that Management and residents worked together in partnership. It is that old "play nicely with others" thing we were supposed to learn in kindergarten. Well guess who was the new kindergarten teacher, Boys and Girls?

What to do? I used my well-honed management skills, worked behind the scenes and found a technical flaw in the Golf Committee's last election. Next thing you know they got a letter from the Council Steering Committee, aka Me, telling them they needed to have a new election. In the meantime I led a few savvy committee members to the realization that they should choose and elect a new chairman from their number, one who could work with the Director of Golf. And they did it! It was a coup! I had pulled off a power play that was transparent to the residents. A good guy, Sam, was put in place as Golf Committee Chairman and was all set to "play nicely" when, two weeks later, he was overcome by a perforated appendix, and he died! In two days he moved across the Departure Table from the Hospital List to the Picture Frame. All that strategy, all that work, and now the committee is not only without a Chair, it is down two people because once Rich was no longer Golf Committee Chair, you might say, "he took his balls," such as they were, "and went home."

I had another Committee Chair who was new that year. She spent three months having back surgery and had not done a darn thing with the Committee. It is understandable, but does the word "resign" ever come to mind? Not for these people! Regardless of what their absence does to the mission, they hold on to every last vestige of usefulness, every title they can – many until they are "framed" on the Departure Table.

I only needed thirty good people – seventeen Floor Representatives and thirteen Committee Chairs. Actually some Reps are Chairs too, so thirty is the maximum number of leaders I would ever need. We have almost 500 residents – that is just 6%. But at the rate they drop, it keeps me hopping. There you have it. I am not busy being President. I am busy recruiting replacements. Furthermore, I can only take my replacements from what seems to be an ever shrinking pool of possibles. I could use some fresh meat, new blood. All my most effective people are young, like they are under eighty-five, and healthy, like they take no more than twenty-five meds a day. I for one am rooting for Marketing to have a really good year because otherwise it's just "Life at the Wrinkle Ranch: Replacements Limited"

Life at the Wrinkle Ranch: Tracking Intruders

Our Wrinkle Ranch is a safe place to live. Visitors come into the Tower through the main entrance and must pass by the Front Desk. The Front Desk is staffed 24/7, and although there is no metal detector and no armed guard, so far in over twenty years there have been no reports of evil intruders.

We have visitors in our building daily. They all must sign in and wear some sort of identification. We also have contractors here on a regular basis. Not only do we renovate various common spaces of the building, there is a natural and expected turnover rate among such an elderly population, requiring an almost constant refurbishing of apartment homes on our halls. We have one or two regular construction contractors, and they seem to have an inexhaustible supply of hard-working Hispanic men to do the labor required. Most of these men speak little or no English, and although they seem to know their jobs, like contractors I have encountered though out my life, they do not seem to notice much of anything except their own project. They routinely manage to track up the floors, get dirty fingerprints on the doors, and leave a trail of debris behind them as they move through our building. They do not realize that this building is our "Forever Home," and they are intruders.

My floor lost four residents over a short period of time. Two died, one moved to a higher level of care, and one moved to another apartment on a different floor, one nearer the elevator to accommodate her ambulation issues. So it was no surprise that we had workers on our floor, redoing kitchens, replacing floor tile and carpets, and painting.

One day I was walking down the hall when I noticed white footprints on our orange carpet. A more careful inspection showed me the footprints were not paint, but rather some sort of white powder! We have a shortage of drug dealers in this building so I was pretty sure it was not cocaine, but I bent down and took a good sniff, just in case. Unless modern dealers are cutting their product with powdered grout, it was just as I expected, some sort of residue from a construction site. By now all my readers must know I have a vivid imagination so you will not be surprised to learn that feeling like Sacajawea during the North West Expedition, I carefully tracked the footprints back to their source.

Along the way, although I did not encounter any wolves, bear, or buffalo, I did see two strange birds and an Indian lookout: See the photographs in "The Butler Battles."

Predictably, the footprints were coming from a recently vacated apartment; furthermore, there was a 3M sticky mat outside the door, one designed to catch such substances as the white powder now marking a trail to our elevators. Apparently our worker had managed to get across the mat and still leave forty feet of footprints down the middle of the hall, proving once again that technology does not take the place of adult supervision!

As I headed for the office of the Director of Maintenance to report this intrusion in the form of a lack of respect for our carpeting, I saw a young worker exiting the apartment in question carrying the ubiquitous construction workers' white plastic five-gallon bucket. From the look of his posture, the bucket was full of something heavy, and to my distress he was headed right for our laundry room!

I had places to go, things to do, bridge to play, and little time to continue to track this issue, but I stopped by the Maintenance office. First I reported the footprints. The Maintenance Director looked at me politely but his eyes said, "Not my problem. Call

Housekeeping." Then I said, "And one worker was headed toward our laundry room with a big bucket full of something." And suddenly the Maintenance Director's eyes were focused on action. He grabbed his phone and started dialing!

Workers are strictly forbidden to use the resident laundry room facilities for disposal of materials and cleaning of tools. More than one laundry room sink had to be replaced when a worker decided to take a short cut and cleaned his tools or paint brushes and then dumped paint or some liquefied construction material down the drain. Over the last few years I have spearheaded a campaign to get our management to run herd on the construction company supervisors to control this abuse of our amenities.

When I returned later in the day, I stopped by the laundry room. Sure enough there was an inch of grey, sandy sludge in the sink, and the sink looked stained. I wrote to Maintenance and reported the laundry room intrusion and to Housekeeping and asked for a cleanup.

This morning I was copied on a strong note from Management to the on-site contractor manager regarding the sink subject. I wrote to all our Council members and told them to keep their eyes peeled for such activity.

So maybe I'm not qualified to flush out wild game or lead a party of explorers into uncharted territory like Sacajawea; still I think I'm successful here. It's just "Life at the Wrinkle Ranch: Tracking Intruders."

Life at the Wrinkle Ranch: A Toothy Luncheon

tooth y - adjective
1. having or displaying conspicuous teeth: *a toothy smile.*
2. savory; appetizing; toothsome
3. possessing a rough surface: *toothy paper.*
4. *Archaic.* sharp or caustic: *toothy commentary.*

Being a floor leader is a cross between being a "sunshine lady" and a "town crier." It is important that you care about your residents and keep up with their comings and goings – especially if those goings are to the hospital! And it is necessary that you make sure your residents know the news about happenings in the community as well as what is going on with their neighbors on the hall.

One of the easiest ways for a floor leader to have a meeting is to hold a floor luncheon or dinner. The Dining Services organization does everything. You just tell everyone when to show up, give them all the news, eat, drink, and have a good time along with the rest of your neighbors. One might say the whole thing is "a piece of cake!"

But sometimes the most unexpected things happen, and the Floor Leader's ability to cope in the face of emergencies and frustration is sorely tested.

Take for example this floor luncheon: We have lovely, lovely people on our floor. They all happily come to parties, luncheons, and dinners. Everyone is positive and cooperative, everyone that is except, old Mr. You-Know-Who. There is one in every group – the person who is never happy, criticizes everything, and claims health issues prevent him from doing anything, anything that is except what he does best – criticizing and complaining.

In this case Mr. You-Know-Who had a wife who was wheelchair-bound. Somehow he talked their way into Independent Living when he first came here, and at the same time he almost always uses a walker himself and vows he cannot stand or walk unassisted for more than a few feet.

So there we were in the midst of a splendid luncheon. I had made a little speech, a positive exposition listing all the good things that had happened recently in our community and on our floor. I had brought up the problem of the dryer lint on the hall carpet – again. The wine had been poured and our entrees served.

We were all eating, and drinking, and chatting. It was an ideal Senior scene, when all at once Mrs. You-Know-Who leaned forward and threw up in her plate! The first casualty was her large cloth napkin, which she brought to her face immediately. Then in turn each of us seated near her proffered our napkins, and they too were caught up and drowned in the effort to cover the situation.

Someone said, "Get some ginger ale. It will help." So I ran to find our server who had efficiently produced a tray and whisked away the disaster from the place in front of Mrs. You-Know-Who, plate, napkins, and all.

When I caught up with the server, Mr. You-Know-Who was right beside me – strange, I thought he was movement-impaired, well, maybe not in cases of emergency. "Don't dispose of that tray," he demanded in a desperate voice. "Her upper plate is in there somewhere!"

The server immediately shoved the tray in his direction. Management regulations prohibit staff from digging through such bodily ejections, and I knew this well-trained associate was not going to fly in the teeth of such a directive. And then Mr. You-Know-Who said, "I can't take that tray. I can't stand up long enough to go through it."

Annoyed but determined to play the part of the composed and competent Floor Leader to the bitter end, I took the tray, carried it to a bussing stand at the end of the hall and starting shaking out the napkins one at a time. I was stunned to see Mr. You-Know-Who standing right by me. I thought he just said he was not able to stand. I must have misheard him. At the shaking of the last napkin full of the remnants of Mrs. You-Know-Who's lunch, the sought after upper plate fell into the luncheon plate.

The plot thickened. "That has to be washed," said the man who was rapidly rising to the top of my special list or at least some list starting with "S," "and I can't do it," he whined.

Clenching my teeth – all natural, and fully and permanently attached to my gums – and making sure I did not touch anything "personal," I scooped the upper plate into a nearby Styrofoam container and hurried down the hallway to the public bathroom. As I was running water and squirting soap onto the recently expelled denture, who should appear by my elbow – in the bathroom – but, ta dah – Mr. You-Know-Who! As I dried off the clean, shiny denture, he said, "I'll take that now," and off he went, denture in hand, to impress the neighbors with what a dedicated husband he was and to claim the gratitude of his wife.

So you see, even once the speech is made, the wine is poured, and the food is served, the dedicated Floor Leader cannot just relax. You just never know what might come up next. It's just "Life at the Wrinkle Ranch: A Toothy Luncheon."

Life at the Wrinkle Ranch: An Alarming Event!

The following is a real e-mail exchange between the two parties identified, namely me when I was Resident President and our excellent Executive Director on one Saturday morning right after the new fire alarm system was installed. Note the increasing frustration on my part and my loss of any appreciation for the humor of this situation as time and the incessant alarming went on. Contrast that with the consistently calm, polite, and restrained management responses from the Director. Note the e-mails have been numbered for your reading convenience.

1. **From: Resident President**

To: Executive Director
Time: 9:48
Subject: Fire Alarm Sounding!
We are defending in place. Hope we don't lose Internet!

2. From: Resident President
To: Executive Director
Time: 10:01
Subject: Still Alarming!
The system works! Can we turn it off now? It is getting annoying.

3. From: Executive Director
To: Resident President
Time 10:05
Subject: Re: Still Alarming!
Attempting to learn what the issue is....

4. From: Resident President
To: Executive Director
Time: 10:09
Subject: Re: Still Alarming!
Twenty-one minutes and counting. This now rates hazard pay!

5. From: Resident President
To: Executive Director
Time: 10:10
Subject: Re: Still Alarming!
The SOBs cannot find the key. How do I know this? We called Front Desk and they, eager to provide TMI, blurted it out. How stupid and inept do we look now?

6. From: Executive Director
To: Resident President
Time: 10:10
Subject: Fire Truck Has Arrived!

7. From: Resident President
To: Executive Director
Time 10:11
Subject: Re: Fire Truck Has Arrived!
Do they have a key?

8. From: Executive Director
To: Resident President
Time 10:15
Subject: Re: Fire Truck Has Arrived!
Someone pulled a pull station and they are having challenges resetting it.

9. **From: Resident President**
To: Executive Director
Time: 10:16
Subject: Re: Fire Truck Has Arrived!
Front Desk needs to get their story straight. "We can't find the key" is a bad message to put out to residents. Forgive us if we do not feel "safe" when protected by such associates.

10. **From: Executive Director**
To: Resident President
Time: 10:21
Subject: Status
Director of Maintenance is entering campus to support/handle.

11. **From: Resident President**
To: Executive Director
Time: 10:22
Subject: Re: Status
Him, I trust

12. **From: Resident President**
To: Executive Director
Time: 10:25
Subject: Hooray for Dir. Maintenance. Alarm is off!

13. **From: Executive Director**
To: Resident President
Time: 11:31
Subject: Re: Hooray for Dir. Maintenance. Alarm is off!
Apparently, an unknown resident pulled the fire pull station versus pushing the button to exit the side door. Further education and communication required. Will also install covers on 1st floor pull stations as well to avoid.

14. **From: Resident President**
To: Executive Director
Time: 11:32
Subject: Re: Hooray for Dir. Maintenance. Alarm is off!
Then we need to have someone on duty at all times (not 1/2 hour away) who is able to turn off the alarm. Your other precautions are sensible. I'm just sorry we didn't think about these problems, and solutions, in advance.

15. **From: Executive Director**
To: Resident President
Time: 11:32:30
Subject: Re: Hooray for Dir. Maintenance. Alarm is off!

Also, reset key was in key box in closet at Front Desk. More training and re training

16. From: Resident President
To: Executive Director
Time: 11:33
Subject: Re: Hooray for Dir. Maintenance. Alarm is off!
These things, like children's ear infections and high fevers, never happen during "prime time" when the right people are available. The trick is how to be covered at night and on weekends, but sadly we have our 3rd string on duty then. The residents' perception is that they are not competent to keep us safe. Please think about this. After 38 minutes of being bombarded by the relentless alarm, my systolic which had been 111 an hour before (and quite reasonable for days) was 141. This is just one example of what sort of problem this situation can cause. I was not worried in the least for my safety nor was I angry or nervous; but the constant noise has a deleterious effect on residents, and does not provide an acceptable environment for anybody, much less old people who frequently have medical conditions. I'm sure there are studies available which detail the effect of continuous, loud noise on heart rate, respiration, and blood pressure. Certainly the CIA uses noise to assist in interrogation and some identify that practice as "torture." Perhaps you can prepare a memo for distribution to our residents to explain and reassure them after this unfortunate occurrence. There is bound to be blowback.

17. From: Resident President
To: Executive Director
Time: 11:35
Subject: Psy Ops

Music in psychological operations

From Wikipedia, the free encyclopedia "Music has been used in psychological operations. The term **music torture** is sometimes used by critics of the practice of playing loud music incessantly to prisoners or people besieged.

The United Nations and the European Court of Human Rights have banned the use of loud music in interrogations.[citation needed] The term torture is sometimes used to describe the practice. While it is acknowledged by US interrogation experts that it causes discomfort, it has also been characterized by them as causing no 'long-term effects.'

Music and **sound** have been usually used as part of a combination of interrogation methods, today recognized by international bodies as amounting to torture. Attacking all senses without leaving any visible traces, they have formed the basis of the widely discussed torture in Guantanamo and Abu Ghraib. They were, however, devised much earlier in the 1950s and early 1960s, as a way to counter so-called Soviet 'brainwashing.' They include:

- **sensory deprivation**
- **stress positions**
- **sleep deprivation**
- **food and drink deprivation**
- **continuous music or sound** [underline added for emphasis]"

Interestingly, there was no response to my sending of the article which clearly defined our morning experience as torture. Where is the Geneva Convention for Seniors when we need it? It's just "Life at the Wrinkle Ranch: An Alarming Event!"

Life at the Wrinkle Ranch: Persistence Revisited

During the three years that I was president of the Wrinkle Ranch, I developed a good partnership and working relationship with our Executive Director with whom I met for an hour every week. He was an excellent manager and had a splendid sense of humor. He quickly learned how to process my brand of humor, which a lesser man might have misconstrued as disrespectful. Although he never responded in writing with anything stronger than "Thank you for the information," an intelligent move for a person in his position, I know that he found many of my missives entertaining and even useful.

One of my pet projects during my term as President was to persuade him to divest our community of a propane fueled vehicle we residents referred to as "the Whale."

The Whale was purchased at some astronomical price by the ED who managed our community over ten years ago. It looked much like an old fashioned street car or trolley with a tandem carriage. It has removable windows and was envisioned as an ecologically responsible way to move groups of residents around the campus, especially those living in the apartment homes a quarter of a mile from the Tower and the Dining Rooms.

I had many successes as President, and although the ED and I were in total agreement that the Whale was the wrong vehicle for us, and he abandoned its use on a regular basis, I could not persuade him to donate it to a worthy cause or sell it to the first bidder who offered to take it off our hands. Instead he insisted that he had a fiduciary responsibility to the corporation, and it was incumbent on him to get a reasonable sum for the sale so that he could buy a large and sturdy tram for our campus from the proceeds.

Although no longer President, I persisted in my desire to get this monstrosity out of our parking lot and off our campus. Finally, I thought I saw a window of opportunity, and I wrote the following letter to him, firmly tongue in cheek. I did not know how he would react, but my guess is he laughed as he tossed my recommendation into the circular file, and then responded, "Thank you for your comments."

Dear Executive Director,

You know that I admire persistence. Indeed, I practice it regularly myself. I also admire the decision to change directions when one has exercised the available means to one's end. We might view that approach as "persistence revisited."

Three years ago when you came here you vowed to get another bank to replace the one which abandoned us. You worked long and hard to do that. When it became apparent that no bank, not even a proper ATM, would locate here, you rethought the situation and wisely repurposed the space. The residents admired that decision, that demonstration of "persistence revisited."

Three years ago you had another excellent goal: the goal of selling the Whale, clearly an expensive "white elephant" on our campus. You intended to put the money to good use for more appropriate campus transportation – a splendid idea. I know that you and our Transportation Director have worked diligently to sell the Whale, and as in the case of the bank project, all that work has been to no avail. The fuel for the Whale is not readily available, so even using it for special occasions is becoming increasingly more difficult. Every month it depreciates further. Perhaps it is time to revisit persistence in this case as well.

We are about to spend thousands of dollars of capital funds to create additional parking spaces, certainly something necessary and important for our community. As you explained it, a parking space generated by this project costs us $1,333.33.

Since the Whale is 45 feet long, my engineering consultant tells me it occupies, at a minimum, the equivalent of four parking spaces. At a cost of $1333.33 per space that means that the Whale will soon cost us at least an additional $5333.32 if we allow it to continue to hulk in our valuable parking area.

Surely you have fought the good fight here. Surely it is time to go to Plan B. Can't we please make the Whale, which was a bad idea in the first place, just go away? If someone would haul it out of here for $5,000.00, according to my reckoning, we would save $333.32! As a charitable donation and a tax write off, we would probably save even more.

As Herman Melville chronicled, obsession with a white whale did not turn out well for Captain Ahab, and even though this particular white Whale has not yet cost you an arm, much less a leg, perhaps it would be wiser and less expensive if we just allowed it to depart our parking area quietly.

It's just "Life at the Wrinkle Ranch: Persistence Revisited."

Epilogue

My Life at the Wrinkle Ranch is not over. Even those pessimists, the actuaries, would give me a minimum of another eight years.

So as I conclude this volume My Hero and I are still here, and I am still involved in community life. Our splendid Executive Director has moved on to the "next level" of his career, and unless my fellow Ranchers discover what I have written, I am not ostracized – yet.

Will there be another volume of Wrinkle Ranch stories? Who knows? Maybe I will succumb to the basics of WR life and take up bingo instead, but somehow I doubt it.

Virginia

Made in the USA
Lexington, KY
29 November 2018